BILL SEVERN'S COMPLETE BOOK OF MAGIC

GALAHAD BOOKS
NEW YORK

Previously published in three separate volumes as:
MAGIC IN MIND Copyright © 1974 by Bill Severn. Illustrated by Katherine Wood.
MAGIC MONEY Copyright © 1977 by Bill Severn. Illustrated by Elizabeth Green.
MAGIC WITH ROPE, RIBBON & STRING Copyright © 1982 by Bill Severn. Illustrated by John
Garcia.

First Galahad edition published in 1995.

Galahad Books
A division of BBS Publishing Corporation
450 Raritan Center Parkway
Edison, NJ 08837

Galahad Books is a registered trademark of BBS Publishing Corporation
Published by arrangement with Stackpole Books.

Distributed by Sterling Publishing Co, Inc.
387 Park Avenue South
New York, NY 10016

Distributed in Canada by Sterling Publishing
Canadian Manda Group
165 Dufferin Street
Toronto, Ontario, Canada M6K 3H6

Distributed in Autralia by Capricorn Link (Australia) Pty, Ltd.
PO Box 704
Windsor NSW 2756 Australia

Distributed in Great Britan by Chrysalis Books Group PLC
The Chrysalis Building
Bramley Road
London W 10 GSP, England

For information about special sales, premium and corporate purchases, please contact
Sterling Special Sales Department at 800-805-5489 or specialsales@sterlingpub.com

Library of Congress Catalog Number: 95-75034
ISBN: 0-88365-898-4
Printed in United States of America.

CONTENTS

I

MYSTIFYING MENTAL TRICKS

CONTENTS

1

THE MENTAL MAGICIAN

The magician who pulls a rabbit from a hat deceives the eye. But the mental magician deceives the mind. He creates the illusion that he is able to read minds, that he can transfer thoughts from his mind to the minds of others, can predict future happenings, and can perform other demonstrations of psychic phenomena.

What he does is no part of the serious scientific and psychological research into such things. Whether performing for a few friends or for a larger audience, he is an actor playing the role of a mentalist, an entertainer presenting a rehearsed show of mental magic. It is a form of theatrical make-believe that audiences have enjoyed since the beginnings of theater itself and is part of the fun thousands of amateurs have found in the hobby of performing magic.

The mental magician doesn't say it is all a trick, any more than the magician who takes a rabbit from a hat would break into a performance to explain that there is no real magic in what he does. He claims no supernormal powers, but he suggests the possibility that they may exist for some people, demonstrates what might be accomplished if someone did possess such powers—and leaves it to the audience to decide how it is done.

Unlike the magician who displays his skill at deception, the mentalist avoids the appearance of trickery. He presents no visual magic show. His illusions are with thoughts, not with things.

He depends more on showmanship, personality, and acting ability than on the mechanics of what he does or the props he uses. If he is convincing, the audience centers its attention entirely on him and is not concerned with the apparently ordinary pads of paper, pencils, cards, envelopes, and other incidental things he has or the way in which he handles them. He *seems* to do it all with his mind.

The basic secrets

Most of the secrets of mental magic are simple ones, far simpler than the audience imagines. Some of the props are tricked, of course, but seldom in any elaborate manner. The mentalist relies more on subtlety than on apparatus. Because everything must be made to look as innocent as possible, the less there is to hide the better. Simple, bold, direct methods allow him to concentrate on the presentation, and that is what counts—not the trick as a magical puzzle designed to fool the spectators, but the illusion he can build around it in their minds, the effect that he can create of some psychic happening.

He has an advantage over other magicians in that his props can be carried in his pockets or in a briefcase. There are no suitcases filled with equipment, no boxes, tubes, and other bulky devices to set up and repack afterward. Most of his routines, no matter how small the things used in them, can be adapted for presentation to audiences of any size, almost anywhere.

Another advantage is that his audiences are often in a less challenging mood than they are when they watch an ordinary magic show. People know the usual magician is a trickster and they watch for every clue to his tricks with a fool-me-if-you-can attitude. But the mental magician presents no visible tricks as such, no obvious display of sleight of hand. The audience may guess that what he does is a trick and yet be less certain that it is, more willing to suspend disbelief, to go along with the illusion that he creates.

Everything he presents is an experiment, a test or an attempt, never with results guaranteed in advance. If he fails, he can always say that that particular experiment didn't work, that he just couldn't "get the thought clearly." As a mentalist, he is not expected to be right all the time. In fact, he may deliberately make minor mistakes, just to be more convincing.

Of course, if he is caught, even once, doing something tricky with his props, then the whole illusion of mental magic is gone as far as that audience is concerned. As simple as a trick may seem when reduced to its bare bones, the mechanics of it must be practiced until it can be done surely every time, naturally and almost automatically.

The mental magician must also avoid the *suggestion* of trickery in his handling of things and in what he says. He doesn't make a finger-waving exhibition of showing that his hands are empty; he merely lets it be seen that they are. He doesn't elaborately display a pocket handkerchief on both sides as a magician might before covering a glass with it; he simply takes it from his pocket, shakes it out, and drops it over the glass. He makes no attempt to "prove" that things are "ordinary and unprepared." It will be assumed that they are, unless he arouses suspicion by suggesting otherwise.

Many mentalists avoid the use of playing cards, or even manufactured alphabet and number cards, because they call to mind the card-manipulating magician. Some also contend that mental magic and other kinds of magic should never be mixed in the same program. On the other hand, there are any number of successful magicians who have included mental effects in their magic shows, and quite a few mentalists who combine both. It is something each performer must decide for himself.

Visibility and dramatic effect

One thing the ordinary magic show has that the mental magic show greatly lacks is visible entertainment, something for the audience to see. That is a disadvantage the mentalist must try to overcome. He must create a sense of something always happening, keep things moving, dramatize his effects, and build each routine to a climax to maintain the interest of the audience.

For the most part the audience can participate only indirectly, through a few spectators chosen to join in the experiments as representatives of the whole audience. The others can't see for themselves what is printed on the selected page of a book, for instance, or what may be written on a small slip of paper. They are asked to accept what happens on the basis of what a few spectators say is happening.

Whenever possible, the spectators who do take part in an experiment should be asked to read things aloud. Large cards or slates may also be used so things can be written for everyone to see and to give the entire audience something to watch. The plots of mental effects should be easy to follow, and the mentalist should make sure that the whole audience does understand exactly what is happening, or at least what he wants them to *think* is happening.

Setting the stage

The effects in this book are for solo performance. That is, the mentalist works alone, without seen or unseen assistants, confederates, or stooges, but rather with spectators chosen from the audience to take part.

When the audience is small, the performer can invite spectators to join in various experiments as he goes along, or he can go to where they are seated. But in a large room, or when he is working from a platform, he may want to select a "committee" of half a dozen spectators at the start. The group can be seated in chairs at the front, so he doesn't have to leave the platform or delay the performance to bring spectators up individually.

He will need a table, such as a card table or whatever other small table may be available, and if he is presenting more than one or two effects, he probably also will need an attaché case or briefcase to carry things in. But equipment generally should be kept to a minimum, since the whole idea is to suggest that what he does is with his mind alone.

The mentalist usually will position his table so that he can stand at the front of a room, with no spectators seated behind him. But he can't fuss over such arrangements. If he does happen to find himself surrounded by an audience, he may have to eliminate some routines from that particular program rather than risk exposing his secrets.

Dealing with spectators

When he gives any instructions to spectators, he must make sure that they understand exactly what he wants them to do. He should show them, if possible, and repeat the instructions if necessary. But their help should always be politely requested, never commanded, and if something goes wrong, no spectator should be openly criticized for it.

The mental magician's attitude should never be one of challenging the audience in a boastful or superior manner, and he should avoid being drawn into arguments or debates. Even if the performer can prove that he is right, he is not there to prove anything—only to entertain by offering in a modest and friendly way to "attempt" some interesting experiments that he wants to share with the audience, with their help and just for fun.

Practice and rehearsal

Aside from the necessary practice to learn the working of a trick, each effect should be carefully rehearsed, just as an actor would rehearse his part in a play. All the props should be set up and the words and movements acted out before an imagined audience. The mentalist should know exactly how the smallest thing will be picked up, displayed, handled, what will be in which pocket or in a certain position on the table, and where he will put it when he has finished using it. More than that, he should try to imagine what could go wrong and to plan in advance how he would handle the situation.

Planning the show

When the chosen effects have been individually practiced and rehearsed, they will have to be put together in a planned program, balanced and with good variety. The performer probably will want to start his show with something quick, direct, and impressive that requires very little buildup or handling of things by members of the audience. Each effect after that should be like one act in a play, with its own climax, but building in interest from one to the next, with what he considers his best effect to end the show.

Which effects he selects and how many he includes will depend in part on where he intends to perform and on the size and kind of audience. If he is going to entertain a small group of friends, two or three effects that use things he can carry in his pocket should be enough. For a larger audience, he will want to include props that are more visible from a distance, and perhaps four or five effects. He should know from rehearsal how long each effect will take to do, and allow for the time it will take spectators to handle things and carry out instructions.

He may find, when he puts a show together, that the props for one effect fill a pocket and leave no room in it for the things required for the next effect. In that case, he will have to rearrange the setup, decide which things are most essential to have in that particular pocket, and perhaps have the others in order in his briefcase or on the table.

Whatever show he gives, even if only for a few friends in his own living room, it should be planned and rehearsed. It is only from such rehearsals that he can gain the assurance and confidence he needs when he performs. And rehearsing tricks, trying them in various ways to achieve the best possible effect, is a good part of the fun of doing magic.

Experience and personality

Of course, no amount of rehearsal will replace the trial and error of actual performance before a real audience. It is only by giving shows, trying things, testing the audience reaction to them, that a performer learns what should be left out, what needs to be added, and how to point up each routine with words and actions to get the most from it in terms of impact and entertainment.

All the directions given in this book for what to say and do should be considered as suggestions, to be followed only to the extent that they may fit the performer's own style. He will want to find his own best ways of presentation, and he should translate the patter into his own words. Above all else, he should be himself in his role as mental magician. What he has to put across is not the tricks, but the convincing illusion he can create with them out of his own personality.

2

EXTRASENSORY DECEPTIONS

Symbolic Sight

How it looks:

"The standard symbols for scientific testing of extrasensory perception are a circle, a cross, three wavy lines, a square, and a star," you say. "I have printed those symbols on these office file cards." You show each of the symbols and then hand all the cards to a spectator and turn your back.

"Mix them, please," you tell him, "and when you're satisfied that they are thoroughly mixed, spread them all out face-down on the table so it will be impossible for me to see what is on them. Then just take any one—look at it and hold it with its face against your forehead while you think of that symbol."

You turn around and face him. After some effort, you announce which symbol he has in mind, and ask him to hold up the card and show it to everybody. Then you tell him:

"Please put it back with the others and mix them on the table again. This time, while my back is turned, take three—any three you wish. Look at them, hold them against your chest, and then turn your own back to me."

When he says he has done that, you face the spectators while he stands with his back toward you. Again, you concentrate, and then say: "One of the symbols you have is the star (or whatever it may be). . . . Will you hold it up, please—and then the cross that you have—and the square?"

For a final ESP experiment, while your back is turned again, you have him mix the symbols and spread them facedown on the table as before. You turn around, go to the table, take a red pen from your pocket, and draw a symbol on the back of each facedown card. Then you hold them up, one at a time, to show that your drawings match the hidden symbols on the faces of all five.

What you need:

Five office index file cards, the standard kind with printed lines on one side and the opposite side blank. These come in various sizes. Small 3-by-5-inch cards, which are easy to carry in the pocket, may be used for closeup performance. For a larger group, 4-by-8-inch cards should be used, with bigger symbols drawn on them.

A black marking pen and a red marking pen.

A typewriter eraser.

The secret and setup:

This routine is strong, direct, and can be presented almost anywhere. Its secret depends on the use of the file cards. The fact that they are manufactured with lines printed on what will be used as the backs allows for marking them in a way that can be seen from a fair distance. The performer quickly knows, from the back of a card, which symbol is on the face of it.

First, for those unfamiliar with the standard ESP symbols, a coding system that is often used by mentalists should be learned. It is an easy one to remember. The circle is one continuous line, so it is thought of as 1; the cross or plus sign is made with two lines, so it is thought of as 2; the three wavy vertical lines are 3; the four-sided square is 4; the five-pointed star is 5. Memorize them in that order and always think of them that way: circle, cross, lines, square, star — 1, 2, 3, 4, 5. Thus, if you see a mark that indicates "1" it is the circle card, "3" is the wavy-lines card, and so on.

The lined sides of index cards are manufactured with a *red* line at the top and *blue* lines spaced down the rest of the card. The red line will be your key. No matter in what position a card is held or placed on the table, you will look first for the red line, then for the blue lines, to count them mentally from the red-line starting point.

Put one of the cards on a table with the *red* line at the top. Make sure the typewriter eraser is clean and erase a full inch from each end of the *first* blue line beneath the red one. Erase it thoroughly, so no trace of the printed line remains at the ends.

Turn the card over so the blank face is up and so the narrow edges of the card are now at the top and bottom. With the black marking pen, draw a circle as large as will fit on the card.

Put that card aside and take another. Erase an inch from both ends of the *second* blue line beneath the red one, then turn it over and draw the cross vertically on the face of that

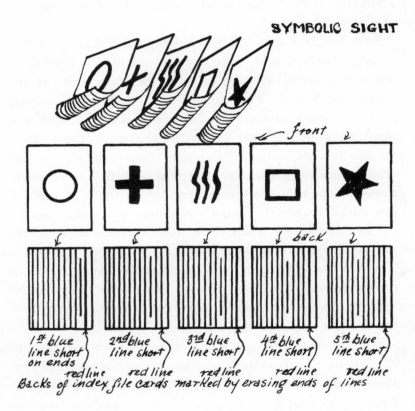

card. From the back of a third card, erase the ends of the third blue line and draw three wavy vertical lines on its face. Erase the ends of the fourth blue line from the fourth card and put a square on its face; the fifth blue line from the fifth card, and a five-pointed star on its face.

Now try this: turn all the cards facedown, spread them on the table and mix them around any which way, then look at the back of one of them. Count to yourself from the red line (no matter whether it is now at the left, right, top, or bottom) to the first blue line that has no ends. If it is the first line from the red one, the face of that card has a circle on it; if it is the fourth line from the red one, it has a square on its face.

Try it from a distance. Prop up one of the cards against the back of a chair, as though someone might be holding the card, then stand several feet away from it. You still should be able to see the erased line clearly, so as to tell which one it is from the back.

The reason for erasing both ends of the blue lines is that one end may be partly covered by a spectator's fingers when he holds a card against his forehead, or ends may be overlapped when cards are spread on the table. Don't worry about the fact that the markings seem obvious to you once you know where to look for them. The spectator is kept busy doing things and looking at the faces of the cards. He won't be holding the cards long enough to compare the backs carefully, and even if he should notice that part of a line is missing it will appear to be an imperfection in the printing.

There is no setup for performing. Just have the stack of cards and red marking pen in your pocket or on the table.

What you do:

Explain about the standard ESP symbols and show each of the cards. Hand them all to the spectator, move away, and turn your back, and have him mix them and spread them facedown on the table "so it will be impossible to see what is on

them." Ask him to take any one, look at it, and hold it with
its face against his forehead while he thinks of that symbol.

Face him and look for the red line on the back of the card
he is holding. Mentally count from that to the first blue line
with missing ends. Announce what the symbol is, but don't
make it seem too easy, and have him hold it up to show it to
everybody. Ask him to return that symbol to the table with
the others and to mix and spread them around facedown
again. Turn your back and invite him to take any three
symbols he wishes, to look at them, hold them against his
chest, "and then turn your own back to me."

Turn to face the audience while his back is to you. Pretend
to be having trouble sensing his thoughts. Close your eyes
and put the palm of your hand to your forehead a moment.
Partly cover your eyes to prevent the audience from seeing
the direction of your downward glance as you look down at
the table. Look at the backs of the two cards that remain
on the table. If you see from their backs that those are, for
instance, cards 1 and 3, you know that the spectator is holding 2, 4, and 5 — cross, square, and star. Call each of them and
have him hold them up to show them.

Now turn your back once more while he spreads the facedown cards around on the table to mix them. Then go to the
table, remove the pen from your pocket, and read the back of
each of the cards in turn as you draw red designs on them.
You have plenty of time to figure out each marking. Don't
rush it. Hesitate as you start to make a design on one. Scratch
it out and start over. Say: "I can't get them clearly. . . .
I'm afraid I missed on this — but maybe I got a few."

Finally pick up one of them. Show the audience the face

and then turn it to show your matching symbol on the back. Continue with the others. When you come to the last two, lift them together, one in each hand, with their faces toward you. Glance from one to the other to build suspense, then quickly turn them and hold them up high to show them.

Two Out of Three Isn't Bad

How it looks:

"Some people believe that everybody has extrasensory perception—that we use ESP frequently without being aware of the fact," you say. "Have you ever felt almost certain that you could guess what some person was about to say before he said it? That's a common experience. But is it always only a guess, or is it ESP?"

Taking out some blank cards and a pen, you ask a spectator if he would like to test his possible powers of extrasensory perception in a little guessing game. "It's a game of three guesses. I'll think of three different things and ask you to guess each of them. I don't expect you to get all three. If you could do that, you'd be a mind reader. But perhaps you'll be able to guess one of my three thoughts—or come close to it. Shall we try?"

Holding the cards so he can't see their faces, you write on the top one. "I'm writing the name of a friend of mine, someone I'm sure you don't know," you explain, "the person's first name. . . ." You put that card facedown on the table without revealing what you have written. "It's a rather common first name. Of course, the person might be a man or a woman. Will you just make a guess? What name came into your mind?"

He may say: "John." You repeat it aloud, write it on the second card you are holding, show it to him, and put that on the table on top of the first card you wrote. "That's your first guess," you say. "Next, I'm going to think of a big city. It might be an American city or a foreign one." You write on the next card and without showing the writing put that on the table. "What city do you guess I have in mind? I'll tell you this much — it's among the one hundred largest cities in the world. Which city do you guess?"

He may guess: "Chicago." You write whatever he says on a card, show it, and put it with the others. "All right. Now the third guess. I'm thinking of a television show — not the name of a particular show, but a much broader category. The kind of a show it is, the type of program, such as comedy or sports, but not those. It's a certain kind of show millions of people watch every night." You write what you are thinking and add that card to the others on the table. "What's your guess?"

He may answer: "The weather report."

You write what he says on the last card you have, pick up the rest of them from the table, and say, "Let's see how well you've done. The television show was the broadest category, so we'll check that one first." You show his card. "You guessed the weather program. . . . No. I'm afraid you missed that one. What I had in mind was the news." You show your card with NEWS on it. "You were very close. I suppose the weather report could be considered part of the news — but to be fair, I think we should call that one wrong."

Putting those two cards aside, you take the next two. "I

thought of a friend's name. Your guess was 'John.' And the name I had in mind *was*—" you show it "—John." Then you take the next two. "You guessed that out of all the cities in the world I was thinking about Chicago. And the city I had in mind *was*—Chicago." The thoughts written on the cards again match. "Two out of three," you say. "That's rather remarkable. Congratulations. Were you only guessing—or did you use your ESP?"

(There is a chance that the spectator may correctly get all three. But at the least, two of his "guesses" will be right.)

What you need:

Six blank cards. These may be any size from business cards to large pieces of poster board, since the routine can be shown close up or to a large audience.

A pencil, pen, or colored marking pen, depending on the visibility required.

The secret and setup:

This is a very simple way of using what is known as the "one-ahead" principle, upon which countless mental-magic effects have been built. Usually the mentalist first asks the spectator to think of something and then appears to read his mind. This presentation is in reverse, in that the performer first writes something and then invites the spectator to "guess" what he has written.

That is done partly to dress up the effect and partly to put the "blame" on the spectator for missing one of three tries. After all, the audience doesn't expect a spectator to be as good at reading minds as the mentalist might be, and the very fact that he may miss one out of three adds to the credibility. It also avoids the use of a direct force, such as with playing cards, dice, or some other device, which is necessary in many "one-ahead" routines.

Sort of a verbal force, which may or may not work, is used. When it does work, the spectator is right all three times. But it isn't essential. The basic principle remains the same. What you write on the first card really matches your third question, and you keep one step ahead of the spectator all the way along, writing his answer each time on the next card instead of what you say you are writing. This will become clear from the presentation.

There are no tricky moves at the end and nothing to prepare in advance. All you need are the six cards and the pen or pencil. You can have them in your pocket or on the table.

What you do:

After introducing the ESP "guessing game," hold the stack of blank cards in your left hand, close to you, and with their faces toward you. Explain that you are writing a friend's name but instead, on the first card, write: NEWS. Be careful not to reveal the writing, and put that card facedown on the table. Say: "It's a rather common first name." This is to keep the spectator from thinking of long or exotic names. "Of course, the person might be a man or a woman. Will you just make a guess? What name came into your mind?"

Repeat aloud whatever name he says, write it on the next card in your hand, show it to him, and put that card facedown on the table on top of the first card. Now tell him you are thinking of a big city. Hold the cards close and write, not the name of a city, but the name of the person that you just wrote on the previous card. Put that card facedown on top of those on the table, continue to talk about the city, and ask him to make his second guess.

Write whatever city he says on the next card in your hand, show it to him as you call it aloud, and put that card facedown on top of the ones on the table. Then tell him you are thinking of a television show, not a particular program, but the kind of a show that it is. Hold the cards close and write, not a TV show, but the city he named. Put that facedown on top of the cards on the table.

Go on talking about the category of TV shows you have in mind, "such as comedy or sports, but not those." By ruling out sports and comedy shows, you have eliminated a lot of possibilities. You now strongly suggest a "nightly" show, a kind almost all viewers regularly watch. "It's a certain kind of show millions of people watch every night," you say. "What's your guess?"

If the verbal force works, he will say, "News." But he may say "Weather" or "Talk show" or something else. Whatever he says, write it on the last card in your hand. Show it to him, then turn its face toward you again, and *keep that card in your left hand*. With your right hand, take all the other cards from the table together, lift them with their faces toward you, and just slide the batch of them *behind* the card you are still holding with your left hand.

There is no "move" to be made. You just casually pick up the cards with one hand and put them into the other as you naturally would. The result is that they are now all stacked in pairs: the two TV guesses, the two names, the two cities. But they are not in the order in which you called for the guesses. So you make an excuse to dispose of the pair facing you first, which are also the ones least likely to be correct.

"Let's see how well you've done," you say. "The television show was the broadest category so we'll check that one first." Turn the stack to show the first card, his TV guess. Whatever he guessed frequently can be called "close," but if he guessed anything but a news program, say that he is wrong. "I'm afraid you missed that one. . . ." Show the next card. "What I had in mind was a news program. I think we'll have to call that one wrong."

Of course if he did guess "News" correctly, you build up to the fact that he got all three right. In any case, you take the next two cards and show that he guessed the person's name, then the last two and show that he guessed the city, and say: "That's rather remarkable. Congratulations. Were you only guessing—or did you use your ESP?"

What's Your Bag?

How it looks:

"I've been exploring the practical uses of psychic phenomena," you say. "There are so many everyday ways that mentalism could be applied if the techniques were developed beyond the area of scientific experiment. For instance—why not put extrasensory perception to work at airline terminals, where baggage is always getting mixed up or lost?"

From a small envelope, you remove four baggage tags, which you lay out on the table around the envelope. On the envelope, you draw a picture of a suitcase. "Let's imagine this is a missing suitcase. It could belong to any of you. The problem is to identify the owner quickly. So why not put a mentalist to work at the baggage counter?"

On each of the tags, you write the name and address of one of the spectators, and invite someone to turn the tags facedown so the names are hidden. "Mix them all up so I have no idea which is which," you say, as you step away from the table and turn your back. "Then spread them all out again."

You return to the table, hold a hand above the facedown tags to "sense the vibrations," and correctly identify each tag, which you pick up and hand to the person whose name is on it. "Applied clairvoyance might accomplish it that way," you explain. "But there are other psychic methods that could be used. Paranormal vision, for example."

Someone now is invited to gather up the tags, mix them thoroughly, and hand the batch of them to you behind your back. "I have no eyes in the back of my head," you say, "but mentally I might try to envision each of your names and match a missing suitcase to its owner." You stand before each person in turn, close your eyes to concentrate, and then bring out the proper tag from those you are holding behind you. "This is yours, Mary. . . . I think your name's on this one, Joe. . . ."

Then you say that it also might be done by "direct telepathy," and explain, "That would be the hardest way to sort out the baggage—if the clerk had no contact at all and simply had to read minds from a distance. But let's try."

You walk to a far side of the room and turn your back. Someone is asked to freely select one tag, without showing

the name on it to anyone else, and to put all the other tags
into his pocket. Holding that tag before him, he thinks of
the name written on it. Standing well away, and with your
back to the group, you dramatically reveal the name.

What you need:

Four oblong tags, about 2½-by-4 inches, the kind commonly sold as "household tags." These have a reinforcement
tab around the hole at the top where the string is attached.
   A small envelope to hold them.
   Pen or pencil.

The secret and setup:

This is a combination of three tricks, each accomplished by
a different method, all of which depend on the way in which
the tags are laid out around the envelope on the table at the
start.
   The tags are secretly pencil-marked in clockwise order, so
you can identify them from their backs by sight. Their tabs
are prepared in the same order, so you can tell the tags apart
by feeling them when they are held behind your back. They
are positioned in such a way on the table that when a spectator later holds up one of them to read what is written on it,
he will turn the top of the tag to point in the direction in
which it was originally placed on the table. By stealing a quick
glance at the tag, from across the room, you can immediately
tell which one he holds.
   First remove the strings and put the tags on a table in a
horizontal row, with their holes at the top. Think of the tags,
from left to right, by number: 1, 2, 3, 4. On tag 1, make a

small pencil mark at the very top edge of the hole. Pencil mark the right edge of the hole of tag 2, the bottom edge of the hole of tag 3, the left edge of the hole of tag 4. Mark the holes on both faces of each tag.

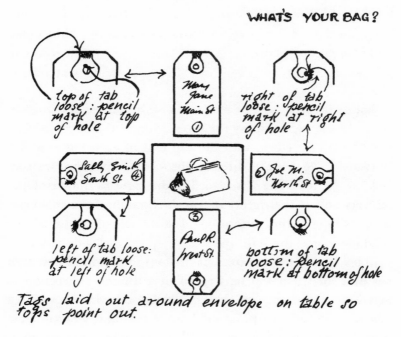

WHAT'S YOUR BAG?

top of tab loose: pencil mark at top of hole

right of tab loose: pencil mark at right of hole

left of tab loose: pencil mark at left of hole

bottom of tab loose: pencil mark at bottom of hole

Tags laid out around envelope on table so tops point out.

Next take tag 1 and work your fingernail beneath the top edge of the reinforcement tab around the hole, so as to pull it away from the tag a little and roughen that edge to the touch. Loosen the right edge of the tab of tag 2, the bottom edge of tag 3, the left edge of tag 4. Do that with the tabs on both faces of each tag.

When they are mixed, you now should be able to tell which

is which by sight from the pencil marks. If you hold them behind your back, you should be able to identify them by feeling around the edges of the tabs with your fingernail. Be
sure the markings are clear enough and the tabs are fixed so
you can sort the tags quickly by sight or by touch.

Stack the four tags in order — 1, 2, 3, 4 — from the top down,
slide them into the envelope, and have that in your pocket
with the pen or pencil.

What you do:

Take out the envelope and put it at the center of the table.
Remove the tags and lay them out around the envelope like
the hands of a clock, with the top end of each tag pointing
outward. Tag 1 goes directly above the envelope, with its
hole at the top. Tag 2 is placed at the right of the envelope,
with its hole to the right; tag 3 at the bottom of the envelope,
with its hole to the bottom; tag 4 at the left of the envelope,
with its hole at the left.

(This automatically positions the tags so that what is written
on each of them will be written in a different direction in
relation to the top of that particular tag. Later, when a
spectator picks one up, he will have to turn it so that the hole
is at the top, right, bottom, or left to properly read what is on
it. From the way he holds it, you will know at a glance which
tag it is:1, 2, 3, or 4.)

Draw a quick sketch of a suitcase on the face of the envelope,
a simple oblong shape with a curved line over it to indicate a
handle. Ask four spectators their names and addresses. Without changing the clockwise position of the tags, write each
name on a tag in turn, starting with the one at the top. Include

the complete name and address, so the writing covers a con-
siderable portion of the tag, and make the writing small but
legible.

As you write the names, remember each person by the
number of his tag. For example, if their names are Mary, Joe,
Paul, and Sally, think of them as "Mary One," "Joe Two," and
so on. There is no need to memorize more than the person's
first name.

Step away from the table, turn your back, and invite someone to turn all the tags facedown so none of the names can
be seen and to mix them thoroughly. When that has been
done, return to the table and hold a hand over the tags without touching them. Pretend to "sense the vibrations" of the
hidden names as you secretly look for the pencil dot that
identifies each tag so you can hand it to the person whose
name is on it.

For the next test, have the tags mixed once more and given
to you behind your back. Feel for the tab on the top tag of the
batch. Run your fingernail around the edges of the tab to feel
where it is loose and secretly learn which one it is. Call the
name, give the person the tag, and continue until all the
names have been revealed.

Finally suggest "direct telepathy" as the most difficult test
of all. Go to a corner of the room, stand with your back to
the group, and ask someone to choose any tag without showing the name to the others and to put the rest of them in his
pocket. Tell him to hold it up so the writing faces him and to
concentrate on that name. Give him time to follow your
instructions and then glance around and ask, "Have you done
that?"

Immediately turn your head away again. All it takes is a brief glance to spot whether the top of the tag he holds points up, to the right, bottom, or left. You know its number from the position in which it is held, the same position that it was in when you laid the tags out on the table at the start, because the spectator has to turn it that way to read the name written on it. Again, you mentally count clockwise, and reveal the name.

The Head and Tail of It

How it looks:

"Some experiments in extrasensory perception have dealt with how accurately a person may be able to predict the number of times a coin will fall heads or tails," you say, as you invite a spectator to join you in such a test. You hand him a drinking glass, ask him to drop a quarter or any coin from his pocket into it, and then show him what you want him to do. Holding your hand over the mouth of the glass, you shake the coin in all directions, then turn the glass upright and call whether it has fallen heads or tails.

"Try it a few times," you say. "Then we'll run a test series of ten consecutive tosses. Meanwhile I'll attempt to make a prediction."

You write your prediction on a small scratch pad, tear off the slip of paper, fold it, and put it in plain view by sticking the end of the slip into the top of a book that you stand upright on your table. When the spectator says he is ready to start the test, you say, "I'll keep score as you call each toss aloud . . . and everybody—please count to yourselves and keep score of the heads and tails with us."

As the spectator shakes the coin in the glass and calls each toss, you write the results on the pad. When he completes the series of ten, you hand him the pad and say, "Please check this. Just add them up in your mind and see if my totals are correct." Then you ask, "How many times did the coin fall heads and how many times tails?"

He says, perhaps, "Seven and three." You give him your prediction to open and read aloud. He reads: "Seven and three."

What you need:

A tall drinking glass.

A 3-by-5-inch white scratch pad.

A pencil short enough to fit easily into your jacket pocket.

A paperback book.

Three paper clips.

A piece of thick cardboard, such as from a packing carton, cut to a size 4 inches long by 1½ inches wide.

(You should also have a quarter in one of your pockets in case the spectator has no coin of his own to use.)

The secret and setup:

Because of the way they are worded, six prediction slips cover all possibilities. Each slip can be interpreted two ways. A slip that says, SIX AND FOUR, for example, could mean a total of six heads and four tails or six tails and four heads. You lead the spectator, by what you say at the end, to call the totals in the order that you want them called.

The "six-four" slip is the one you write as your prediction during the performance. The other five, to cover the rest of the possibilities, are in a simple index device in your jacket pocket. When you put the pencil into that pocket, you secretly get the needed slip into your fingers and then switch it for the original prediction in a way that will be explained. (Of course, if the spectator should happen to throw a six-four total then no switch is needed, but the slips usually must be switched.)

Start by making up the slips of paper. Put the pad lengthwise on a table. On the first sheet, in capital letters, print: TEN AND NONE. Then, on following sheets: NINE AND ONE, EIGHT AND TWO, SEVEN AND THREE, FIVE AND FIVE. You skip SIX AND FOUR because that will be your original prediction. Tear off each sheet and fold it in half from left to right, in half again, and then from top to bottom.

To understand how the book is used to switch the slips, stand the book upright on end, with the spine to the left. Pick up the pad and write on it: SIX AND FOUR. Tear off the sheet and fold it as you did the others. Stick one end of the folded slip into the top of the book, between the pages, and slide it to the left until it is wedged there with most of it sticking up in full view. That is the way the original prediction will be displayed during the performance.

For now, just to try it, put any of the other folded slips into the right-hand pocket of your jacket. Curl your fingers loosely around it, bring out your hand with the slip concealed by your fingers, and drop your hand naturally to your side. With your left hand, pick up the book and bring it in front of you.

Bring your right hand, with the concealed slip in it, over the top of the book, and with your thumb push the original slip to the right and down between the pages, where it becomes

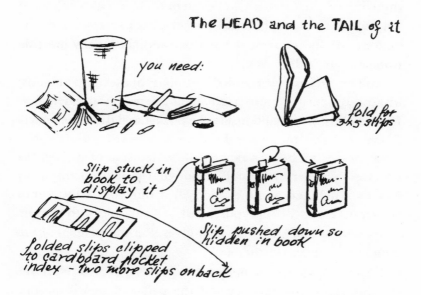

The HEAD and the TAIL of it

you need:

fold for 3×5 slips

Slip stuck in book to display it

Slip pushed down so hidden in book

folded slips clipped to cardboard pocket index - two more slips on back

hidden. Immediately lift that hand to the right and hold it high to show the previously concealed slip, which should be held between your thumb and first finger as if you had merely plucked it from the top of the book. With your left hand, turn the top of the book towards you and drop the book back on the table.

The pocket index to hold the five slips is made with the three paper clips and the piece of thick cardboard. Hold the

cardboard lengthwise and fasten the clips to it by pushing
them up from the bottom as far as they will go, spacing them
left, center and right. Then slide the folded slips into the
clips and against the cardboard in order: 10, 9, 8 on one side
and 7 and 5 on the other. Push them all the way down into
the clips so they remain well-fastened. This index is placed
lengthwise in the right-hand pocket of your jacket, with the
bottoms of the clips at the bottom and the "10, 9, 8" side
toward your body.

Position the index correctly in your pocket and try this:
Take the pencil in your right hand, as you will when performing. Put your hand inside the pocket and drop the pencil.
Bring your thumb down behind the cardboard, towards your
body, and your fingers against the outer side of it. Feel for
the slip you want and pull it out of the clip against your
fingers. Curl them around it loosely, bring your hand out of
your pocket, and drop your hand to your side with the slip
concealed in your fingers. This gives you the proper slip to
switch for the one in the book.

To set things up for performance, have the loaded index
in your right-hand pocket and the pad and pencil in your
left-hand pocket. The glass and book are on your table. The
book should appear to be one that is just lying there for use
in some other routine, not deliberately put there for this.

What you do:

Give the spectator the glass, have him drop the coin into
it, and demonstrate what you want him to do. Say, "Try it a
few times. Then we'll run a series of ten consecutive tosses.
Meanwhile, I'll make a prediction."

Take the pad and pencil from your left-hand pocket. Hold it close so nobody can see what you write and print: SIX AND FOUR. Tear the sheet from the pad, put the pad and pencil on the table, and fold the paper. Glance around as if looking for somewhere to place it. Casually pick up the book, stand it on end, and tuck the folded slip part way into the top and leave it there.

Tell the spectator: "I'll keep score as you call each toss aloud. . . ." Make a score sheet on the pad by printing HEADS at the top left, TAILS at the top right, and drawing a vertical line down the page between them. As he calls each toss, make a mark under the proper heading. When he calls the last one, mark that, and then add them up and write the total at the bottom of each side. Give him the pad and say: "Please check this. Just add them up in your mind and see if my totals are correct."

With your right hand, drop the pencil into your pocket. Think of the higher number of the two totals and get the proper slip from the index into your fingers. Curl your fingers around it, bring your hand out with the slip concealed, and drop your hand to your side. While the spectator is mentally adding the marks on the score sheet to check your totals, pick up the book, make the switch, and hold up the slip that was concealed in your fingers.

The questions you ask him now must be phrased so his answers will match the wording on the slip you are holding. All you have to remember is which total was higher, heads or tails, and ask for that one first.

If he tossed more heads than tails, you ask: "How many times did the coin fall heads?" Wait for his answer. Then ask:

"And how many times did it fall tails?" But if he tossed more tails than heads, you reverse the questions and first ask: "How many times did the coin fall tails?" Then you ask: "And how many times did it fall heads?"

You repeat each of his answers as he gives them, for example: "Seven heads . . . three tails," and then say, "The totals then are seven and three—is that correct?" Hand him the slip. "Will you please read this aloud?—exactly what I predicted?"

He reads: "Seven and three."

Puzzle Me This

How it looks:

"I don't know how many of you are crossword-puzzle addicts," you say, "but for those of you who enjoy doing them the hard way I'd like to suggest this—instead of working out the puzzle with a pencil, try using ESP. . . . I've tried it, but I'll admit that I cheat a little. I need somebody to look at the words and to mentally spell them out for me."

You ask a spectator if he will try it with you and give him a large card on which there is a printed crossword puzzle with its definitions. "It won't be a puzzle for you because all the words are written in," you explain. "You'll see that there are seventy-one definitions and matching words, across and down." From your table, you pick up some cards and spread them in your hands to show them. "On these office file cards, I have printed the letters of the alphabet—two complete alphabets plus a few additional cards for the most commonly used letters."

Turning to the audience, you ask someone to call out any number between one and seventy-one, and then ask the first spectator to look for the word at that number in the puzzle he is holding. "Read the definition to yourself, please," you say, "and then find the proper word, across or down, and concentrate on it. Make sure you have the right one, because I can only get whatever letters are in your mind—and if you are wrong, I will be."

Sorting through the alphabet cards, you remove one, hesitate, and put it back. "I'm not getting your thoughts clearly. . . . So that I will know how many letters I need, will you count the letters in the word to yourself, the number of spaces?—but don't tell me. Let me try to tell you what you're thinking." You close your eyes a moment. "You are thinking seven spaces—a seven-letter word. Am I correct? . . . Good. Now think of just the first letter. I'm getting it now. Think of the next letter, please."

One by one, you draw out letters from the pack of alphabet cards, putting those you choose facedown on the table, and finally putting the rest aside. "I may have missed a letter or two," you say, "but I think I got most of them. . . . First, will you please read the definition of the word aloud—then, very slowly, spell the word for us, letter by letter."

As he spells aloud, you show each of the cards you selected and they match exactly so that you spell out with him the word he had in mind.

What you need:

A fairly large crossword puzzle and its definitions, cut from a newspaper, magazine, or puzzle book. You will also need the printed solution to the puzzle.

Poster board to mount the puzzle upon.

A self-sealing sheet of clear plastic.

A package of 100 blank 3-by-5-inch office index file cards.

A black felt-tip pen.

A rubber band.

Scissors.

The use of a typewriter.

The secret and setup:

All the words of the puzzle are listed by their proper numbers on several typed "cue cards" that are put with the pack of alphabet cards you hold. While searching through the cards for the letters to remove and put on the table, you secretly read the word that matches the number called aloud, and then just draw out the cards to spell that word.

Begin by filling out the crossword puzzle. Work from the definitions and the printed solution. Be careful not to mark over any of the numbers. Write the proper letters with the pen in all the spaces across and down to complete the puzzle. Place the completed and neatly trimmed puzzle, with its accompanying definitions, on a slightly larger piece of poster board. Cut a piece of the self-sealing clear plastic sheet to cover it and smooth that over the puzzle to seal it to the board. This protects it so that the puzzle can be used for many performances.

Make up the pack of alphabet cards, by turning the stack of file cards with their narrow ends top and bottom, and vertically printing one letter of the alphabet on each card. The letters should be large and bold for easy visibility, but there is no need to spend a lot of time drawing them since they are meant to look as though you just quickly penned them. At the top left corner of each card, print the same letter again, much smaller, like the corner index of a playing card, so you won't have to spread out their full faces to find letters you want.

Altogether you will need two complete alphabets of twenty-six letters each, plus two additional *E* cards and one additional card for each of these letters: *A, B, I, O, S.* With those, you can spell almost all words, including the unusual ones often found in crossword puzzles. But add one blank card to the back of the pack. In the unlikely event that you do need some additional letter when performing, just explain to the audience that you have run out of *E*'s, or whatever it is, and take out your pen and make one by printing that letter on the extra blank card.

Use the typewriter to prepare the "cue cards." All the typing should be in capital letters and each line should start at the far left, at the very edge of the card. Take a blank card, roll it into the typewriter with a narrow end at the top, and at the far left type: ACROSS-1. Now look at your completed puzzle, find the first word under the "Across" definitions, space the card down a line, and type the proper number and word, such as: 1-LAMA. Directly beneath that, type the next number and word. Continue until you come to the bottom of the card, then start a second card, and at the top far left of that type: ACROSS-2.

When you have finished all the "Across" words, type cards in a similar way for the "Down" words. All the words in the average puzzle can be typed vertically on four 3-by-5-inch cards, one word to a line. But don't crowd the listings. Use more cards if you need them.

Add the typed cards to the back of all the alphabet cards,

behind the extra blank one. Put a rubber band around the
pack of them and have the cards and puzzle on your table.

What you do:

Give the spectator the puzzle. Explain that all the words
are written in and that there are seventy-one (or whatever
number there are) definitions and matching words, across
and down. Pick up the alphabet cards and show some of their
faces to the audience as you explain what they are, but don't
expose the typed "cue cards" at the back. Square them up
and put them on the table for a moment.

Ask someone in the audience to call out any number between one and the highest number in your puzzle. Tell the
spectator who is holding the puzzle to look for that number.
Repeat the number and say to him: "Look for that number
under the definitions for the words that go across. Is there a
word that goes across for that number?"

Wait for him to answer. If he says that there *is* an "Across"
word for that number, tell him to read the definition to himself, and then to find the proper word in the puzzle and to
concentrate on it. But if he says there *is not* an "Across"
word at that number, you say: "Then please look for that
number under the definitions for the words that go down—
read the definition to yourself and then find that word in the
puzzle and concentrate on it."

This is important, because for some numbers there are
two words, one that goes across and the other that goes
down. By asking him to look first at the "Across" definitions,
you eliminate the duplicated "Down" numbers. In either
case, you learn from his answer whether he is looking at a

word that goes across or down. "Make sure you have the right one," you say, "because I can only get whatever letters are in your mind—and if you are wrong, I will be."

Take up the pack of alphabet cards again and hold them close with their faces toward you. As you pretend to look for the letters of the word the spectator has in mind, spread out some of the cards at the right, then some at the center, then spread the typed cards at the back as far as is necessary to read the "cue" words. Because all the typing is at the extreme left edges, you won't have to spread them much.

Look at the "Across" or "Down" listings, as the case may be, for the number that was called from the audience. You have a legitimate excuse to take your time and look directly at the typed cards, since you are supposed to be searching through the alphabet cards for the letters of the thought-of word. When you find the number and matching word, don't try to memorize the entire spelling at once. Remember the first letter of it and count the total number of letters in it to yourself.

Close up the cards, shake your head, and say: "I'm not getting your thoughts clearly. . . . So that I will know how many letters I need, will you count the letters in the word to yourself?—but don't tell me. Let me try to tell you what you're thinking."

Then announce that it is a seven-letter word, or whatever it may be. Ask him to think of the first letter, tell him his thoughts are coming more clearly, and spread the cards with their faces toward you as before. Remove an alphabet card for the first letter and without showing it put it facedown on the table. Again look directly at your "cue card," memorize the next two letters, and after hesitation and fingering of the alphabet cards, remove those letters and put them on the table, facedown on top of the one already there.

Continue until you have chosen all the letters necessary to spell the word. Square up the rest and put the pack aside. Take the chosen cards from the table, hold them stacked together with their faces toward you, and ask the spectator to read the definition of the word aloud. Then have him spell out the word and stress your request to spell it *very slowly*.

Turn the cards one at a time to show the audience each letter. After you show the first, put it face out behind the others in your hand, and continue to do that with the rest, one by one. Match your cards, letter by letter, to his spelling of the word he has in mind.

3

THE MIND
CONTROLS

The Dice of No Chance

How it looks:

"Does chance alone always decide the numbers that will come up when dice are rolled?" you ask, as you shake a pair of dice and roll them out on the table. "Is there any power of mind that can control the turn of the dice with predictable results?"

Two spectators are invited to join in an experiment and to stand at the sides of the table. Each is asked to take one of the dice. Taking turns, each rolls his single die, calling out the numbers that come up. You write each number as it is called on the face of an envelope in your hand, and show each number written.

"Now let's add all the numbers that turned up by chance," you say, "if it *was* only by chance." You add the column of figures written on the face of the envelope and ask one of the spectators to check your addition and then to call out the total.

He says: "Forty-one."

"Please open the envelope," you tell him. "Inside it, you will find a card. Will you take that out—and read it aloud?"

He removes the card from the envelope and reads: "If the dice *could* be mentally controlled—it might be possible to predict that the total of all the numbers rolled would be exactly . . . forty-one."

What you need:

A letter-sized envelope, about 4-by-7½ inches.
A card that will fit inside it.
Dice with spots large enough to be read easily.
A slip of paper.
A pen that can be clipped into your pocket.

The secret and setup:

You decide on any two-digit number in advance and use that for your prediction. As each spectator in turn rolls his die, you write the number he calls, but you also mentally add them as you go along. Since the highest number that can be rolled with a single die is six, you stop the experiment as soon as the total comes to within six or more of what you predicted. Then when you add the column of figures on the envelope, you secretly write in whatever number is needed so that the total will add up to what you want it to be.

If your predicted number is forty-one, for example, you stop the rolling of dice whenever the total reaches thirty-five or more. At that point the total may be anything from thirty-five to forty. If it happens to be exactly thirty-five, you know you have to add six; if it happens to be thirty-six, you need to add five; if it happens to be thirty-seven, you would add four, and so on. You simply subtract whatever the total happens to be from your predicted total of forty-one and then write in the difference when you add up the column of figures.

But if you wrote it in at the bottom of the column, the spectators might notice that it wasn't the last number rolled. So at the start, when you first begin to write the figures on the envelope, you leave a space beneath the first number. Then when you openly add up the figures, you do it from the bottom of the column up, and when you come to that space near the top, you quickly write in the figure you need. This is covered, as will be explained, by the way you check off each figure with your pen as you add them aloud.

To set things up, choose a two-digit number, somewhere around forty so the rolling of the dice won't be too prolonged. Print your prediction on the card, using that number and the wording given, and put the card into the envelope. Make a note of the predicted total and also of the number that is six less than that so you will know when to stop the experiment. Write them on the slip of paper so you can look at them just before the performance to refresh your memory. Have the envelope and pen in your inside left-hand pocket and the dice in your outer right-hand pocket.

What you do:

(For explanation, the number forty-one will be used as an example of the predicted total.)

Take the dice from your pocket. Shake them and roll them

out on the table as you question whether there is some psychic power that might control the turn of the dice. Have two spectators stand at the sides of the table while you stand between them in back of it. Remove the envelope and pen from your pocket and hold the envelope face up in your left hand with its narrow edges at the top and bottom.

Ask the spectator at your left to pick up one of the dice and tell him to "shake it, roll it out, and call the number."

The DICE of NO CHANCE

number secretly added
prediction envelope
face of envelope
what you need

Write whatever that number is at the top of the envelope and show him what you have written. Then ask the spectator to your right to take the other die and do the same thing. Write his number on the envelope, but down a little beneath the first one, so there is enough space between them to secretly put in your own number later. Turn the envelope so that the spectator can see what you have written.

Mentally add the first two numbers, and continue to total the numbers in your mind as each spectator rolls his die and you write and show the numbers called. This is easy mental arithmetic since all the numbers are single digits. As soon as your total comes to thirty-five or more, stop the experiment with that roll of the die. Write whatever the last rolled number was, show it to the spectator who rolled it, and say, "Now let's add all the numbers that turned up by chance — if it *was* only chance."

Step back a little so the two spectators can't watch over your shoulders, and hold the envelope close as you bring the pen to it. Add the column of figures from the bottom up and make a small check mark to the right of each figure as you add them aloud. "Three and six are nine . . . and five are fourteen," you might say, making a check to the right of each, "and six are twenty, and five are twenty-five, plus three. . . ."

When you come to the space near the top, write your own number into it, make a check, add it in aloud, and without pausing go on to add aloud the final number at the top of the column. Then draw a line at the bottom and write the total beneath it, but don't say what it is. Turn to either of the spectators, give him the envelope, and say, "Will you check my addition and then call out the total?"

He calls: "Forty-one." You tell him to open the envelope, remove the card he will find inside it, and to please read aloud what it says. He reads your prediction that the rolls of the dice will total exactly forty-one.

Do As I Think

How it looks:

There are three chairs positioned at the front of the room, each with a large numbered card to number them 1, 2, and 3. "I want you, if you will, to walk completely around all three

chairs and then sit in whichever you choose," you tell a spectator brought up from the audience. "Just walk around them
once, make up your mind, remove the number, and sit down."

He sits in, say, chair Number 3. "I have something that I
wish you would keep for a minute or two," you say. "In my
pocket, there is a sealed envelope. Will you remove it, please —
and satisfy yourself that there is nothing else in my pocket?"
Pointing to your pocket, you hold out your jacket so he can
remove the sealed envelope.

From your table, you take another, larger envelope, and
explain that it contains a knife, a fork, and a spoon. "One of
them has something about it that is quite different from
either of the others, as you will see in a moment," you say.
"Because of that, I won't show them to you yet. But I want
you to imagine that you're seated at your dinner table, enjoy-
ing a meal. Which one would you choose to pick up—the
knife, fork, or spoon?"

He may say: "The knife." You take it from the large envelope and give it to him. "I'm glad you chose that one," you
say, "because there's something wrapped around the handle
of it—a little note, from me to you." You remove the fork
and spoon from the envelope and show that there is nothing
wrapped around the handles of either of those. "Will you
open my note, please, and read it aloud?"

The spectator unfastens the rubber band that is snapped
around it, opens your note, and reads: "I am writing this
note twenty-four hours before we will begin our experiment.
I have made up my mind that, when we meet, I shall mentally
direct you to choose the knife you now have, rather than the
fork or the spoon. . . . P.S. — There is something more. . . ."

"Yes, there is something more," you say, as he finishes reading it to the audience. "That sealed envelope you have been keeping since we began this experiment—will you open it up now, please? Take out the card you will find inside it and read aloud what I wrote on it yesterday."

He reads: "I am certain that if you have had your mind open to my directed thoughts—you will now be seated in chair Number 3."

What you need:

Three 7-by-11-inch pieces of white poster board.

A bright red marking crayon.

A knife, fork, and spoon.

Six 3-by-5-inch blank index file cards.

A 9-by-12-inch manila clasp envelope.

Three 2½-by-4¼-inch coin envelopes with end-opening flaps.

Three rubber bands.

A pair of scissors.

The use of a typewriter.

The secret and setup:

There are three sealed predictions, one for each chair, in three different pockets of your jacket, and you simply ask the spectator to remove an envelope from the proper pocket, according to which chair he chooses to sit in. There are also three different predictions for the knife, fork, and spoon— one wrapped around the handle of each. You give him the chosen one with the prediction still wrapped around it, but in removing the other two to show them, you slide their predictions off and leave them hidden inside the big envelope.

Because the routine switches the order of reading the two predictions, the audience should have forgotten by the time the spectator opens the sealed envelope that it wasn't given him to hold until after he sat in the chair that that prediction names. One effect strengthens the other and helps to conceal the very simple methods used in both.

DO as I THINK

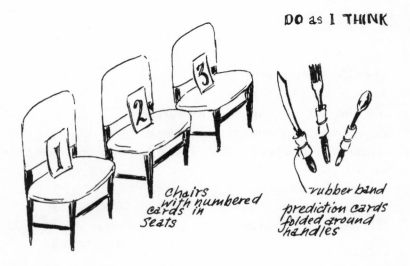

Chairs with numbered cards in seats

rubber band prediction cards folded around handles

Number the poster boards 1, 2, and 3 with the red marker, making each number big and bold. Put one of the blank file cards lengthwise into the typewriter and type the note that will be wrapped around the knife handle, worded as previously explained. Type a second card for the fork, substituting the words ". . . choose the fork you now have, rather than the knife or the spoon," and then type a third card worded to predict the choice of the spoon.

Fold the "knife" card lengthwise from top to bottom, roll

it around the handle of the knife, and fasten it there by winding a rubber band around the outside of the card. Do the same with each of the other cards and the fork and spoon. You will have to experiment a little to discover how tightly the folded cards should be wrapped around the handles so that they won't shake loose and yet can be pushed down off the end easily with your thumb and fingers. The rubber bands provide some "give" for sliding the tubelike cards off the handles. When you have them in place, drop the banded knife, fork, and spoon into the large envelope and fasten the clasp.

Each of the three remaining file cards must be cut to a 2-by-4-inch size with the scissors to fit inside one of the coin envelopes, but it is easier to type the notes on them first and then cut them. Center the typing on them to allow for the cutting. Write the first, with the wording given, to predict that the spectator will be sitting in chair Number 1, the second for chair Number 2, the third for Number 3. Slide one card into each envelope and seal the envelopes.

Put envelope "1" in the outer breast pocket of your jacket, pushed down out of sight, envelope "2" in the inside left-hand pocket, "3" in the inside right-hand pocket. Have the large envelope containing the banded knife, fork, and spoon on your table. Before the performance, position three chairs of any kind so they will be facing the audience, and prop up the number cards in the chairs by resting the bottom end of each card on the seat and the top against the chair back.

What you do:

Explain to the spectator that you want him to walk around the three chairs, make up his mind which he will choose, remove the number card from that one, and sit down. By the time he is seated, you should be standing beside him, holding open the left or right side of your jacket to point to the pocket if the proper envelope is in one of those inside pockets, or else to your outer breast pocket if the envelope you want him to take is there.

Stand at the side of his chair, rather than directly in front of him, so you don't block the view of the audience. Bend down enough so he can reach into your pocket and say, "In my pocket, there is a sealed envelope. Will you remove it, please, and satisfy yourself that there is nothing else in my pocket?" When he has taken it, ask him to keep it "for a minute or two."

Pick up the large envelope from your table and rattle it a little so the knife, fork, and spoon "clink" inside it as you explain what it contains. Turn it so the clasp is toward you and hold the bottom of the envelope with your left hand. Unfasten the clasp with your right hand and spread the top of the envelope wide so you can look down into it but he can't. Tell him one of the three items has something different about it, which is why you won't show it to him yet, and ask him to choose.

When he calls out which one he wants, look down into the envelope, put your hand in, take the chosen one by the end opposite the handle, and bring it out. Hold it up so the audience can see the note banded around the handle as you point it out to the spectator. Ask him to remove the rubber band and unfold your note and read it aloud.

While he is doing that, put your hand into the envelope and take either of the two that remain by the middle of its handle. Inside the envelope, push the banded card down and slide it off the handle with your thumb and fingers, and immediately bring that piece of silverware out. Casually hold it up and show that it has no note wrapped around it, *but don't say anything about it.* Put it into your left hand, which is holding the envelope. Then take out the other one, minus its banded card, to show it in the same way.

When the spectator finishes reading from the note that there is "something more," you say: "Yes, there *is* something more. That sealed envelope that you have been keeping since we began this experiment. . . ." Ask him to open it and read aloud from the card you "wrote yesterday." He reads your prediction that he will be in the specific chair in which he is seated.

Spy Hunt

How it looks:

"Let's imagine we're all secret agents—international spies," you say to four spectators who have been asked to take part in an experiment with you. "We're all hunting for the secret plans that have been hidden among the papers in a hotel room."

You take a paper bag from your pocket, open it up, and spill out on the table five small rolls of paper. "Five little strips of paper, all tightly rolled, each sealed with tape. Please look them over—but don't open any of them yet. You'll see that outwardly they appear identical. But one of these slips— only one—contains the secret plans."

Dropping them back into the bag, one at a time, you mix them thoroughly. "Imagine that the hotel room is dark. It would be too dangerous to turn on the lights. As spies, we are all after the same secret plans — the papers that are somewhere in that room. We all have an equal chance of getting our hands on them — unless one of us somehow might mentally influence the decisions of the others."

You ask each of the spectators in turn to dip his hand into the bag and take out one of the slips of paper. They may change their minds, put back the one taken and choose another, or trade among themselves, until each is satisfied to keep the slip that he holds. "Each of you has chosen one," you say, "and that leaves one for me." You take the last one that remains.

They all unroll their papers and hold them up for the audience to read what is written on them. Printed in large letters on one spectator's strip of paper are the words: LAUNDRY LIST. The others read: SUBWAY MAP, HOTEL BILL, SHOPPING LIST. You unroll yours and show it. On it are the words: SECRET PLANS.

What you need:

Five strips of white paper, each about 15 inches long and 2½ inches wide. You can cut them from a large sheet of paper or use strips from a blank roll of adding-machine tape.

A flat-bottomed brown paper bag, about 5-by-10 inches in size.

Transparent tape.

A broad-tipped black marking pen.

The secret and setup:

Although the strips of paper are rolled and taped so they all look alike to the spectators who casually examine them, the one marked SECRET PLANS is slightly torn so that you can tell it from the others at a glance. When you drop that one into the bag, bend it in half; later secretly draw it up beneath your fingers as you hold the bag at the top. It remains hidden under your fingers while each of the spectators takes one of the other slips from the bag, and at the end it becomes the only one left for you to take.

With the marking pen, in bold black letters as large as will fit on the paper, print the words SECRET PLANS on one of the strips. Roll it up tightly from end to end. Wind a strip of tape around the center to keep it rolled, leaving an end of tape that you can bend down and stick together to form a little tab so it can be pulled loose to quickly open up the roll.

Put that aside a moment and prepare the other strips in a similar way, but print different words on each in turn: LAUNDRY LIST, SUBWAY MAP, HOTEL BILL, SHOP-PING LIST. Now take the SECRET PLANS roll, lift one overlapping end, and tear the paper slightly right along the edge of the tape that binds it. A tiny tear is enough—just a fraction of an inch; it should appear accidental, yet you will spot it instantly when that slip is mixed on the table with the others.

Drop that slip and the others into the paper bag, fold the bag, and have it in your pocket.

What you do:

Invite four spectators to join you in the spy hunt for the secret plans and have two of them stand at each side of your table. Open the bag and spill out the rolls of paper as you explain that each strip is sealed with tape and that only one contains the plans.

Rest the bottom of the opened bag on the palm of your left hand. Pick up the papers one at a time with your other hand and put them into the bag. When you come to the one that you recognize as the SECRET PLANS slip, bend it between your thumb and fingers inside the bag as you drop it to the bottom with the others. Just quickly double it, squeezing hard so the two ends touch, and immediately bring your hand out to pick up another slip from the table to drop into the bag.

When you have dropped them all in, shake the bag as you explain that you want to mix them thoroughly. Put your right hand into the bag again and mix the slips around in the bottom, feeling for the bent one. Draw that into your fingers, bring your hand up flatly against the inside of the bag, and take hold of the bag at the top with that hand. Your fingers remain inside at the top, your thumb on the outside, and the slip stays hidden under your fingers, pressed against the inside of the bag at the top.

Holding it that way, shake the bag again, and ask one of the spectators to put his hand in and mix the slips around at the bottom. Have him take out any slip he wishes and tell him, "You can change your mind. Put that back and take another one, if you'd rather." When he is satisfied with the one he has, ask each of the other spectators to reach in and take a slip.

By the time you reach the fourth spectator, there will be only one slip still in the bottom of the bag instead of the two that he thinks are there, because the secret one is hidden

SPY HUNT

slight tear

rolled strip fastened with tape

bent when dropped into bag

Laundry List

Subway Map

Hotel Bill

Shopping List

Secret Plans

fingers hide slip against inside top of paper bag

under your fingers that hold the bag. You are aware of that fact, but he isn't, and to keep him from feeling around in the bag, you hurry him a bit. "Just dip your hand in and take one," you tell him, "and hold it up high."

As soon as he has a slip, move the bag away, shake it, and let the hidden slip drop from under your fingers so it falls to the bottom of the bag. Put the bag on the table and leave it there while you invite the spectators to swap their slips with each other, if they wish. Then say, "Each of you has chosen one—and that leaves one for me."

Let the audience see that your hand is empty by making a casual gesture with it as you speak. Reach into the bag and remove the slip, straightening it between your thumb and fingers inside the bag as you take it out. Don't worry if it remains slightly bent. Just hold it up high and keep it in plain view.

Have each of the spectators unroll his slip. "Open it out between your hands and hold it up so everyone can read it," you say. "What's yours? . . . Oh, I'm sorry—in the dark, you seem to have picked up the laundry list. . . . And you, sir, have a subway map—but not the secret plans we were after. . . . The next gentleman seems to be on his way to do a little shopping. . . . And you're stuck with the hotel bill—I am sorry about that."

Finally you unroll yours and hold it stretched between your hands to display the words: SECRET PLANS.

Mix-Matched Socks

How it looks:

"This is an experiment you might like to try at home—the next time you sort out your laundry," you say, as you display four pairs of socks: black, white, brown, and green. "I can't promise that it will make your household chores easier, but it might make them more interesting. I'm going to ask several of you to attempt to project your thoughts to me—so as to control a series of decisions I will make."

Four spectators are invited to join in the experiment. While your back is to them, each is asked to step up to the table and to select any pair of socks. He is to hide one sock of the pair in his pocket and give the other one to you, behind your back. When all four have done that, you ask the first spectator to take the whole batch of socks you are holding behind your back.

"I want you to keep one of them," you explain, "but not the sock that matches the color of the one you have hidden in your pocket. Some other color—one that doesn't match yours." That spectator then passes the remaining odd socks to the next person, and so on, until each is holding a sock of a different color from the one he has in his pocket. "Now will you all trade with each other—just swap the sock you have for the one your neighbor has? . . . Have you done that? Are you each holding one sock again?"

You then face them, moving along the line as you attempt to determine the color each is projecting in his thoughts, and you sort out the socks, taking a sock from one and handing it to another, changing your mind and shifting the order a few times.

Each spectator finally is left holding one sock. All together, at your signal, they reach into their pockets and bring out the hidden socks to hold beside the ones you have given them. All four pairs match, color for color, down the line.

What you need:

Four pairs of socks: black, white, brown, and green, or any other distinctive colors. They should be of fairly thick material.

A roll of 1-inch-wide double-faced *cloth* adhesive tape (sticky on both sides).

A pair of scissors.

The secret and setup:

The sticky cloth tape is used to make a bead-sized lump inside each sock of a pair in a known position. When each sock is first handed to you behind your back, you know the color of the matching sock that the spectator has hidden in his pocket by secretly feeling for the little lumps. The rest is buildup and presentation.

Since the sticky tape is easily removed, any socks may be borrowed for use as long as they are not transparent when held in the light. For explanation, they will be referred to here by the colors previously listed.

Take the black pair and turn both socks inside out. Cut a 1-inch piece of the double-faced cloth tape and wad it into a tiny ball. Now cut off another 1-inch piece of tape. Put the little ball at the toe of one of the socks, cover it with the second square of tape, and press that firmly to the sock so it stays in place. Then turn the sock right side out and press the tape with your fingers from the outside so it sticks to both inner surfaces. Do the same thing with the matching sock of the black pair.

Fix small lumps of tape in a similar way inside the *heels* of both socks of the white pair, halfway down the *legs* of the brown pair, nearer to the inside *tops* of the green pair. When that has been done, you should be able to learn the color of any sock held in your hands behind your back by running your hand along the length of it from top to toe, remembering that if you feel a lump in the *toe*, it is the black one, and so on for each of the others according to where the lump is.

Roll up each pair, tucked into a neat bundle, and have them all on your table.

What you do:

Display the socks, opening them out to show them, and replace them on the table in pairs. Ask the four spectators to join in the experiment and have them stand two at each side of the table. Explain to the first spectator on your right that you want him to select any pair he wishes without letting you see them. Move forward a few steps, so your back is toward the table and the four spectators but you are facing the audience. When he says he has chosen a pair, tell him: "Please hide one of those socks in your pocket—either one of the pair—and then hand me the other behind my back."

Take the sock from him, keeping your hands behind you, and instruct the second spectator to do the same thing. While he is following your instructions, feel for the lump in the sock the first spectator has given you. Do it casually, by pulling it through your fingers as if you were unconsciously toying with it as you talk. Mentally tag the first spectator according to the sock you know he has chosen. For example, if you feel a lump in the toe you know it is black and that he has the matching black one in his pocket, so you think of him as "Mister Black."

By now, you have taken the sock from the second spectator, and you feel for the lump in that and mentally think of

him, say, as "Mister Brown" or "Mister Green." Continue in
the same way with the two spectators standing at the left of
your table.

Finally give the whole batch of socks to the first spectator,
keeping your back toward him as he takes them from you.
Tell him you want him to keep one of the socks, but not one
the same color as the sock he has hidden in his pocket. "Mix
them all up and take any one," you say, "but some other
color—one that doesn't match yours. Then please hand the
rest of them to your neighbor."

Have each of the remaining spectators do the same. Then
tell them to trade socks with each other, swapping them down
the line. Give them time to do that and ask, "Are you each
holding one now?"

Turn to face the spectators and say: "Perhaps the one you
are now holding happens to match the one you have hidden
in your pocket. Maybe so—maybe not. But I want each of you
to please think of the color of the sock hidden in your
pocket—not the color of the sock in your hand, but the one
in your pocket. . . . Your thoughts will control the decisions
I make."

Move from one to another. If the sock he holds doesn't
match the one you know he has in his pocket, take it from him
and give it to the person who does have that color in his
pocket, switching them around from person to person until
you know they all match. Pretend to make a mistake. Change
the order a few times.

Step to the side and say: "I believe I have read your
thoughts. I'm not sure. Maybe I haven't gotten all of them."

Hold up your hand. "When I snap my fingers, will you all please reach into your pockets and pull out the socks you have been hiding there?" Snap your fingers. "Now. All together— hold both hands up high, please." Look at them a moment and then turn to the audience. "They do match. All of them. Four out of four."

4

FROM
MIND TO MIND

Telepathy for One

How it looks:

You are alone with one of your friends, someplace where the person can sit at a table directly across from you, and you turn the conversation to psychic phenomena and telepathy.

"If you came up to me on the street and challenged me to read your mind, I know I couldn't do it," you say, "because you might be thinking any of hundreds of different things and I wouldn't know where to start. But if we both agreed in advance that you were to think of something specific—such as somebody's name. . . . Let's try it. Just for fun."

From your pocket, you take out a wallet, and sort through the cards in it until you find one with a blank side. "This will do," you say, pushing the card across to him, and giving him a pen or pencil if he hasn't one. "I'll turn my head and you just print a name on the card. Print the name of someone you're sure I don't know. Then turn the card so the writing is facedown and put it at the center of the table."

You turn your head or stand up and turn your back to him. When he says he has written the name and turned the card over, you sit facing him across the table again. "I'll cover it with this," you say, picking up the wallet and dropping it on top of the card. "I want you to imagine that there is a big red spot, right here." You point to the face of the wallet. "Fix your eyes on that to center your thoughts and then concentrate on the name."

Slowly you begin to "read" his thoughts. You get one letter of the name, then another, and finally reveal the entire name.

What you need:

A large "secretary-type" wallet, about 4½-by-8 inches in size, with a pocket inside that will hold an assortment of cards.

Half a dozen business cards. Preferably these should be cards of various kinds and sizes, some with one side blank and some penciled with notes, such as normally might be carried in a wallet.

Double-faced (sticky both sides) transparent tape.

A pen or pencil.

The secret and setup:

The wallet has a small strip of double-faced tape stuck to one face of it. When you cover the person's card with the wallet and point to an imaginary red spot, the card sticks to the bottom of the wallet. You tilt the wallet up on edge as you explain how you want the person to center his thoughts on the "spot," and the card lifts with it so you can secretly read the name he has written on the card.

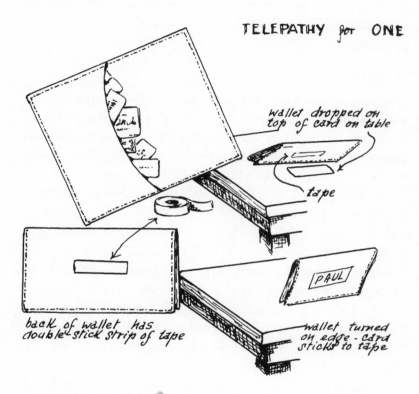

TELEPATHY for ONE

wallet dropped on top of card on table

tape

PAUL

back of wallet has double-stick strip of tape

wallet turned on edge - card sticks to tape

There is little to prepare. Start with the wallet on a table, turned like a book you were about to read, narrow ends top and bottom. Fasten a 1½-inch strip of double-faced tape vertically to the outside center of that face of the wallet. Rub the ball of your thumb over the tape a few times to make it slightly less sticky. Then open the wallet and put the assorted cards inside it.

Put the wallet into the inside right-hand pocket of your jacket, so the taped side of it is toward your body, with the open edges of the wallet at the rear of the pocket. Have the pen or pencil clipped into that pocket.

What you do:

With your friend seated directly across from you at a table, remove the wallet from your pocket with your left hand. Keep it upright, tape at the back. Transfer it to your right hand and put it on the table with its taped side down so that its *long* edges are at the top and bottom. Open it, sort through the cards, select one with a blank side, close the wallet, and leave it in that lengthwise position.

Slide the card, blank side up, across the table to him. Ask if he has a pen or pencil, and if he hasn't, give him yours. Turn your head or stand with your back to him and say, "Just print the name on the card. Print the name of someone I don't know." You are telling him twice to "print" the name, to avoid handwriting that might be difficult to read quickly. "Then turn the card so the writing is facedown and put it at the center of the table."

When he has done that, sit facing him again and say, "I'll cover it with this." Pick up the wallet with your right hand at the long edge that is toward you and drop it on top of the card. As you do, glance to see that the tape will come in contact with the card. The wallet should lie horizontally, covering the card lengthwise.

"I want you to imagine that there is a big red spot right

here," you say. Point to the center of the wallet and press down with the tip of your finger so that the card beneath it sticks to the tape. With your left hand, tilt the wallet up without lifting it off the table, and continue to tap the face of the wallet with your right finger, pointing to the imaginary "spot." Tell him, "Fix your eyes on that to center your thoughts and then concentrate on the name."

As you speak, secretly look at the card that is stuck to the back of the up-tilted wallet and read the name he has printed. You should be able to gain the information at a glance, even if the printing appears upside down to you, which sometimes happens. The instant you know what the name is, immediately drop the wallet flat so that it lies over the card again.

Pretend to get one or two letters and finally reveal the entire name. With your left hand tilt up the wallet, and bring your right hand underneath to flick the card free of the tape with your fingers. Lift the wallet away with your left hand, pick up the card with your right hand, and turn the card over. Read the name aloud as if to confirm that you "read his mind" correctly, and put the wallet away in your pocket as you hand him the card, to keep if he wants it.

Needle in a Mental Haystack

How it looks:

"In this dictionary there are more than seventy-five thousand words," you say, as you show a paperback dictionary and hand it to one of a group of spectators. "In a

moment, I will ask you to open it to any page at all . . . and
to choose any word at all from that page. When you have
decided on a word—don't say it aloud, don't even whisper
it. Just point to it on the page and show it to the person
seated at your right."

You turn to that person seated next to him. In your hand,
you have a self-erasing Magic Slate, the kind with a plastic
face on which things that are written can be erased simply
by lifting up the top plastic sheets. "What I want you to do is
to copy down that word he points to and show it to a few of
the others around you, so that you will all have it in your
minds," you explain. "Then erase what you have written—
like this—so the word remains only in your minds."

To demonstrate, you write something on the Magic Slate
and lift the top sheets to erase it, then give him the slate and
move away with your head turned. "All right. . . . Open the
dictionary. Any page—any word. Have you found one? Point
to it on the page so your neighbor is sure which one you
mean. . . . And you, sir, will you copy it on the slate, please,
and show it to the others near you—then erase it? Have you
done that?"

You take back the dictionary and plastic slate and return to
the front of the room. "I'm sure you'll agree that for me to
search through your minds to find one word out of seventy-
five thousand is a little like searching for a needle in a mental
haystack—which is why I wanted more than one of you to
think of that word. Will you think of it now, please, as I turn
these pages, and try to guide me to it mentally."

Opening the dictionary, you turn it to a page, glance at
the words, shake your head, and turn to another page.

"Let's try it another way," you say, putting down the dictionary. "Just think of the first few letters in the word."

You pick up the slate, show it blank, write a letter or two,
then erase and start over. You write several more letters, show
them, and ask, "Am I right so far?" Taking the dictionary
again, you turn the pages, finally run your finger down a
page and stop. Aloud, you hesitantly begin to spell out the
letters. Quickly, you take up the slate and print the correct
word across it. "One word in seventy-five thousand," you say.
"Is that the word?"

What you need:

A self-erasing plastic surfaced Magic Slate, about 6-by-8
inches. These are available in stationery stores and at toy
counters. You will also need the plastic writing stylus that
comes with it.

A paperback pocket dictionary.

Some facial tissues.

The secret and setup:

Although lifting the top plastic sheets instantly erases the
visible writing on a Magic Slate, a clear impression of it
remains on the black waxed backing directly beneath. By
gently rubbing and polishing that waxed black surface with a
tissue before the performance, all previous marks can be
removed. When the spectator writes the word and erases it,
the impression of the word remains, hidden under the top
plastic sheets.

Each time you attempt to write a few letters while trying to
"read" the spectators' thoughts, you naturally lift up the top

sheets to clear the slate, and you secretly glance at the impression of the word on the backing beneath. This can be done several times if necessary when the word is a long one and the spelling difficult to remember.

Try the slate by writing any word with the stylus, then lifting the top sheets to clear it. Hold the plastic sheets up and you will see the impression of the word on the waxed black backing. By tilting the slate very slightly, depending on the light, you can make the writing seem to stand out even more boldly.

When performing, hold the slate with your left hand, upright with its surface facing you. With your right hand lift the top sheets straight up all the way to erase the slate and also to give you a clear view of the backing, and then release the sheets so they fall down into place again.

To clear the slate of the practice word you wrote, crumple a tissue and gently rub it over the black surface, polishing the wax clean. Have the slate, stylus, and dictionary on your table.

What you do:

Take the slate and stylus in your left hand and the dictionary in your right hand and approach the group of spectators. Give the dictionary to one of them and explain that in a moment you will ask him to open it to any page and to select any word. Explain that he is not to say the word aloud, but is just to point to it on the page and show it to the person next to him.

Turn to the second spectator and explain that you will want him to copy the word that is pointed out to him, to show it to those around him, and then to erase what he has written. Demonstrate by printing a short word at the top of the slate and to the side, and then lift the plastic sheets to erase it. Give him the slate and stylus, move away and turn your head.

Ask the first spectator to open the dictionary "to any page—any word" and repeat your instructions that he is to say nothing, but just to point to the word and show it to his neighbor. Tell the second spectator again to copy that word, show it to those around him, and then erase it. When they say they have done that, take back the dictionary, slate, and stylus and return to the front of the room.

Keep the dictionary in your hands, but toss the slate on the table as if it were no longer of any importance, and drop the stylus into your pocket. For the next few moments ignore the slate entirely. Open the dictionary and turn the pages, pretending to try to read the thoughts that will guide you to the word. Admit you are having difficulty. As if the idea just occurred to you, say, "Let's try it another way." Put down the dictionary and pick up the slate. "Just think of the first few letters in the word."

Take the stylus from your pocket. Hold the slate upright and facing you. Lift the top sheets as if to clear it and glance at the impression of the word on the waxed black backing beneath. Try to catch at least a letter or two at first glance, but don't stare at it. Immediately drop the sheets again, turn the slate to the audience to show it blank, and print any letters on it that *do not* suggest the chosen word. Print them up high or down low, not over the area of the slate where you know the hidden impression is.

Show what you have written, questioningly look out at the

spectators, and then say, "No. I'm wrong—that's not how the word starts." Turn the slate to face you, clear it again, and steal a second glance at the word. Then print the first few letters of it. Show the slate and ask, "Am I right so far?"

When you are sure of the word, put the stylus and slate on the table and pick up the dictionary. Look for the word in it. Turn the pages, run your finger down the columns, turn another page or two. Finally stop at the right page.

Point your finger to the word. Start to spell it aloud. Throw down the dictionary, quickly pick up the slate, hold it towards the audience, and boldly print the correct word across the slate for everyone to see as you say: "One word in seventy-five thousand. . . . Is that the word?"

What's in the News?

How it looks:

You pick up a newspaper and give each of three spectators a double-page sheet of it, keeping one yourself to demonstrate what you want done. "Just tear a piece about this size from any part of any page," you explain as you rip a piece from your paper. "Top, bottom, front, back. It doesn't matter what pieces we use. Then crumple the piece into a ball like this."

To show them, you crumple yours into a ball and drop it into a glass, in which you collect the rest of the pieces. One of the spectators is invited to return to your table with you. You pour the balled-up pieces out of the glass, and he chooses one, which he opens and reads to himself while you stand well away from him.

You then "read his mind" to reveal what the news story is about. He concentrates on the headline, and you tell what it is. He is asked to think of the name of any person who happens to be mentioned in the news item, and you reveal that name. Finally, he mentally spells out one of the words to himself, and you spell it aloud with him, letter by letter.

What you need:

A newspaper, preferably tabloid size for easy handling.
An "iced-tea" glass, about 6 inches high.
A large pad and broad-tipped marking pen.
A pencil.

The secret and setup:

Although the presentation leads the audience to imagine that any part of the newspaper might have been chosen, you actually do the "choosing" yourself, and the spectator gets a news item you have read and made notes from in advance.

Start by looking through the paper you intend to use for a news item that meets these conditions: It should be at the top of the outside column of a right-hand page as you open the pages before you; the item should have a solid advertisement or picture on the back of it, not another news story or reading material; it should mention the names of only two or three people.

When you have found the news item you want, read it through a few times and remember as much about it as you can. At the top of the first sheet of the large pad, lightly pencil the headline, then list the personal names mentioned in the item with a one-word reminder for each to indicate who they are or what they do, and finally make a note of the very last word in the item.

Now remove the outside front double page of the paper and three more pages. Put the double sheet that contains your news story inside those, and then put the rest of the paper inside your page at the center. Refold the paper and have it on your table with the glass, the facedown pad and the marking pen.

What you do:

Show the newspaper and discard the front page as you explain: "We won't use the big headlines for this. Let's get down to the fine print." Peel off the next three double pages from the outside of the paper, one at a time, and give one to each spectator. Remove the fourth double page and put aside the rest of the paper.

As you demonstrate what you want the spectators to do, open out the double page you are holding. Unknown to the audience, the piece you want to save is at the top of the right-hand column. Just tear it out as you say: "Tear a piece about this size from any part of any page. Top, bottom, front, back. It doesn't matter what pieces we use." Don't try to be precise or fussy about the tearing. Make it seem casual, as if you were merely ripping any piece from the paper. Hold the piece up for them to see its size and crumple it up into a ball at least as big as a golf ball as you continue to show the spectators what to do.

While they are doing that, pick up the glass and drop your ball of paper into it. Then take the glass to the spectators and have each of them drop in their balled-up pieces. Because you put yours in first, it naturally remains at the bottom, so there is no difficulty in remembering which it is. Invite one of the spectators to return to your table with you. Tip the glass and spill the balls of paper out on the table, watching to see where yours falls.

Ask the spectator to pick up any two of them. If one of the two he picks up is yours, say: "All right. Now hand me one of those—either one you choose." But if neither of them that he first picks up is yours, say: "All right. We've eliminated two. Just throw those away. Now pick up the other two and hand me one of them—either one you choose."

Whichever way he starts, you have now brought him to the point of handing you either the piece you want or of keeping that and handing you the other one. If he hands you the one you want, you say: "Okay. We'll use this one then. You can throw the other one away." But if he gives you the other one, simply throw it away yourself and point to the one he still has in his hand as you say: "That's the one you've chosen to keep."

Tell him to unroll the ball of paper as you turn away from him. "Open it up and read either side of it to yourself," you say. "It doesn't matter which side you choose as long as there's a news item on it—a few paragraphs of information of some kind." Since there was only a picture or solid advertisement on the back of the chosen piece, he is forced to read the side you want him to read. "Is there enough of the story there so that you can get an idea of what the news item is about?"

Close your eyes a moment and then, haltingly and in general terms, begin to reveal the subject of the news item aloud. Talk around it and gradually describe some of the details you remember. Pick up the pad and marking pen and say, "It may help if I try to jot down some of your thoughts as they come to me."

Hold the pad upright facing you and scribble a few words as you continue to talk about it. As you do, glance at your penciled notes at the top of the pad. Ask if the item includes a headline. Have him concentrate on it. Scribble again and then tell him what the headline is, not word for word, but the gist of what it says.

Ask him to glance through the item and to think of some person whose name may be mentioned in it. If there are three names, you will now have to fish a little to find out which one he is thinking about. From the notes on your pad you know the three possible names, so you call out an initial or describe who a person is or what he does — keeping it vague until you know you have hit on the one he has in mind. Then quickly reveal the full name as you scribble it on the pad. While you are doing that, memorize the final note on your pad, the spelling of the last word in the news item.

"Now please look at the last sentence — the very last word," you say. "In your mind, spell that word slowly — to yourself."

Throw the pad facedown on the table. Face him directly and spell the word aloud as if you were receiving his thoughts one letter at a time. Repeat the word and ask: "Am I right? Was that the exact word you had in mind?"

First the Answer— Then the Problem

How it looks:

You tell the audience that all evening long you have been receiving a strong mental impression of a number. "It keeps popping into my mind. I can see it clearly, but I don't know what it means." You write the number on a slate and show it to them.

"Does it have any special meaning to anybody?" you ask. "Somebody's phone number—part of the license number of somebody's car?" There is no response. "No? . . . I guess not." You shake your head and put the slate, number side down, on the table. "Never mind. Let's forget it. We'll go on to something else. . . . I'd like to try an experiment dealing with the years of your birth–your birthyears."

Three spectators are asked, in turn, to write the year they were born on the first page of a small memo book that they pass from one to another while your head is turned so that you can't see what is written. The last spectator is asked to close the cover. Holding the closed notebook high in your hand, you return to your table.

"I'm going to attempt to get a mental impression of each of these three years," you say, "and mentally add them together so that the unknown total—" You interrupt yourself. "Wait a minute. This is very strange. There's something happening here that I don't understand. It's like having an answer before I know the problem."

Quickly you go to a fourth spectator, open the notebook, and ask him to add the three birth years, and then to call the total aloud. He does and it is the same number you wrote on the slate at the start.

"That's where that number came from," you say, as you pick up the slate and show it. "The number that kept popping into my mind all evening—before I knew the years when any of you were born. You weren't consciously thinking of those dates when I started to see that number in my mind—but perhaps the years of our lives are always subconsciously in our thoughts."

What you need:

Two identical small (about 3-by-5-inch) memo books, the kind with a spiral wire binding at the top and with stiff, but fairly thin, brightly-colored covers.

Slate and chalk.

Double-faced (sticky both sides) transparent tape.

A pencil and scissors.

The secret and setup:

The memo book is prepared so that you can switch pages. The years the spectators write are on a page that will be hidden by a double-cover device. On another page are three dates you have secretly written in advance. Those are the ones that are finally added up to give the total first shown on the slate.

Start by removing the colored cover from one of the memo books, tearing through the perforations that hold it to the spiral wire at the top. Discard the rest of that memo book. With the scissors, carefully trim away the torn perforations at the top edge of that cover. Then trim a tiny edge from the sides and bottom so that the entire duplicate cover is just slightly smaller than the paper pages of the second memo book.

Open the second book flat. Turn back four of the paper pages. With strips of the double-stick tape fasten the loose

FIRST the **ANSWER** - then the **PROBLEM**

duplicate cover to the *rear* of the fourth paper page. When the duplicate cover is in place, it should look like the inside front cover of the memo book. But between it and the real cover there are four paper pages. Those pages should hide the fake cover when the book is opened to the first page.

On the fifth page of the prepared memo book write any three years you choose, one beneath another so they may be added up later. Keep them within a reasonable age range and try to make it look as if the three numbers had been written by different persons, by making the sets of figures seem in different handwriting. On a separate scrap of paper, add the three dates. Lightly pencil the total on the wooden frame of the slate.

Close the memo book and have it on your table with the pencil and the slate and chalk.

What you do:

Secretly glance at the penciled number on the slate frame as you pick up the slate. Talk about the number that keeps "popping into my mind." Write that number in chalk across the face of the slate and ask if it has any special meaning to anyone in the audience. When you get no response, put the slate on the table with the number side down, and pretend to go on with another experiment.

Pick up the memo book and pencil and approach the first spectator. Open the real cover, turn it underneath the pad, and hand him the book and pencil. Ask him to write the year he was born while you turn your head away. Then have him pass the memo book to a spectator next to him. Tell that person to jot his birth year down directly beneath the first one. Have him hand the memo book to a third spectator, who is asked to write the year of his birth "right under the first two." Instruct the third one to close the cover of the book so that you can't see what has been written.

Take it from him, hold your hand high so the memo book remains in full view, and return to your table. Explain that you are going to attempt to get an impression of each of the three years and then add all three together mentally to reach a total. Break off your explanation. Say that "something strange" seems to be happening, as though you were getting an answer before you know the problem. Act puzzled about it and quickly approach a fourth spectator, one who is *seated at a distance from the first three.*

As you do, open the memo book to the *duplicate* cover. It is easy to locate because of its thickness beneath the extra pages on top. Swing that duplicate cover right over the top of the spiral binding and bring it underneath the book, turning the extra top pages and real cover with it, as if merely opening the book again. Don't make a tricky move of it; just open the book there, give it an outward flip, and the real cover and top pages will all flip over together with the fake cover.

The audience has a brief glimpse of the back of the duplicate cover and assumes that you are opening the real cover to the first page. Actually the page you now show the fourth spectator is the one on which your own set of figures was written. Turn the memo book so the figures face him, with the covers held under it. Give him the pencil and have him add the numbers while you hold the book for him. Ask him to write down the total and call it aloud.

Take the memo book with you and go back to your table. Read the total aloud again from the book. Turn the slate and show the number on it as you say, "That's where that number came from. . . . The number that kept popping into my mind all evening—before I knew the years when any of you were born."

A Walk Through the Yellow Pages

How it looks:

"You can find almost anything in the yellow pages of the phone directory—hundreds of all kinds of products and services," you say as you show a phone book and hand it to someone in the audience. Pointing to another spectator, you ask, "Will you please call out any letter of the alphabet from *A* to *Z*?"

He calls out, say, the letter *C*. The person holding the book is asked to open it to the yellow pages that start with that letter. "Just look through them for the first main heading that begins with a *C*—whatever type of business that may be. Turn the pages until you find that first heading with the names and phone numbers of various companies of that kind listed beneath it."

You hold up a large card that has a rough sketch of a telephone dial drawn at the top. "I want you to look at this phone dial and imagine that you are dialing the number of the first company listed under that heading," you explain. "Don't say anything aloud. Dial it mentally. Think of one number at a time—and dial it slowly, please."

Taking a pen from your pocket, you print a phone number on the card in large red numerals and ask, "Is that the number you dialed in your mind?" When he says that it is, you ask him to think of the kind of business or service he is calling, and you print on the card, say, CABINET MAKER. He again confirms that you are correct.

"Now when somebody answers your mental phone call," you say, "what name will you ask for? What company or person are you calling? Will you please think of that name—but don't tell me." After a moment's concentration, you write on the card, say, PAUL GREGORY & SONS. For the third time, the spectator agrees that you have correctly read his thoughts.

What you need:

A classified phone directory or a phone book with a classified yellow page section in the rear.

A large blank white piece of cardboard, about 8-by-14 inches.

Two 3-by-5-inch blank index file cards.

A broad-tipped black marking pen.

A red marking pen that can be clipped into your pocket.

Transparent tape.

The use of a typewriter.

The secret and setup:

The listings are limited to a total of twenty-six by the fact that one letter of the alphabet is called for and the first category, number and name under that letter are used. The information for all twenty-six possible choices is typed on two cards taped to the back of the large one, on which the phone dial is drawn.

When you hold the large card in front of you so the spectator can "mentally dial the number," you read the information to yourself from the back of the card. The routine gives you a logical excuse to hold up the "phone dial" card three times, so you don't have to remember everything at once.

Turn the large card so its narrow edges are at the top and bottom. Near the top draw a rough sketch of a phone dial with the black pen. Start by making an outer circle about 5 inches in diameter. Inside that draw another circle about 3½ inches in diameter. Between the two circles print large numbers from 1 to 0, spaced around from right to left as they are on a phone dial. Beneath each number, inside the smaller circle, draw another little circle of about ½ inch in diameter. These represent the finger holes of the dial. At the center of the whole thing, where the head of the screw that holds the dial would be, mark a black dot.

Roll one of the file cards, with its narrow edges top and bottom, into the typewriter. Open the phone book and find the first *main heading* in the yellow pages that starts with the letter *A* and that has a listing of companies and phone numbers directly beneath it. (Ignore any minor cross-index headings in small print that may refer to listings on other pages.)

At the top of the file card and as far to the left as the typewriter will allow, type the letter *A* and then the kind of business given in the heading, for example: A-ACCOUNTANTS-CERTIFIED PUB. Space down a line and type the first listed name and phone number, such as: ADAMS, GORDON-528-2873.

Then look in the book for the first main heading that starts with *B* and type that information — and so on until all twenty-six listings for each letter of the alphabet are typed on the two file cards.

Turn the large "phone dial" card facedown and attach the two typed file cards, side by side, to the back of it near the top. Attach them with short strips of tape top and bottom so

A WALK THROUGH the YELLOW PAGES

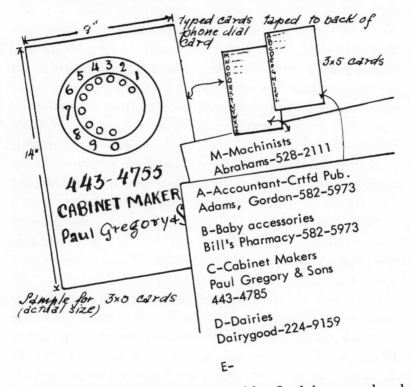

7"

typed cards taped to back of phone dial card

3x5 cards

14"

5 4 3 2 1
6 0 0 0 0
7 0 0 0
8 0 0
9 0

443-4755
CABINET MAKER
Paul Gregory&S

Sample for 3x5 cards
(actual size)

M-Machinists
Abrahams-528-2111

A-Accountant-Crtfd Pub.
Adams, Gordon-582-5973

B-Baby accessories
Bill's Pharmacy-582-5973

C-Cabinet Makers
Paul Gregory & Sons
443-4785

D-Dairies
Dairygood-224-9159

E-

you can remove them later to use with a fresh large card and won't have to retype all the information for each performance.

Have the prepared "phone dial" card faceup on your table and the red pen clipped into the inside left pocket of your jacket.

What you do:

Show the phone book and give it to someone in the audience. Have someone else call out any letter of the alphabet,
then ask the person with the book to look in the yellow pages
for the *first main heading* for any kind of a business or service that begins with that letter. Make sure he understands
that you want him to find a heading with a listing of company
names and numbers beneath it. Wait for him to locate it and
say again, "The first main heading that begins with a *C*,"
(or whatever letter may have been called from the audience).

Ask him to look for the phone number of the first company
listed under that heading. Pick up the large card and hold it
upright in front of you so the dial faces the spectator and the
audience. Hold it so you have a clear view from the back of
the small cards with the information typed on them.

"Now I want you to look at this phone dial and imagine
you are dialing that number," you explain. "Don't say anything aloud. Dial it mentally. Think of one number at a
time—and dial it slowly in your mind."

While you are speaking, look at the back of the card and
memorize the phone number listed under that letter of the
alphabet. Look only for the number, not the rest of the
listing yet. Turn your body a little to the left and hold the
card, still upright and facing the audience, with your left
hand so that the back of the card is cradled against your
left arm. With your right hand remove the red pen from your
pocket.

Pretend to "receive" the number the spectator is mentally
dialing. Print it with the red pen in large numerals across the

face of the card and beneath the drawing of the dial. Ask: "Is that the number you dialed?"

When the spectator says that it is, ask him to look at the dial again and to think of the kind of business or service he is calling. Hold the card in front of you so he can "concentrate his thoughts" on the dial. Glance at the back of the card for the proper listing, remember it, and then hold the card as before against your left arm while you print the kind of a business across the face of it, beneath the phone number. Ask him to confirm it.

"Now when somebody answers your mental phone call," you say, "what name will you ask for? What company or person are you calling?" Hold the card in front of you again so the dial faces him. Look on the back for the listing of the name and remember it. "Will you please think of that name?"

Shift the card so its back is against your left arm. Write the name beneath the number and kind of business, then ask once more if you are correct. For the third time, the spectator says that you are.

The Silent Commercial

How it looks:

Showing a folded slip of paper, you ask a spectator who is standing beside you, "May I put this in your pocket?" Tucking it into the top of his breast pocket, you say: "We are about to conduct a marketing survey. . . . But first — we'll have to take time out for a commercial."

You stand silent for a moment with your eyes closed, and

then open them and say: "There—the commercial's finished. You didn't hear it because it was a silent commercial. There were no pictures to watch because it was an invisible commercial. It was in my mind—and perhaps it is now in your mind, too, even though you may not be aware that you heard any commercial message at all."

From your pocket, you take four metal-rimmed cardboard discs and explain that on each of them you have written the name of a breakfast cereal. You ask the spectator to take them and read them aloud, and he reads: "Flakes, Crackles, Toasties, Crunchers."

"My sponsor is the manufacturer of one of those four brands," you say, "and our survey is to test whether silent commercials work—whether you have been mentally influenced to buy that brand instead of one of the others—so that you will reach for my brand by some blind impulse."

You drop all the discs into the side pocket of your jacket and hold it open wide as you invite the spectator to dip his hand in and take one of them. "Mix them up. Don't take the first one you touch—unless you want to. . . . You have one? Will you please read the name on it aloud?"

He reads: "Toasties." You then ask him to remove the slip of paper that you put in his breast pocket at the start and to read that aloud. He reads: "Thank you for listening to my silent commercial. My sponsor will be pleased that you bought—Toasties."

What you need:

Eight round metal-rimmed blank cardboard tags, 1¾ inch in diameter, with their strings removed.

A sheet of paper from a small scratch pad.

A black felt-tip marking pen.

A jacket with a small "ticket pocket" just inside the top of the right-hand pocket. Most men's jackets are made with such a pocket.

The secret and setup:

There are four duplicate tags, all with the same name on them, in the bottom of your right-hand jacket pocket. The other four, with various names on them, are shown to the spectator and then are dropped into the little "ticket pocket" inside the top of your right-hand pocket. You hold your hand over that as you spread the rest of the pocket wide so that he may dip his hand into it. He is forced to "choose" one of the four duplicates from the bottom of the pocket, which bears the name that was written on the slip of paper given to him at the start.

Print the four breakfast cereal names, or any other product names you may wish to use, on four of the tags. Then print one of those four names, TOASTIES for example, on all four of the other tags. Write the prediction note, worded as explained, on the sheet of paper from the scratch pad and fold it in half.

Drop the four duplicate tags, all with the same name on them (TOASTIES), into the bottom of your right-hand pocket. Put the other four, all with different names on them, into the little "ticket pocket" along with the folded slip of paper.

What you do:

Have the spectator stand to your right. Remove the prediction slip from your pocket. Show it without opening it and ask if you may put it in his pocket. Tuck it into the top of his breast pocket so part of it remains in view.

Say that you are about to conduct a marketing survey, "but first — we'll have to take time out for a commercial." Stand with your eyes closed and silently count to twenty. Then open your eyes and explain that he didn't see it or hear it because it was a silent and invisible commercial — "in my mind — and perhaps it is now in your mind, too. . . ."

Remove the bunch of four different tags from your "ticket pocket." Show him what is on them, give them to him, and ask him to read each of the names aloud. Take them back, stack them together in your right hand, and show them again. Turn your body a little to the left so everyone can see, and openly drop them into the right-hand pocket of your jacket — but really into the "ticket pocket" at the top of it.

Don't put your hand all the way into your pocket. Just spread the "ticket pocket" with the backs of your fingers, let the tags fall into it, and immediately remove your hand. This should be done with seeming carelessness, not as though you are being cautious about where they go.

Explain that your "sponsor" is the manufacturer of one of the four brands and that the survey is to test "whether silent commercials work," whether he will reach for one brand instead of the others "by some blind impulse." This is said to give a reason for having him choose blindly from your pocket, instead of simply looking at them and choosing one.

Without deliberately showing that your right hand is empty, let it be seen that it is. Put that hand just far enough into the top of your right-hand pocket so your fingers cover the "ticket pocket." Hook your left thumb into the top of the whole pocket at the opposite side, the side toward the spectator, and spread the pocket wide.

Hold it open that way as you shake it, as though mixing the tags that rattle in the bottom of it, and say, "Just dip your hand into my pocket and take one of them. Mix them up. Don't take the first one you touch—unless you want to. But take just one—any one—and bring it out."

As soon as he takes one, remove both your hands from the pocket. Ask him to read aloud the name on the tag he has "chosen." Repeat it. Then say: "You have had a note in your pocket since we began this survey. Will you open it now, please, and read it to everyone?"

He reads your thanks for listening to your silent commercial and the prediction that he would choose "Toasties."

Telepathy à la Carte

How it looks:

"Have you ever been in a restaurant where you just couldn't get the attention of the waiter and had to sit for what seemed hours before he finally took your order?" you ask. "Someday perhaps we'll solve the problem—by telepathy. Can you imagine a restaurant with a cook who's a mind reader? As soon as the patron reads the menu, they know in the kitchen exactly what he wants for dinner."

A spectator is asked to imagine himself in such a restaurant and is given a menu to look over so he can mentally decide what he would like to eat—appetizer, main course, dessert. When he has made up his mind about each, you ask him to write his choices on a slip of paper while you turn your head away, and to fold the slip and give it to another spectator "so we can check your order later if there's any question."

You read aloud the menu list of appetizers, ask the first spectator to concentrate on the one he has in mind, and you reveal what it is. Then you announce what he has chosen as the main course of his imaginary dinner. But when you come to the dessert, you find that you can't read his thoughts—so you turn to the other spectator, who has been holding the written slip, and read his mind instead.

What you need:

A 9-by-6-inch piece of *white* transfer paper, the kind sold at sewing counters for tracing dress patterns.

A 9-by-12-inch sheet of black construction paper.

Several slips of thin paper from a small scratch pad.

A hard lead pencil with a freshly sharpened point.

A paper clip.

The use of a typewriter.

The secret and setup:

The white transfer paper serves the purpose of carbon paper, but it doesn't look like carbon paper. The menu is typed on it, and its innocent appearance permits it to be openly displayed inside a black menu cover, which contains nothing but that typed menu. When the spectator is given a slip of paper to write down his mental choices, he rests it on the menu cover, and a faint white impression of the writing is transferred to the inside black cover so that later you can secretly read it as you consult the menu.

The menu cover is simply made by folding the sheet of black construction paper as you would close a book. Put the paper lengthwise on a table, bring the left side over to the right until those two edges exactly meet, and crease the center fold.

At the top of the *shiny* side of the white transfer paper, type the word: MENU. Space down a few lines and type the heading: APPETIZERS. List several choices, but keep them short and simple, such as Tomato Juice, Fruit Cup, Melon. Avoid unusual foods, foreign spellings, anything that would be difficult for the spectator to remember or to write.

Under the next heading, MAIN COURSE, list such plain things as Steak, Chops, Roast Beef, Shrimps, Fish. Under the DESSERT heading you might list Pie, Ice Cream, Cake. Don't be tempted to add other courses—three choices will be enough for the spectator to keep in mind.

Paper-clip the top of the menu to the *left* inside cover of the black folder and have it on your table with the slips of paper and pencil.

What you do:

After you have invited the spectator to imagine himself in a restaurant where telepathy is used, display the menu, hand it to him, and ask him to choose what he would like to start the meal, then his main course, and then dessert. "Keep the choices in your mind," you say. "Appetizer, main course, and dessert." Walk back to your table as you give him time to make his mental selections, pick up a slip of paper and the pencil, and return to him again. "When you have done that, just close the menu."

As he closes it, you should be right beside him to hand him the pencil and to place the slip of paper on the front of the folded menu cover. "Now please write down your order so

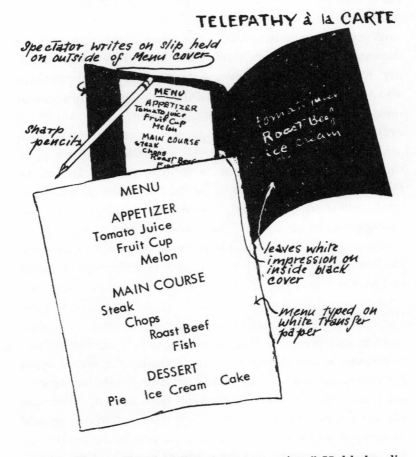

we can check it later if there's any question." Hold the slip of paper on the cover so he can take it and then immediately turn away.

When he has written his choices on the slip, you say, "I'll ask you to fold it, please, and give it to that lady next to you." Look at the second spectator and ask, "Will you be kind enough to keep it for us?"

Take the menu from the first spectator, casually tuck it under your arm, and move well away from him. "I get the impression that you're a man who really enjoys his food," you say. "You're not on a diet, are you?—I hope not. Anyhow, you don't have to worry about calories. This is strictly a mental meal. I guarantee you won't gain a pound."

Open the menu and start to read aloud from the list of appetizers, enlarging a bit on the simple typed descriptions. "You might have chosen the Tomato Juice Cocktail, the California Fresh Fruit Cup, or the Iced Persian Melon to start your meal. Then, for a main course . . ."

As you continue to read the possible menu choices, glance to the right of the inside cover; there the "carbon" impression of what he wrote on the paper slip will appear in white against the black. Depending on the lighting in the room, you may have to tilt the menu a little so the impression shows clearly. This is a matter of moving the cover very slightly until it catches the light at the right angle.

Memorize the three choices and toss the menu on your table as you begin to reveal his thoughts. "You decided to start with Tomato Juice," you might say, "and then you mentally ordered the Prime Roast of Beef. . . . That was rare, wasn't it—or do you prefer it well done?" Look at him and ask, "Have I been right so far—Tomato Juice, Roast Beef?" Wait for him to say so, then say, "And now, what for dessert?"

Pretend to be having difficulty. Finally admit that you can't get his thoughts clearly. Turn to the other spectator who has been holding the written slip and say, "I'm afraid I'll have to read your mind instead. Will you please look at the slip of paper you have and concentrate on what he wants for dessert?"

Then announce, for instance: "Oh, of course — Ice Cream. I thought first of chocolate — chocolate cake. But it is Ice Cream." Look at the first spectator and ask, "Is that correct? Did I get your order exactly right? Tomato Juice — Roast Beef — Ice Cream?"

5

MENTAL VISIONS

Toll the Hour

How it looks:

You take an envelope from your pocket and remove a card from it, on which there is a drawing of a numbered clock dial without hands. One of a group of spectators gathered around a table is asked to think of something that happened to him yesterday or that will happen tomorrow.

"It could be something trivial or something important," you say, giving him a pencil. "I want you to think of the hour of that happening—never mind the minutes—and draw in a hand to that hour on this clock. Just draw a straight line—an arrow—from the center of the dial to the hour."

While he is doing that, you turn your head so you can't see, and then ask him to place the drawing facedown on the table. Facing the group again, you slide the card flatly across the table and put it into the envelope, which you seal. Both sides of the envelope are shown so there will be no doubt that the clock dial is entirely covered from view.

"Your thought of that hour exists in two dimensions—in your mind and in the physical expression of it on the drawing sealed in this envelope," you say. "If I were to tear up the drawing, the thought would be physically destroyed." You tear the envelope and the drawing inside it into small pieces and discard them by dropping them into your pocket. "In a strictly physical sense, the hour is now lost. But, of course, the thought of that hour still remains in your mind."

For a moment, you stand silent, and close your eyes. "In *my* mind," you say then, "I hear a clock tolling—chiming the hour." You slowly tap the end of the pencil on the table, sounding it one, two, three times. Opening your eyes, you tell the spectator: "The hour in your mind is three o'clock."

What you need:

A 2½-by-4¼-inch manila coin envelope with an end-opening flap. It should be of good quality paper, thick enough so it cannot be seen through.

A blank card, cut slightly smaller than the envelope.

Pencil, pen, and scissors.

The secret and setup:

Although the envelope is convincingly shown on both sides so it appears to have no openings, it does have a hole cut in the face of it. But the hole is so small that it can be covered by the ball of your thumb when the envelope is held in a way it normally would be held to display it. Through the hole you are able to see the center of the clock dial and enough of the "hand" that the spectator has drawn on it to tell the hour to which it points.

Start by drawing the clock dial on the card with the pen. In the center of the card, make a circle about 2¼ inches in diameter. The size need not be exact, but the dial should be large enough so the numbers will be well spaced around it. Number it from 1 to 12 as a clock is numbered, with the numbers positioned carefully where they would be on the face of a clock.

At the center of the circle make a fairly large dot. Then enlarge the dot just a bit more at the top, so the top of the dot points upward toward the 12. This is done so that when the numbers are covered by the envelope you can tell from looking at the point of the dot whether the dial is upside down.

With the scissors, cut a small "window" in the face of the envelope so that the dot of the clock dial will be at the center of this opening when the card is in the envelope. Cut it only in the face of the envelope, not through the back. The "window" should be about ½-inch-square so your thumb will cover it entirely. All you need to see is the bottom end of the line the spectator will draw, starting at the dot, to tell which hour the "hand" points to.

To understand how it is handled, have the envelope containing the card lengthwise and facedown on a table, flap end of the envelope to the right. Pick it up by bringing the tips of your right-hand fingers against the back of the envelope and sliding the envelope toward you off the edge of the table, where you naturally grip it by bringing your thumb up underneath. As you take the envelope, your thumb comes up right over the hole. You can feel the opening to make sure it is well covered.

Now turn your hand over from left to right and show the face of the envelope. With the "window" hidden by your covering thumb, the face looks as unprepared as the back. After you have shown it, turn your hand from right to left and drop the envelope on the table, facedown as before.

Later, when you take it again to tear it, you pick it up almost the same way, but with your hand more toward the right end of the envelope as you slide it back off the edge of the table and grip it from underneath with your thumb. That way your thumb does *not* cover the "window" and you can see the center of the clock dial through it as you hold up the envelope, its back toward the spectators.

Have the envelope, with the clock dial inside, in the right-hand pocket of your jacket and the pencil with it. The "window" face of the envelope should be toward your body.

What you do:

Reach into your pocket for the envelope. Feel for the "window," cover it with your thumb, and bring out the envelope. Casually show the face of it, turn it over, and drop it on the table with its back up.

Ask the spectator to think of something that happened or may happen to him, to think of the hour of that happening. Keeping the envelope flat on the table, open the flap and draw out the card. Show the clock dial on it and slide the card over to him. Take the pencil from your pocket.

"In a moment, I'll ask you to draw in a hand to that hour

on this clock—while I turn my head so that I can't see what hour you're thinking about." To demonstrate what you want him to do, you turn the pencil to its unpointed end so it won't make a mark and draw an imaginary straight line from the dot to one of the hours. "Just draw a straight line—an arrow—from the center of the dial to whatever hour you have in mind." You give him the pencil and turn your head away. "Have you done that? . . . Please turn the dial facedown on the table."

You face the group and slide the card over to the envelope. Open the flap and put the card in. Moisten the tip of your finger, wet the flap with it, and seal the envelope without lifting it from the table. Now pick up the envelope as previously explained, by sliding it toward you off the edge of the table so your thumb comes up underneath to take it and covers the hole.

Feel to make sure it is well covered, and then turn the envelope to show the face of it. Don't say anything about it, but give everybody a good chance to see it. Hold it that way a moment and then turn your hand over and drop the envelope facedown on the table.

"Your thought of that hour now exists in two dimensions— in your mind and in the physical expression of it on the drawing sealed in this envelope." You point to the envelope and slide it back off the edge of the table so that your thumb coming up to take it from beneath does *not* cover the hole.

Lift the envelope that way, with its face toward you and its back to the spectators, and glance through the "window" to see in which direction the dot at the center of the dial is pointed. If it points up, the dial is positioned correctly. But if the dot points down, the 12 on the dial is at the bottom. In that case, turn your hand and bring the point of the dot to the top.

Look at the spectator and say, "If I were to tear up the drawing, the thought would be physically destroyed." With

TOLL the HOUR

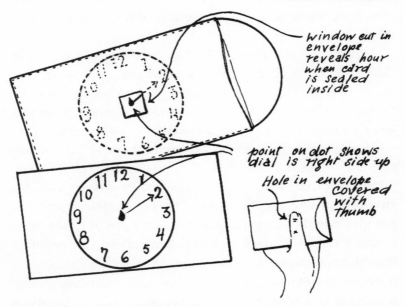

Window cut in envelope reveals hour when card is sealed inside

point on dot shows dial is right side up

Hole in envelope covered with Thumb

both hands, start to tear the envelope, and as you tear it look through the "window" to see where the clock "hand" is pointed. Imagine the clock dial and think around it—12, 3, 6, and so on—until you have mentally fixed the position of the pencil line at the right hour. Continue to tear the envelope to pieces, show the scraps in your hand, and drop them into your pocket.

"In a strictly physical sense, the hour is now lost," you say. "But, of course, the thought of that hour still remains in your mind."

Pick up the pencil the spectator has left on the table. Stand silent for a moment and close your eyes. Then say, "In *my* mind I hear a clock tolling—chiming the hour." Tap the pencil on the table to sound whatever the hour is. Open your eyes, look at the spectator, and tell him the hour that is in his mind.

Psychic Fingerprints

How it looks:

"May I have your autograph?" you ask a spectator as you give him a pen and a small card on which to write his name. "When you have written it, will you please put the card in this envelope and drop it on the table. I have a special reason for not touching that card again myself."

You then show two other cards and explain: "On one of these I have written the name 'George Washington' and on the other one 'Abraham Lincoln.' But the only genuine signature is the one you have just written. That would be obvious to anyone who could examine the writing. But with the cards hidden in envelopes it becomes impossible to see the writing, to identify yours from the others." You put your two cards in two similar envelopes and drop them to the table next to his.

"When you handled that card," you continue, "you gave me more than just your signature. You left your fingerprints all

over it. Not visible fingerprints, but the touch of your fingers—
what psychometrists might call the impression of your personality on the object you handled—psychic fingerprints. . . .
Please put all the envelopes in your pocket—and then remove
any one of them and hold it out before you."

He takes one of the envelopes from his pocket. Without
touching it you hold your hand above it, as if sensing the
vibrations. "No," you may say, "that's not yours. Try another
one, please." He removes them from his pocket, one at a time,
and when he holds the envelope containing the card he has
signed, you are able to tell him so. "Yes. That's the one that
bears your touch. Will you please open it and see if your
signature is on the card?"

You offer to try another experiment and ask him to put the
card back into the envelope and then to put all three envelopes
into his pocket again. "I want you to mix them up, shift them
around inside your pocket, until you are satisfied neither of
us could guess which is which," you say. "Now remove two of
the envelopes and toss them on the table—so there is just
one left in your pocket. It could contain the card with your
signature, or it could be one of the others."

Without touching the two envelopes he has tossed on the
table, you hold your hand over each in turn and then close to
the outside of his pocket. You then reveal which of the three
envelopes, whether on the table or in his pocket, contains the
card with his signature and have him open it to confirm your
discovery.

"Psychometry might explain that much," you say. "But it
doesn't explain what I will try to do now—because you
haven't touched the other cards at all, not since I put them

into their envelopes. There are no psychic fingerprints of yours on those." You point to one of the envelopes on the table and announce: "On the card in that envelope, you will find the name of George Washington. And on the one still in your pocket, the name of Abraham Lincoln."

You ask him to open each of the envelopes and read aloud the names, which prove to be exactly as you called them.

What you need:

Three 2½-by-4¼-inch manila coin envelopes with end-opening flaps, made of paper thick enough so there is no suspicion that writing can show through.

Three blank cards that will fit easily into the envelopes.

A pen and a rubber band.

The secret and setup:

The envelope into which the spectator puts his signature card is not marked in any way, but the other two are prepared so you can identify each of them at a glance no matter how they are held or tossed on the table. One is slightly creased at the sides and the other has its corners bent. These markings appear accidental, as if caused by handling the envelopes, and the routine centers the spectator's attention on the unmarked envelope.

To prepare the envelopes hold one at the bottom between your thumb and finger and strike the side edge of it sharply against the edge of a table. Tap it hard to leave an "accidental" crease and then smooth it out a little with your fingers. Do the same thing with the opposite side edge of that envelope. Take a second envelope and strike one of its bottom corners sharply on the top of a table so that the corner is bent, and then do the same with the opposite bottom corner.

Write the name "George Washington" on one of the cards and "Abraham Lincoln" on another. Then stack the cards and envelopes so the one with the creased sides is at the bottom, the one with bent corners next, then the "Washington" card, the "Lincoln" card, the third envelope, and the blank card on top. Put the rubber band around them and have them in one of your pockets with the pen.

What you do:

Take out the stack of cards and envelopes and remove the rubber band. Give the spectator the blank card and pen so he can write his signature. Hand him the plain envelope, ask him to put his signature card into it and to drop the envelope on the table. Say, "I have a special reason for not touching that card again myself."

Show him the "Lincoln" and "Washington" cards. Put the "Lincoln" card into the next envelope with the bent corners, then put the "Washington" card into the last envelope with the creased sides. Drop those to the table next to his. Point out that it is impossible to see the writing on the cards and identify his signature, then have him put all three envelopes in his pocket.

Ask him to take out any one. Hold your hand above it and pretend to sense the vibrations. Glance at the side edges and corners. If there is no crease or bend, you know the envelope is his.

If the first one he takes from his pocket isn't his, tell him so and have him drop that to the table and remove another. By glancing at it you will know whether that is it or whether the signature card is in the one still in his pocket. Reveal which one it is and have him open that envelope to confirm that you are right.

Ask him to put his signature card back into its envelope and put all three in his pocket again. Have him take out any two and toss them on the table. Once more, you discover where the correct envelope is and have him open it and verify his signature.

At this point, after his signature card has been eliminated, there may be two envelopes on the table, or only one on the table and one still in his pocket. In either case you know which is which and where each of them is. All you have to remember is that the envelope with bent corners has the "Lincoln" card in it and the one with creased sides contains the "Washington" card. If "Lincoln" is on the table, for example, then "Washington" must be in his pocket.

Announce that you are going to carry the experiment beyond what might be explained by psychometry or "psychic fingerprints." Then point in turn to each card on the table, or one on the table and one in his pocket, and say: "On the card in that envelope you will find the name of George Washington. . . . And on this one—Abraham Lincoln."

The Bagged Bill

How it looks:

You ask if someone will please take out a dollar bill and hold it up. "Fold it in half so George Washington is on the inside—and then fold it a couple of times more," you say. "You'll remember that George Washington never told a lie . . . so I might as well admit the truth. What I really want—is to borrow your dollar for a few moments, if you'll be kind enough to bring it up to me. But keep it tightly folded that way, please."

Taking the folded bill between your thumb and finger, you hold your hand up high. With your other hand you pick up a paper bag, shake it open, and drop it upside down over the hand holding the bill, so that the bag completely covers your hand and part of your upheld arm.

You give the spectator a slate and chalk. "What I'm going to attempt to do is read the serial numbers on your dollar bill," you explain, "but with my mind instead of my eyes. As I call out the numbers, will you write them on the slate—large enough for everyone to see?"

With some hesitation, and a mistake or two that you correct, you call out the numbers. You remove the paper bag that covers your hand, crumple up the bag with your free hand and toss it aside, and return the still-folded bill to the spectator, as you take the slate and chalk from him.

"Open your dollar and check the numbers with me, please," you say, "to see how close I came. Read them slowly, so we can check each number."

As he reads the serial numbers from his bill, you point to each digit on the slate, and then make a large check mark as the total number proves to be entirely correct.

What you need:

A dollar bill that is in average condition, neither crisply new nor badly worn.

A flat-bottomed brown paper grocery bag, about 4-by-7-by-13 inches when opened out.

A slate, about 8-by-12 inches.

Chalk and a pencil.

Double-faced (sticky both sides) transparent tape.

The secret and setup:

The paper bag, which apparently serves to keep you from seeing the bill in your hand, also allows you to switch the borrowed bill for one of your own with serial numbers that have been copied on the side of the bag in advance.

Your own folded dollar with its known numbers is stuck to a piece of tape inside the bag at the start. With your hand inside the bag you switch it for the borrowed one. At the end, when you pull the bag off your hand, you pinch the borrowed bill in one corner of it and it stays hidden in the bag as you crumple up the bag and toss it aside on your table. You are left holding your own bill, which looks like the still-folded bill the spectator gave you. He opens that one to read the numbers you have called as you check them off on the slate.

Open out the bag and put it on a table with its mouth towards you. On the left side panel, right at the mouth of the bag, print the serial numbers of your dollar bill with the pencil. Keep the bag in the same position and fasten a short strip of double-faced tape *inside* that left side panel about an inch from the bottom of the bag.

Turn the dollar bill lengthwise with Washington's picture face up and fold it in half from left to right, again in half, and then from top to bottom. Stick the folded bill to the tape inside the bag. Close the bag flat and have it on top of the slate and chalk on your table, with the mouth of the bag to the rear.

What you do:

Ask if someone will please take out a dollar bill and hold it up. If several spectators hold up bills, try to choose one that nearly matches the condition of your own bill that is hidden inside the bag, neither brand new nor badly worn. In any case, hurry things along so the person won't have much chance to examine it carefully. Tell him to fold the bill "so George Washington is on the inside" and then to fold it a couple of times more. By wording the instructions that way, you avoid saying anything about the serial number that might cause him to look at it before he folds the bill.

Have him bring it to you. Stand at the right of the table with the spectator to your right. Take the bill from him with the thumb and finger of your right hand. If he hasn't folded it enough, give it another fold so it somewhat matches the bill hidden in the bag. Then hold that hand high, with your arm outstretched and your fingers open wide so it can be plainly seen that there is nothing else in your hand.

With your left hand take the bag from the table. Shake it open, turn it upside down, and pull it down over your upheld right hand to cover it with the bag. Keep your left hand at the mouth of the bag a moment, as if adjusting it, but really to hold the bag so it won't twist around.

With your right hand up inside the bag pull your bill from the sticky tape. Just scoop it off the tape with your free fingers and close them around it. The borrowed bill remains held between your thumb and first finger, as it was, with your own bill closed in your other fingers to keep the two apart.

Drop your left hand to your side. Turn your right arm around slowly to show all sides of the bag so it can be seen—

without your saying so—that there are no holes or slits of any kind in it. Then bring your hand back to its original position and keep it held up that way with the bag upside down over it.

Take the chalk and then the slate from the table with your left hand. "What I'm going to attempt to do," you say, "is to

The BAGGED BILL

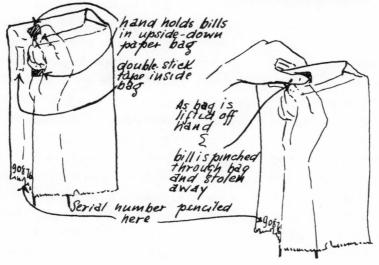

hand holds bills in upside-down paper bag

double-stick tape inside bag

As bag is lifted off hand

bill is pinched through bag and stolen away

Serial number penciled here

read the serial numbers of your dollar bill—but with my mind instead of my eyes." Give the chalk and slate to the spectator. "As I call out the numbers, will you write them on the slate— large enough for everyone to see?"

Glance at the numbers penciled at the mouth of the bag and memorize the first few. Turn your head away, pretend to concentrate, and call out two of the numbers. Then call a wrong number and quickly correct yourself. "No—that's not right. Make that a two—not a seven. Five, three, two . . . ."

Look at the spectator, as if to see if he is writing them correctly on the slate. Steal another glance at the penciled numbers on the bag. Turn your head away again and slowly call out the rest of the numbers.

When you have called all of them, bring your left hand to the top left corner of the bag to pull it off your right hand. Inside the bag, push the borrowed bill into that corner with your right fingers. Pinch it through the bag with your left first finger and thumb and lift the bag straight up off your right hand, taking the borrowed bill with it. As you do that, bring the other bill up to the tips of your right fingers so that hand can hold up what appears to be the still-folded bill borrowed from the spectator.

Crumple up the paper bag with your left hand and carelessly toss it aside on the table. Give the spectator the folded bill and take the slate and chalk from him. Tell him to open the dollar and to "check the numbers with me, please, to see how close I came — read them slowly, so we can check each number."

Hold the slate facing the audience and touch each digit with the chalk as he calls the number aloud. When he has called the whole number, read it off the slate again and make a big check mark. (And don't forget, after the show, to retrieve the other dollar from the crumpled paper bag.)

Crystal Vision

How it looks:

"Have you ever gazed into a crystal ball?" you ask a spectator. "No? Would you like to attempt to discover for us something that hasn't happened yet?" You pick up a drinking glass from your table. "I haven't brought along a crystal ball. But perhaps we can imagine this drinking glass is one."

Holding the glass on the outstretched palm of your hand, you slowly lift it into the spectator's direct line of vision. "I want you to think of some simple geometric figure—perhaps a circle, a triangle, a square. If you do imagine that you see anything, don't tell us what it is—not *what* you see. Just tell us whether you see any figure at all. . . . You do? There's an image in your thoughts?"

You snap your fingers and then hand the glass to the spectator. "Look into it now. Do you still see something? Nothing at all? Then the vision must have been entirely in your own mind. . . . But please remember what you think you saw. We'll both keep that thought a secret from everybody else for a moment."

Turning to a second spectator, you show him a series of geometric designs on a set of cards, which you display one at a time. "I want you to make an entirely random choice," you explain. "Nothing that could be a preconceived thought. I'll turn these so that you can't see their faces. As I hold each up, please just call out which one you want. Any one at all. . . . This one?"

Without showing the design he has chosen, you rest the card face down on top of the glass on your table. To the first spectator, you say, "A moment ago, you had a brief vision of something. Will you please tell everybody now what it was? When you did your crystal gazing, what figure did you see?"

He says: "A triangle."

"You saw it in your mind before the gentleman over there

made his choice," you say. "A mental vision of something that hadn't happened yet. . . ."

Lifting the card from the glass, you hold it to show that the design the second spectator chose was—a triangle.

"Congratulations," you say. "For a first try as a crystal gazer—I think you deserve our applause."

What you need:

A clear, straight-sided drinking glass.

White transfer paper, the kind sold at sewing counters for tracing dress patterns.

Fifteen 4-by-8-inch blank index file cards.

A ball-point pen and a broad-tipped black marking pen.

Transparent tape.

A pair of scissors.

A rubber band.

The secret and setup:

A white transfer paper impression of a tiny triangle is marked on the side of the glass ahead of time. This sort of paper leaves a waxy mark that can be erased with a quick rub of the thumb, so that when the spectator looks into the glass a second time there is nothing to see. The stack of design cards shown to the other spectator includes six duplicate triangles and they are stacked so he is forced to choose one of those.

Wash the glass and dry it thoroughly. Cut a 1-inch square from the white transfer paper. Stick the waxy side of it firmly to the side of the glass, about halfway down from the top, with small tabs of tape. Draw a triangle on it with the ball-point pen, pressing hard so the design will transfer to the glass.

Leave the square of transfer paper taped to the glass until you are ready to use it, to avoid smudging the design. The glass can be carried that way in a briefcase with other props.

Turn the file cards with their narrow edges at the top and bottom. With the black marking pen, making the designs as large as will neatly fit, draw a triangle on seven of the cards, a circle on two of them, then a cross, a square, a rectangle, an oval, a right angle, and a star.

Stack the cards *faceup* in this order: Put six of the triangles together, one of the circles on top of those, then the cross, square, rectangle, the seventh triangle, the oval, right angle, star, and finally the second circle. Fasten the rubber band around them to keep them in proper sequence.

To set things up for performance remove the taped paper from the glass and place the glass on your table with the waxed triangle design to the rear. Have the design cards beside it.

What you do:

Have the first spectator stand at the left of your table while you stand in front of the table facing him. Pick up the glass by its top rim with your left hand and rest the bottom of it on your outstretched right palm. Raise it until you have brought the glass level with the spectator's eyes. At this point, the design is at the rear of the glass, so the spectator will see nothing as he looks through the sides of it.

Tell him to concentrate on the glass as if it were a crystal ball and to think of some simple geometric figure — "perhaps a circle, a triangle, a square." But caution him not to reveal what he sees. Say: "If you do imagine that you see anything, don't tell us what it is—not *what* you see. Just tell us whether you see any figure at all—not what that particular figure may be. Do you understand?"

As you speak, slowly turn your outstretched hand to revolve the direction of the glass a half-turn so as to bring the side with the waxed design toward yourself. This brings the little triangle directly into the spectator's line of vision as he looks through his side of the glass. Ask: "Are your thoughts begin-

CRYSTAL VISION

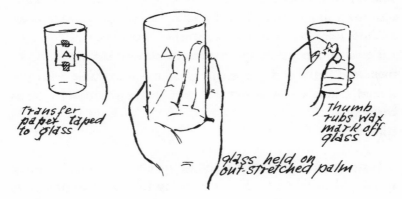

Transfer paper taped to glass

Thumb rubs wax mark off glass

glass held on out-stretched palm

ning to form around some image that is becoming vivid in your mind? . . . Don't describe it yet. You do see something? There's a clear image of some figure in your thoughts?"

As soon as he says that he sees what it is, bring your left hand up to the glass so that your thumb comes right over the waxed mark, and lift the glass away with that hand. There's no need to hurry the action. Look at the glass yourself as you talk and just bring your thumb over the design as your left hand picks up the glass from your right palm.

Drop your left hand to your side, carrying the glass with it, and secretly rub your thumb across the side of the glass to erase the design. This takes only a sweep of your thumb. At the same time, raise your right hand and snap your fingers, as if to clear the spectator's mind of his "vision."

"Look into it now," you say, as you hand him the glass. "Do you still see something?" Give him time to look over the glass, on which he will find no trace of the triangle he saw. "Nothing at all? Then the vision must have been entirely in your own mind. But please remember what you think you saw. We'll both keep that thought a secret from everybody else for a moment."

Take the glass from him, put it on your table, and pick up the design cards. Point to a second spectator in the audience and ask, "Will you please join in our experiment, sir? . . . There's no need to leave your seat. I just want you to look at these symbols that I have." Remove the rubber band and hold the stack of cards facing the audience, with the first circle design showing at the front.

Point to that front card and say, "A circle." Remove it and put it at the back of the stack behind all the others. Point to the next card and say, "A star." Put that at the back and continue showing them that way and calling out what each design is until you come to the second circle card. Say, "The circle again—which brings us back to where we started."

Leave that where it is at the face of the stack. Turn the whole stack around so the backs of the cards are toward the spectator and the circle card faces you. "I'll turn these so that you can't see their faces," you explain, "because I want you to make an entirely random choice of one of these symbols— nothing that could be a preconceived thought."

Lift off the circle card, keeping its back to him, and hold it up to demonstrate as you say, "I'll hold them up one at a time and I want you to call out—whenever you want me to stop. Choose any one you wish." Put that behind the rest of the stack. The first of the six duplicate triangle cards now faces you. Hold it up, with its back to him, and ask, "This one?" Put that at the back of the stack, take the next triangle, hold it up back outwards the same way, and ask, "This?"

Continue until he calls out to choose one. Without showing it rest it face down on top of the glass on your table and put the other cards aside. Turn to the first spectator and say, "A moment ago, you looked into this glass and had a brief vision of something. When you did your crystal gazing you saw some figure—some design. . . . Will you please tell everybody now what it was that you saw?"

He says: "A triangle."

"You saw it in your mind before the gentleman over there made his choice." Lifting the card from the top of the glass, you hold it to show the triangle. "A mental vision of something that hadn't happened yet. . . . Congratulations. For a first try as a crystal gazer—I think you deserve our applause."

Comic Strip Clairvoyance

How it looks:

"I've clipped a bunch of comic strips out of the newspapers," you say, holding up a batch of them. "All your favorite funny characters—and mine. Different papers, different strips, different days." You show them to one of the spectators as you read off some of the names. "Plain Jane, Momma, Broom Hilda, Steve Roper, Judge Parker, Rex Morgan. . . ."

Turning them all facedown, you give him some, invite him to choose one of them, but caution him not to let you see it. You also give him a small envelope. "I want you to read that comic strip to yourself," you explain. "Read the name printed at the top and think about the character and the events that are pictured. Then please fold it up, put it into the envelope, and seal it."

While he is doing that, you go to two other spectators, have them choose comic strips and give them envelopes to seal them in. You then collect the three envelopes, put them into your pocket, and return to the front of the room.

"I have no way of knowing which comic strip each of you chose to put into the sealed envelopes that are still in my pocket," you say. "But in my mind the characters I see most clearly are—Li'l Abner . . . Mutt and Jeff . . . Andy Capp. If I have correctly named the comic strip any of you is thinking about—will you please hold up your hand?"

You look at the three spectators, all of whom have raised their hands. "All three of you? All three correct. . . . I am getting your thoughts clearly. Let's see if I can get any of the pictures in your minds."

Removing one of the sealed envelopes from your pocket, you hold it to your forehead and describe the events that are pictured on the comic strip sealed within it. Repeat this procedure with the second and third envelopes, each in turn. Once more, you ask the three spectators: "If I have correctly described the pictures that were in your minds — any of you — will you hold up your hands?"

Again all three hold up their hands. "All three," you say. "Thank you. That is unusual."

What you need:

Three duplicate copies of the same issue of a daily newspaper that contains a page of comic strips. These should be full comic strips, each with several panels of pictures, not single-frame cartoons. They should be black and white, not Sunday color comics, with plain newsprint on the back of them.

A few newspapers with different comic strips, to provide a variety.

Six 2½-by-4¼-inch manila coin envelopes with end-opening flaps.

A pair of scissors.

A pen or pencil.

A rubber band.

The secret and setup:

Although a lot of different strips are shown, all three spectators are limited to choosing one from identical sets of three strips. It doesn't matter which of those three they choose, or if they all happen to choose the same strip, since you reveal all three possibilities before you ask whether theirs was among the three you named.

The same principle applies when you reveal the details of what is pictured in the strips. You don't know or care who chose what or which envelope he put it in — it has to be among the three you describe—and none of the three spectators knows which strip any other spectator chose.

You are able to describe the strips in some detail without having to memorize them because the information is written on the faces of three dummy envelopes that you take from your pocket instead of the sealed envelopes that you had put there. As you hold the envelopes before your eyes, you just read what is secretly written on them.

Start by deciding which three comic strips you intend to have the spectators select. Cut those out of the duplicate newspapers and make up three sets, each of which contains all three strips. Put those three sets aside for a moment. Now cut a batch of different comic strips from the various newspapers, so that altogether you have about twenty, with different names and characters.

Put one of the envelopes lengthwise and faceup on a table, with its flap end to the left. On the face of that envelope, print a brief description of one of the three comic strips you have chosen for the duplicate sets. The information should be printed at the center of the envelope in several short lines. You might print, for example: MUTT-JEFF/ JEFF PLAYING CARDS/ GETS HOME 2 A.M./ WIFE WAITS WITH ROLLING PIN/ JEFF SAYS: "DON'T TELL ME YOU'RE UP THIS LATE BAKING A CAKE."

Write similar short descriptions on the faces of two more envelopes for the other two strips. Then take any three *different* comic strips, not strips from your duplicate sets, and fold them up. Put one of those into each of the three envelopes on which you have written descriptions and seal them. That is done to give the dummy envelopes the appearance of having comic strips sealed inside them so the envelopes will have some bulk.

Lay the three sets of duplicate strips *faceup* on a table. Put the rest of the different strips faceup on top of those. Fold all the strips together into a small bundle and fasten the rubber band around them.

Have the bundle of comic strips in the right-hand pocket of your jacket, along with the three empty unsealed envelopes. The three dummy envelopes go into your left-hand pocket. Stand them stacked together on end, flap ends at the top, with their written faces toward your body.

What you do:

Take out the bundle of comic strips, remove and discard the rubber band, and open them out full length. Display them and explain what they are and hold them faceup in your left hand. Show them to one of the spectators by thumbing them off one at a time into your right hand, as if you were counting dollar bills from hand to hand. Read aloud the names of the strips as you show them. When you have shown the spectator about a dozen, put them all back on *top* of the stack in your left hand.

"I'll turn them all over so we don't know which is which," you say. Turn the whole stack over together with your right hand so they lie facedown in your left hand. The first identical set of three preselected strips is now facedown on top of the stack. "Will you please take some?" You don't say how many, but just count off three and give them to the spectator. "Keep them turned down so I can't see them. Mix them up if you like. You have a free choice. Please choose one of them—any one you wish—and then give me back the rest."

Hold out your right hand to take the two he returns and put those at the *bottom* of the whole stack in your left hand. Say: "I want you to read the comic strip you have chosen. Read it to yourself. Read the name printed at the top of the strip and think about the characters and the events that are pictured. Then please fold it up and seal it in this envelope." Take one of the empty envelopes from your right-hand pocket and give it to him. "While you're doing that, I'll give some of the other comic strips to somebody else."

The second set of preselected strips is now facedown on top of the stack. Go to a second spectator who is at some distance from the first one. As you approach him, count three strips off the stack and give them to him as you say: "Will you take some, please, and hold them so I can't see them—keep them turned down. Then choose one and give me back the others."

Again, put the two that he returns on the *bottom* of the stack, which leaves the next preselected set on top. Instruct him to read his chosen strip to himself, as you did the first spectator, and hand him an envelope to seal the strip in after he has read it. Move on to a third spectator, who isn't too close to the second, and repeat the same thing.

Collect the three envelopes and as you take each one say, loudly enough for the whole audience to hear, "Thank you. I'll put it in my pocket." Openly put them into your left-hand pocket, but lengthwise, so that they don't mix with the three dummy envelopes that are endwise in that pocket. Return to the front of the room.

"I have no way of knowing which comic strip each of you chose to put into the sealed envelopes that are still in my pocket," you say. "But the characters I see most clearly in my mind are . . ." Call out the names of the three you have pre-selected, for example, "Li'l Abner . . . Mutt and Jeff . . . Andy Capp." Look quickly from the first spectator to the second and third. "If I have correctly named the one any of you is thinking about—will you please hold up your hand?" Wait for the audience to realize that three hands are raised. "All three of you? I am getting your thoughts clearly. Let's see if I can get any of the pictures in your minds."

With your left hand take one of the dummy envelopes from your pocket, holding the top end of it between your thumb and first finger. Being careful not to turn it, bring it straight up against your forehead and keep it there a moment. Then lower it a little so it is in front of your eyes and you can read the writing on it. When you have read enough to have the information fixed in mind, bring the envelope straight down against your chest, still without turning it, and hold it there as you describe what is pictured in one of the comic strips.

Take that envelope with your right hand and put it away in your right-hand pocket. With your left hand remove another envelope from the pocket on that side and bring it up in front of you to secretly read what is on it. Then put that away in your right-hand pocket. When you have described all three comic strips, say: "If I have correctly described the pictures that were in your minds—any of you—will you hold up your hands?"

Wait for all three to raise their hands as before. Then say: "All three of you again. Thank you. That is unusual."

Double Image

How it looks:

"I want you to picture something in your mind—not a word or a number, but a visual image of some simple object or design," you say to a spectator. "It could be a face . . . ." With a piece of chalk you draw a face on a slate and erase it. "Or it might be a geometrical figure such as a square with a circle inside it." You draw that to show him, then erase it and give him the slate and chalk. "Will you stand facing me, please, and hold the slate so I can't see what you draw— with your back to the others so that they *can* see?"

He faces you with his back to the audience and draws on the slate. When he has finished drawing, you say, "I'll put it into this envelope to cover it." You take the slate from him at arm's length, and without looking at it you keep it upright and slide it into a large envelope. Fastening the flap shut, you show both sides of the envelope. "Please think about what you have drawn—picture it again in your mind."

Holding the envelope, the slate sealed inside it, you take a black crayon and begin to draw on its face. "Please understand that I won't attempt to duplicate exactly what you have in mind," you explain. "I'm certainly no artist, and, as I said, we're dealing not with words or numbers but with a mere image of something. I can only draw whatever I may see in my own mind. . . . What I do see is this. . . ."

You describe some features of it as you draw a sketch on the envelope. Then you turn the envelope so the audience can see what you have drawn. Unfastening the clasp, you remove the slate and hold the two side by side. Your drawing on the envelope roughly matches what the spectator drew on the slate.

What you need:

A piece of Silver Mylar, cut with scissors to a size about 5 inches long and 1¼ inches wide. This is thin paperlike metallic film with a silvered mirror finish, which is available at art supply stores. It is manufactured in rolls and usually sold by the yard.

A wooden-framed "school" slate, about 8-inches-square.

White chalk.

A few facial tissues.

A 9-by-12-inch manila clasp envelope of good quality paper that cannot be seen through.

A dark black wax crayon.

Double-faced (sticky both sides) transparent tape.

The secret and setup:

The Silver Mylar strip is fastened to the inside of the envelope flap where it serves as a mirror so that you can see a clear reflection of the drawing as you slide the slate into the envelope. Being light in weight and with no bulk, it in no way interferes with the natural handling of the envelope, and it is entirely hidden from view when the envelope flap is closed.

Turn the envelope so the flap is at the top and attach the strip of Silver Mylar lengthwise to the inside of the flap, centered directly beneath the clasp hole. Attach it with double-faced tape, fastened to the back of the Mylar along its top and bottom edges. The long bottom edge of the mirrored strip should just clear the fold, so the flap can be opened and closed easily.

To see how it works make a simple drawing on the slate with the chalk. Stand the slate on end, upright against some-

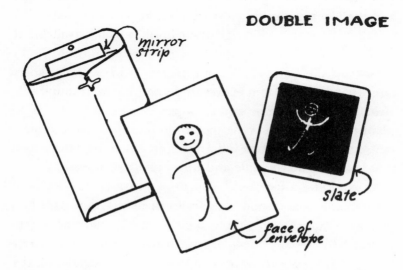

DOUBLE IMAGE

mirror strip

slate

face of envelope

thing on top of a bookcase with the drawing faced away from you. Take the envelope with its back toward you and unfasten the flap. Bring your left hand to the top of the opened flap, thumb at the rear and fingers in front, and hold the envelope that way so it hangs down from that hand.

Stand at arm's length from the slate and take it with your right hand, between your thumb and fingers at the top, keeping it faced away from you. Hold out the envelope with your left hand, lower it a little, and with your right hand *slowly* slide the slate down inside it. As you do that, tilt the flap out slightly—as you naturally would to insert the slate. By looking at the mirrored strip you will see a reflection of the drawing as the slate goes into the envelope.

To set things for performance, have the envelope on your table, back upward and with the flap fastened by the clasp. Put the slate, cleaning tissues, and chalk on top of the envelope and the black crayon in your right-hand pocket.

What you do:

Pick up the slate, chalk, and tissues. Explain to the spectator that you want him to picture something in his mind—"a visual image of some simple object or design." This is to plant the idea that it is the picture in his mind that is important, not the fact that he will draw it on a slate, and to suggest that it should be a simple and uncomplicated drawing.

"It could be a face. . . ." You draw just a circle with lines for eyes, nose, and mouth, again to stress that you want him to make a quick and simple sketch. "Or it might be a geometrical figure. . . ." You draw a plain square with a circle inside. Erase each drawing with a tissue. Then give him the slate and chalk and ask him to stand facing you with his back to the audience and to hold the slate so you can't see what he draws.

While he is drawing on the slate, turn to your table, pick up the envelope, casually show both sides of it, and tuck it under your left arm as you return to face the spectator. "Please tell me when you have finished," you say to hurry him a little. "Keep the back of the slate to me. . . . That's right." When he says he has finished, show both sides of the envelope again. Turn the back of it toward you, open the clasp, and lift the flap as you explain, "I'll put it into this envelope to cover it."

Hold the envelope with your left hand, as explained, between your thumb and fingers at the top of the flap so the envelope hangs down from that hand. Stand at arm's length from the spectator and take the slate from him with your right hand at the top of it. Slowly and deliberately, without turning the slate, insert the bottom end of its wooden frame into the envelope. Lower your left hand a bit for this and tilt the flap outward just a little. The weight of the slate going into the envelope makes tilting the flap almost automatic.

Look directly at the top of the envelope—as you naturally would to see that the slate goes into it properly. As you slowly slide the slate down past the flap, the drawing will be reflected in the mirrored strip. If you don't see it well enough at first glance, pull the slate back up a little, as if you were having slight difficulty getting it into the envelope, and steal another glance at the mirror, but don't overdo this. You don't have to remember every line of the drawing precisely, only enough to duplicate a rough sketch of it.

With both hands fold the flap shut and fasten the clasp. Take the envelope with your left hand at the left side of it, turn the envelope to show the audience the back of it again, and say to the spectator, "Please think about what you have drawn—picture it again in your mind." With your right hand remove the black crayon from your pocket.

Hold the envelope upright, face toward you so the audience can't see what you are drawing, and explain that you won't attempt to duplicate exactly what the spectator drew on the slate. Say: "I can only draw whatever I may see in my own mind. . . . What I do see is this. . . ." Then as you make your sketch, describe it in very general terms, as if you were trying to visualize the spectator's mental image.

If he pictured a simple sailboat, for instance, you might say: "I have an impression of an outdoor scene, a landscape. . . . No, I'm wrong. It's a seascape—the ocean or a large lake, a great expanse of water. There's a boat sailing on the water. . . . Yes, a sailboat. . . ." This is partly to build the effect but also to keep the audience interested while you stand drawing something that they can't yet see.

When you have finished, turn the face of the envelope to show your sketch to the spectator and the audience and say, "I don't know how close that is. . . . The strongest picture in my mind was of a boat of some kind."

Open the envelope and leave the metal clasp squeezed open. Hold the envelope with your left hand and with your right hand pull the slate up out of the top of it. Put the slate in front of the envelope for a moment. Close the envelope flap and fasten the clasp. Then hold the envelope and the slate side by side, one in each hand, to compare your sketch with the picture from the spectator's mind.

6

I PREDICT

Some Predictions Do Come True

How it looks:

"For centuries there have been seers and soothsayers who claimed the ability to foretell the future by gazing into crystal balls, sifting sands through their fingers, reading cards and tea leaves," you say. "There is palmistry, numerology, and, of course, there is astrology. Whether it's by luck, coincidence, or whatever you want to believe—some predictions at times do seem to come true."

You show a spectator a number of metal-rimmed tags with strings attached. "Each tag has a different color," you explain. "Ten different colors. And on the other side each bears a number—from one to ten." After you have spread them out and he has had a chance to look them over, you ask him to select one. "You have an entirely free choice. Take them in your hands if you wish. Decide which one you will keep. All I ask is that once you have decided — don't change your mind."

He is requested to fasten his chosen tag by looping the string through a buttonhole of his jacket, "so it will remain in full view where everyone can see it." You then pick up a newspaper that has been lying on the table. "I've been reading the horoscope column in the paper," you say as you open it and fold it back to the proper page. "I don't know whether you believe in astrology or not, but these predictions are fun to read."

Handing him the paper, you ask if he will first look through the column for his astrological sign. "The birthdates are given there. Will you please read aloud what it says for you—just the part printed under your birthdate."

He reads his brief horoscope from the paper, and you say, "Whatever happens, please don't blame me for your horoscope. I didn't make the predictions printed in the paper. They aren't mine. . . . But if you'll look now at the bottom of the page, you'll see two lines written under all the rest, written with pen and ink. I did make those two predictions. I wrote them there. Will you read just the first one aloud?"

The spectator reads: "Your lucky color is green." You point to the color of the tag hanging from his jacket. "And it *was* green," you say. Turning the tag so he can read it, you ask, "What is the number on it?"

He answers: "Eight." You ask him to read aloud the next line from the newspaper and he reads: "Your lucky number is eight."

What you need:

Ten metal-rimmed white cardboard tags, 1¾ inch in diameter, with strings attached.

Ten copies of a newspaper that has a daily horoscope column. These may be ten different issues of newspapers that have been saved or ten copies all purchased at the same time. It makes no difference as long as they are the same size and each has a horoscope.

Paints or crayons in various colors.

A felt-tip black pen.

A small coin envelope in which to keep the tags.

The secret and setup:

The spectator's choice of a tag is entirely free, but the newspaper is prepared. It is made up of ten double pages, each of which includes a horoscope column, with a couple of other pages of any kind at the outside. Beneath each of the horoscope columns you write a prediction to match the color and number of one of the tags so that there are ten different predictions. You simply open the newspaper to the page with the prediction for the color and number of the chosen tag and have it read aloud.

These colors are suggested for the tags: white, blue, green, yellow, pink, red, orange, purple, brown, black. The white one is left plain, but on its back print a large number "1" with the black pen. Each of the others should be solidly colored on one side, and a large number should be printed on the reverse side in the same color. It makes no difference which number goes on what tag as long as they are numbered from one to ten.

From the ten newspapers remove all the double pages that include the horoscope column. Open out the first one on a table or on the floor so the horoscope faces you at either the left or right, wherever it happens to be printed in that issue. (You may have to turn the double page over to get the horoscope facing you.) Then put the next double page with a horoscope faceup on top of that, and so on with all the rest until you have stacked all ten. Close all the pages together, then take any other two or three double pages from one of the newspapers and put those at the outside around the others.

Open the prepared paper to the first horoscope page and at the top, where the page numbers are printed, write a small "1" with the pen. In the white margin at the bottom of that page print: YOUR LUCKY COLOR IS WHITE. Move down a space and print: YOUR LUCKY NUMBER IS 1.

Turn to the next horoscope page and at the top (left or right as the case may be) write a small "2." Take the tag numbered "2" and write the corresponding number and color predictions for that in the bottom margin. Continue to number and write predictions on each of the other horoscope pages in turn. When you have finished all ten, close the newspaper and fold it.

Stack all the tags together, straighten out their strings so they are not tangled, and slide them into the coin envelope. Have that on your table with the prepared newspaper.

What you do:

Make your opening remarks, invite a spectator to join you, and spill the tags out of the envelope to the table. Spread them out separately, hold up one or two by the strings so the audience can see what they are, and turn a few over as you explain: "Each tag has a different color. Ten different colors. And on the other side each bears a number—from one to ten."

You want both the spectator and the audience to be convinced that the tags are exactly as you say they are and that he does have a completely free choice. When he is satisfied and has chosen one, ask him to fasten it by the string to a buttonhole of his jacket so it will hang in full view, and help him to do that.

Take the newspaper, open it toward you, and as you make your comments about astrology, look for the page with a number at the top that matches the number of the tag he has chosen. Do this openly, as if you were going through the pages to find the one with a horoscope column. When you have the page you want, fold its opposite page and the rest back around behind the paper, then give it to the spectator as you point out the horoscope column to him.

He may notice the writing in the bottom margin, but you instruct him carefully. "First look through the column for your astrological sign," you say. "The birthdates are printed there. Will you please read aloud what it says for you—*just the part printed under your birthdate.*"

When he has read his brief printed horoscope from the

paper, you explain that you have written your own prediction "in pen and ink" at the bottom of the page. Point your finger to it and show him where you mean as you say, "I did make those two predictions. I wrote them there. Will you please read *just the first one* aloud?"

He reads it and you point to the tag hanging from his jacket. Take it by the edge and lift it with the color facing out for the audience to see. Say: "And it *was* green (or whatever the color is)" and then turn the tag so he can read the number and ask, "What is the number on it?" Repeat the number he says. Then ask him to read aloud your second prediction. Point your finger to it on the newspaper he is holding. He reads: "Your lucky number is eight" (or whatever it is).

Take the paper from him and toss it on the table. Thank him and say, "However you explain it—sometimes predictions do come true."

Let him keep the tag that is fastened to his jacket. You can easily make another one, and it is something that will encourage talk about your performance afterward when he shows it to his friends.

Symbolic Choice

How it looks:

You display three large cards, one with a red circle drawn on it, the second a square, and the third a triangle. Pointing to someone in the audience, you say: "Will you please look at each of these symbols intently for a moment without expressing any conscious thought?" After showing him each card separately, you turn to a second person in the audience and say: "Will you do the same thing, please? Just look at each of these. First the circle . . . now the square . . . and the triangle. Thank you."

"I'll make a record of my own thoughts," you explain as you take a pen from your pocket and write something on the back of one of the large cards without showing the audience what you write.

Facing the first spectator again, you say to him, "When I snap my fingers, will you please call out whichever one of these first comes to your mind — the circle, square, or triangle?" You snap your fingers and he says, perhaps, "The square."

You remove that card and prop it against a drinking glass at one side of your table. Then you ask the second spectator to choose one of the two remaining symbols in the same way, by calling out whichever one first comes to his mind when you snap your fingers. He may say, "The triangle." You remove that card and prop it against a glass at the other side of the table.

"The square . . . and the triangle," you say, pointing to each in turn. "And this is what I wrote before either choice was made. . . ." You show the audience the back of the one card still in your hand. On it you have written the words SQUARE AND TRIANGLE.

What you need:

Three 6-by-8-inch pieces of blank cardboard.
Two drinking glasses.

A red marking pen or crayon.

A black marking pen that can be clipped into your pocket.

The secret and setup:

Unknown to the audience, predictions have been written on the backs of two of the cards in advance. Because of the way they are held and handled, the backs of all three appear to be blank. The prediction you openly write on the back of the third card completes all the possible choices. Since two cards are removed by the successive choices, the pairing and elimination works out automatically, thus you are left at the end with the card that has the correct prediction on its back. That, of course, is the only prediction the audience ever sees.

With the red marking pen or crayon, draw a large circle on the face of one of the cards, a square on the second, and a triangle on the third.

Turn the "circle" card facedown. On its back, starting at a point about halfway down from the top and slightly to the right of center, print these words, one under another, with the black pen: SQUARE AND TRIANGLE. Make them large, but keep them to the lower right of the card and print the letters as you might have had you quickly jotted them down during the performance. Then draw a circle around the words.

In a similar position on the back of the "square" card, printed and circled in the same way, write: CIRCLE AND TRIANGLE. Leave the third card, the "triangle," blank on the back for now. That is the one on which you will openly write your prediction during the performance. When you do, it will be worded: CIRCLE AND SQUARE.

Stack the three together with their symbols faceup—the triangle at the bottom, then the square, and the circle on top. Turn them over with their backs to you and hold them upright, as though showing their faces to the audience. Now spread them in a fan so the backs overlap like a hand of play-

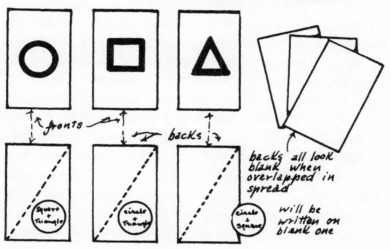

SYMBOLIC CHOICE

ing cards. You will see that you can spread them quite far without revealing the writing on the backs of the first two. Keep them in that overlapping spread and you can turn your hand around to show the apparently blank backs to the audience.

Nothing should suggest that the cards are being held in any special way to hide the fact that two of them already have predictions written on them. Just spread them casually, show the backs, then turn their faces to the audience and square them up again. When you display the faces separately, be careful to hold each card upright and close to you so nobody catches a glimpse of the writing on the back.

Have the cards properly stacked, faceup on your table, one drinking glass at each side of the table, and the black pen clipped into an inside pocket of your jacket.

What you do:

Pick up the cards, hold their backs toward you, and fan them out so the backs overlap to hide the writing. Turn them to casually show the backs and square them up again. Remove one card at a time to show the faces individually.

Choose someone in the audience, face the person, and say: "Will you please just look at each of these symbols intently for a moment, without expressing any conscious thought?" Show him the face of each card again. Then move over to a second spectator and ask that person to do the same thing. "Just look at each of these. First the circle . . . now the square . . . and the triangle."

After you show the three cards to the second spectator, square them together and pretend to concentrate for a moment as you explain, "I'll make a record of my own thoughts." Take out the black pen, casually turn the stack to show the back of the rear card, and turn them towards you again. Hold the stack up so nobody can see what you write, and on the back of that card, about where the predictions were written on the other ones, print and circle the words: CIRCLE AND SQUARE. Then mix the three cards, keeping their backs toward you.

Face the first spectator and ask him to please call out when you snap your fingers whichever first comes to his mind—the circle, square, or triangle. Repeat the name of whichever he calls. Remove that card, its face still to the audience, and stand it upright on the table with its back leaning against one of the drinking glasses.

Go to the second spectator, show the two remaining symbols, and ask him to please call out when you snap your fingers either of the two that are left—whichever one first comes to his mind. When he calls it, remove whichever one he names and prop that upright with its back against the second glass on the table.

On the back of the one card still left in your hand is the prediction that names the two that were chosen and removed. Glance at the prediction, but don't reveal it yet. Point to each of the cards standing on the table, and call out the names of them *in the order in which the prediction is worded.* Finally, turn the card that is in your hand around and hold it so the audience can see what you wrote "before either choice was made."

To the Highest Bidder

How it looks:

Holding up a small package brightly gift-wrapped in red tissue paper, you say: "Hours ago I put something in this package. It could be something valuable—a watch, a set of earrings, a ring, a pair of cufflinks. . . . And then again, it could be worthless. I'm about to auction it off."

You put the package on your table and take a card and

pencil from your pocket as you explain, "I'll keep a record of your bids. Would anybody like to start things off? Come on, folks—for all you know this may be the opportunity of a lifetime. Isn't somebody willing to bid just one penny? . . . You, sir? Do I hear two? . . . The lady over there. I have two cents. Will somebody risk a whole nickel?" You raise the penny bidding as high as it will go. "I have sixteen cents then—is that all? Going once, going twice—gone for sixteen cents!"

When the final bid has been made, you write it on the card and put the pencil in your pocket. Shaking your head, you stare down at the card. *"Sixteen cents?* Sorry, lady—but I just won't sell it to you for that." You crumple up the card. "I refuse to accept your bid!" Then you smile. "Because if I took your money—I'd be cheating you. Instead, I'll give you what's inside the package absolutely free."

Taking the package from the table, you show it again and tear open the tissue paper. "You'll remember that I said I wrapped something in it hours ago? But all I put in the package was this price tag—the price of the highest bid." You remove a metal-rimmed price tag from the torn-open package and take it to the final bidder. "Will you please read it aloud—tell everybody what it says?"

She reads from the tag: "I predict that the highest bid will be . . . exactly sixteen cents."

What you need:

A round metal-rimmed cardboard tag, 1¾ inch in diameter, with its string removed.

A blank card about the size of a business card.

Red tissue paper and decorative tape of a contrasting color.
A pencil small enough to carry in a jacket pocket.
A pair of scissors.

The secret and setup:

There is nothing in the tissue paper package at the start. The card you hold in your hand as you write the bids has a hole in it and the tag is secretly held beneath it. When you write the final bid, you simply pencil in the amount on the tag itself, through the hole in the card. The card is crumpled up in order to dispose of it. Then you rest the package on the hand that holds the tag, tear through the tissue paper, and appear to take the tag from inside the package.

To prepare the card turn it with its narrow ends top and bottom, and about an inch up from the bottom cut a round hole approximately an inch in diameter.

Take the metal-rimmed tag and print on one side with the pencil, spacing out the words: I PREDICT THAT THE HIGHEST BID WILL BE . . . . After the last word draw an arrow that points to the other side. Turn the tag over and on the other side print the word EXACTLY right at the top, then leave the rest blank. Hold the top of the tag between your thumb and fingers and bend the metal rim outward very slightly to leave a small bump at the top. That is so you can tell which is the blank side by feeling the rim with your fingers later when the tag is in your pocket.

Use a piece of red tissue paper about 10 inches square to make up the dummy package. Keep folding it upon itself until you have a neat bundle about 3 inches square and then fasten it with a strip of decorative tape. Work the tissue with your fingers to pull out the sides and puff it into a shape that reasonably might contain some small item of value.

Put the pencil into the left-hand pocket of your jacket. Turn the tag so that its partly blank side faces you. Rest the card on top of the tag with the hole in the card to the bottom. Put them both into the same pocket with the pencil, the card lengthwise and the tag at the outside against the back of the card. They may shift around in your pocket before you get to use them, but that makes little difference since you can easily reposition them, as you reach into the pocket to take them out, by feeling for the bump in the tag's metal rim.

Have the dummy package on your table.

What you do:

Pick up the package and show it as you explain that hours ago you put something in it which might or might not be valuable and that you intend to auction it off. Place the package back on the table and leave it in plain view. Say that you will keep a record of the bids, then put your left hand into your jacket pocket as you ask if someone would care to start the bidding.

Inside your pocket feel for the little bump in the metal rim to reassure yourself that the partly blank side of the tag is still faced the right way in back of the card. With the tag toward the palm of your hand close your fingers around the card and pencil and bring them all out together.

Don't look at that hand or make any immediate attempt to adjust the position of the card and tag. Take the pencil with your right hand and let your left hand, the card and tag in it, drop to your side as you gesture with your right hand and call for bids.

If the audience is slow to start bidding, simply start things off yourself by pretending that someone has made a bid. Look toward the rear of the room and say, "You, sir? Thank you. The gentleman bids a penny — one cent is bid. Do I hear two?"

Bring your left hand up in front of you as you naturally would to write on the card, so the backs of your fingers are toward the audience. With the pencil in your right hand scribble "1¢" somewhere on the card. It makes no difference where since what you write on the card will never be shown. As you get bids of two cents and then three, jot down those numbers.

There is plenty of time as the bidding goes along to adjust the card and tag. You can turn your hand a little or move the card up or down with your other hand, as if to position it better for writing the bids. Part of the letters of the word "EXACTLY" will be visible through the hole in the card so you can make sure that is at the top.

When you have raised the bidding as high as it will go, say: "I have sixteen cents then" (or whatever the amount may be). ". . . Is that all? Going once, going twice — gone for sixteen cents!" Quickly write down the amount, but this time write through the hole in the card to print on the face of the tag. When you have finished writing it, keep the pencil in your right hand and tuck it into your outer breast pocket to leave it there; then let your left hand, holding the card and tag, drop to your side.

Look out at the audience and shake your head as if you were disappointed by the low bidding. Bring your left hand up and stare down at the card. *"Sixteen cents?* Sorry—but I just won't sell it to you for that." With your right hand crumple up the card and lift it away in that hand as you again drop your left hand to your side.

To the HIGHEST BIDDER

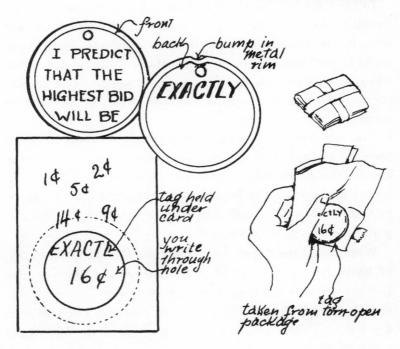

The tag remains in your left hand, loosely held there by the curl of your fingers and concealed by the back of your hand, which naturally falls into that position at your side. Don't make any attempt to "palm" the tag or to do anything tricky with it. Pay no attention to that hand at all.

Look at the crumpled card in your right hand, shake your head again, and say, "I refuse to accept your bid!" Crush the card and put it into the right-hand pocket of your jacket. Then smile and explain: "I won't accept your bid because if I took your money—I'd be cheating you. Instead, I'll give you what's inside the package absolutely free."

Pick up the package with your right hand and show it. Bring your left hand up in front of you and put the package into that hand right on top of the concealed tag. With your right hand tear open the tissue paper, spreading it wide. There is enough of the paper so it will pretty well cover your left hand, which now can be shown quite freely as you continue to tear the package open.

Just tear through the bottom of the paper. Pull the tag out through it a little. Turn your left hand to let the audience see the tag against the torn paper. Take the edge of the tag with your right thumb and first finger, slowly draw it the rest of the way out of the paper, and hold it up high. Crumple the paper in your left hand and toss it aside.

Hold your right hand with the tag above your head as you go to the spectator who made the last bid. Ask the person to read aloud what you wrote on the tag "hours ago." Glance at the tag to make sure you hold it so he will begin reading from the side that starts with the words, I PREDICT THAT . . .

As he finishes reading that side aloud, turn it over and give him the tag to read the other side, which completes your prediction that the highest bid would be . . . EXACTLY 16¢.

Weather Forecast

How it looks:

"One thing everybody tries to predict is the weather," you say, as you hold up a large card and read aloud the weather conditions printed on it in red. "Warmer, colder, cloudy, stormy, fair."

Turning to one of the spectators, you invite him to try to predict what tomorrow's weather will be. "Just make a guess. But don't tell us yet what it is. Look over this list of possibilities and decide in your own mind what kind of a day you think tomorrow will be. Let's see if I can pick up your mental forecast."

When he says he is thinking of one of the listed weather conditions, you turn the card so it faces you. "I'll make a little circle and put an X in it." Taking a black pen from your pocket, you mark the card without showing it to the audience. "All right. I've marked what I believe your forecast will be. . . . You can tell us now. What's your guess — warmer, colder, cloudy, stormy or fair?"

He calls out his mental choice, perhaps, "Stormy." You show the audience the card. The word you have marked with an X is STORMY.

"You were very positive about that, sir," you say. "I got the thought clearly. If you're as good at predicting the weather as you are at projecting your thoughts, we'd better expect a stormy day tomorrow."

What you need:

A 7-by-11-inch sheet of white poster board.

A red marking pen.

A broad-tipped black marking pen that can be clipped into your pocket.

A package of white, round, self-sticking "removable" labels, 1 inch in diameter. These are available at stationery stores, sold under various trade names such as Pres-a-ply.

A pair of scissors.

The secret and setup:

You only pretend to mark the card. The circle and X mark are drawn ahead of time on one of the labels. This is hidden, in a way that will be explained, so that your thumb secretly rolls the label into place and sticks it on the card after the spectator has called out what he is thinking. It looks as if you had marked the card itself, right opposite the word he had in mind.

The list of weather conditions should be printed so as to leave a wide margin at the left of the words. Start with the large card on a table, narrow edges top and bottom. With the red marking pen print WARMER in letters about 1 inch high, beginning about 2 inches down from the top and the same distance in from the left. Print each of the other weather conditions directly beneath the one above, with a good space between them. Turn the card with the printing face down and put it aside for a moment.

Take one of the self-sticking white labels and with the

scissors trim a tiny edge off the top and one side so it is no longer a perfectly round circle. This is done to give the label a slightly irregular shape, such as you would make if you quickly drew a circle with a pen. With the *black* pen draw a circle on the label, all the way around just inside the edge of it. Then mark a large X in the center.

Stick the *left half* of the label firmly to the *back* of the large card, about 1 inch down from the top left corner, but leave the right half of the label unstuck. Bend that free right-hand edge leftward and crease it slightly at the center of the label, so that right edge of it remains unstuck to the card and retains an inward curl. (If it later accidentally does become stuck flat, you can easily peel it free with a lift of your thumbnail.)

Have the card faceup on the table and clip the black pen into the outside breast pocket of your jacket.

What you do:

Pick up the card and hold it at the sides between both hands to show the audience what is printed on it. Your left hand is at the top left side of the card and your right hand at the lower right side of it, and the fingers of both hands are at the front and thumbs at the back. The ball of your left thumb should be touching the label that is hidden on the back of the card.

Read the printed list of weather conditions aloud and invite one of the spectators to try to predict what tomorrow's weather will be. "Just make a guess. But don't tell us yet what it is," you say. "Look over the list and decide in your own mind. . . . Let's see if I can pick up your mental forecast."

While you are talking, secretly press the ball of your left

thumb against the free edge of the label so that the label sticks to your thumb. Roll your thumb to the left and the label will peel off and remain attached to your thumb. The patter allows time to do this slowly, and the slight movement of your thumb is concealed by the card and by your fingers at the front.

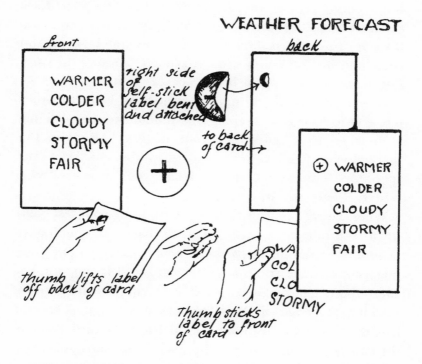

When the spectator says he is thinking of one of the weather conditions, draw your left thumb, the label stuck to it, in toward the palm of that hand. Keep the hand held up as it is. With your right hand turn the card around so it is facing you and grasp the top of the card again with the left hand.

Hold the card up with that hand and drop your right hand to your side. This is the natural way you would turn the card around, and it should look like nothing more than that.

Keep the card facing you, held by your left hand. The fingers are at the front of it and thumb behind, the label still stuck to your thumb. Bring your right hand over to your breast pocket and remove the pen. Move the pen up and down the list behind the card as if debating which word to mark. Scratch your fingernail on the card as you pretend to make a circle and put an X in it without actually marking the card. Put the pen away in your breast pocket again.

Now take the card with your right hand and drop your left arm to your side, keeping that thumb and the label that is attached to it hidden by your fingers. "All right. I've marked what I believe your forecast will be," you say to the spectator. "You can tell us now. What's your guess — warmer, colder, cloudy, stormy or fair?"

When he calls out his mental choice, bring your left hand up to the side of the card again so that your thumb goes behind the card *directly opposite the word he has chosen* and your fingers are at the front. Hold the card, still facing you, between both hands. Secretly roll your thumb to the right, catching the edge of the label against the card. This will peel the label off your thumb and stick it to the card. Smooth the label with your thumb and press it firmly into place.

You can look down at the card as you do this, as if checking the prediction. Take your time and transfer the label properly. Finally turn the card so the audience can see what appears to be the circle and X mark in front of the chosen word.

MAGIC WITH COINS AND BILLS

CONTENTS

INTRODUCTION

This is a collection of some of my favorite magic tricks with coins and paper money. I have included many that the beginner should be able to do with a minimum of practice, and for the more advanced magic hobbyist there are novel money magic plots and subtleties of presentation, as well as updated versions of tricks that have become classics of magic.

There are no feats that require unusual skill or expert manipulation, but a section of the book is devoted to basic sleight of hand, clearly explained so that after a little learning even the novice should be able to put it to use for the performance of puzzling magic with coins.

Some of the tricks can be performed almost anywhere, with the coins and bills that you normally carry in your pockets or that you can borrow from someone in your audience. Others require trick coins and bills, other small props, and advance preparation; but everything needed for them can be assembled at home, and simple step-by-step directions are given for putting them together and performing them. There are tricks for showing to small groups of friends, and others for public performance before larger audiences.

The use of play-money bills, instead of real money, is specified for all tricks that involve cutting, marking, gluing, coloring, or otherwise mutilating the bills. Using transparent tape or other temporary adhesives on real coins and bills is not illegal if they can be removed, but it is against the law to deface currency so as to make it "permanently unspendable." Inexpensive play-money bills, available at toy and game counters, come in many varieties, so it is a good idea to shop around to choose those that are well printed on paper of good quality, and in sizes that are somewhat the same as real money. You won't be trying to convince the audience you are using dollar bills; it is enough in these tricks to suggest the use of money.

As with all forms of magic, tricks with coins and bills should be rehearsed not only individually but in sequence. Even a seemingly "impromptu" showing of just a few simple tricks should be well planned in advance, so that you know not only exactly what you are going to do next and how you will do it, but also where everything will be arranged for the whole performance. Otherwise, you may be embarrassed to discover that a pocket you want to be empty is already stuffed with things used in a previous trick, or you may have to fumble around to fish out the things needed and get them into position. Careful planning and rehearsal also give you the confidence that will let you concentrate on the presentation of individual tricks, which should be practiced until you no longer have to think consciously about each secret move you are making.

The basic methods of magic are a common heritage of all magicians. No claim of originality is made for the methods used in the tricks explained here. Although some have been put to new uses, the methods generally are those that have become accepted as standard and practical. Credit for them belongs to a long line of magicians, who through trial and error have worked them out over the years.

The secrets of tricks, especially of good tricks, are often far more simple than the audience imagines. But for the magician, knowing how a trick is done is not at all the same as knowing how to do it, how to present it interestingly and entertainingly. It may be fun to be fooled, but it certainly is a lot more fun for those who are watching if they are entertained while they are being fooled.

Good presentation is the real secret of magical entertainment, and it comes only through practice, by gradually learning how to please your audiences with what you do. It cannot be taught by any book; it grows out of the personality and style of each performer, and from experience. But I hope that the routines in this book may at least suggest how the secrets of magic can be built into presentations that clothe mere "tricks" with real entertainment.

1

HAND MAGIC
WITH COINS

While it is true that advanced sleight of hand with coins requires long practice and much skill, there are a dozen or so basic moves that are comparatively easy to learn. Once learned, they equip the magician to perform many tricks with just his hands and the ordinary coins that are available. They also provide him with a know-how that can be applied to more elaborate tricks.

Some practice is needed, but that is so with all kinds of magic. For simple hand magic with coins, the most important thing to be learned is not intricate manipulation, but a knack of handling the coins naturally and easily. You also need to do a bit of acting to be convincing.

What is sleight of hand?
Sleight of hand is really just pretending. You pretend to catch a coin at your fingertips, to vanish it, to make it fly invisibly from hand to hand, to magically change a penny to a dime or change a quarter to a half-dollar. You put on an act. Like any actor playing a role, you pretend to be a magician.

What you secretly do with your hands is only part of that act. Like the backstage props in a theater that are hidden from view, sleight of hand is the hidden part of magic, but it is not the whole show. It must be done well enough so that the audience is not aware of it, but what you should always try to keep in mind is what you are *pretending* to do.

What makes magic entertaining to watch and fun to perform is the way you use its secrets to create illusion. You secretly do one thing while you pretend—with your hands, your voice, your eyes, the expression on your face—to do something else. As you learn the moves that are about to be explained, think of the *effect* that you want them to have, what it is that you want your audience to believe.

All of magic is theater. Even when you do something as simple as showing a friend a penny in your hand and then making it disappear, you are putting on a little theatrical performance. You don't have to make a big thing of it. In fact, the more casually you seem to do it, the more surprising it may be. But you do have to act it out, not just go through the fingering.

If you move one hand away from the other, people usually will look at the hand that is moving. If you look down at one hand instead of the other, they will look where you look. That is all part of what magicians call *misdirection*, doing things to lead people's thoughts and attention to what you are pretending and away from the real secret of the trick. The success of magic depends much more on skillful misdirection than any secret moves and devices.

But a lot of it comes naturally. Most people are apt to think in terms of what they would normally expect to see, unless you give them some reason to think otherwise. If the palm of your hand is toward the floor, they tend to think there is nothing in it, because normally anything in your hand would fall out. By habit of thought, they assume that an upside-down hand is an empty hand—unless you hold it in a stiff, unnatural position that makes them take a second look.

A good general rule for hand magic is to manipulate the hands as slightly as necessary to accomplish whatever you are pretending to do with them. If you are hiding a coin in one hand while you pretend to put it into the other hand, the more naturally you can do it, the more convincing it will be.

The object is not to demonstrate how clever you are at hiding the coin by wiggling your fingers around or showing your hand this way or that, but simply to keep from arousing suspicion that you are doing anything "tricky" with it at all. If you go through a lot of elaborate manipulation to try to prove that you aren't hiding something, you may only call attention to the fact that you are.

Practice and rehearsal

Watching yourself in a mirror can help with practicing, but it may also make you self-conscious when you are first trying to learn a new move, so that you become fussy, tense, or timid. Probably the best way to begin is to read the directions and then just go about trying it. Run through it a few times, fumbles and all, until you think you can do it fairly well. Then stand before a mirror and watch yourself as an audience would. Watch the angles, correct the faults, and try it again without the mirror.

If you have a coin palmed in your hand, try doing other things with the fingers of that hand. With the coin concealed, pick things up, carry them, put them down. Try using those fingers to turn the pages of a magazine, to open a bureau drawer, to button your jacket. You can have fun making a sort of game of it, to get used to the natural handling of things while you keep the coin hidden.

But as you practice, also remember that the move itself is only part of the act of pretending. Put it to use in some trick you intend to do and go through the whole trick just as if an audience were really watching. Speak to the people in your imaginary audience, look up at them, smile, look down at the hand you want them to look at. Do it as an actor would rehearse a part in a play.

What coins to use

Most of these basic moves can be done with ordinary coins of any size, but the larger ones are easiest to hold and to get into place. For the person with hands of average size, the best coins to use for learning are half-dollars. They are big enough to grip properly and have good weight and milled edges, which helps in handling them. If your hands are rather small, you may want to begin with quarters. Once you are confident that you can do a move fairly well, try using coins of all sizes.

Remember that coins are light. You don't have to grip them forcefully, squeeze them tight, or hold on to them for dear life. Gently does it!

THE FINGER-PALM

The purpose

Finger-palming is used to hold coins or other small things in the partly closed fingers of either hand so that the back of the hand hides them from view of the audience. It has many uses and leaves the hands and fingers fairly free to pick up and hold other things. Finger-palming looks very natural and is probably the easiest method of palming.

The handling

When a coin is properly finger-palmed, it is held at the base of the partly closed second and third fingers, between the middle joints of those fingers and the edge of the palm.

But to understand why the finger-palm looks so naturally deceptive, first try this, without any coin in your hands: Stand in front of a mirror and drop your hands to your sides, so they hang loosely as they usually do when you're not using them. You will see that your fingers normally curl inward because of the natural curve of the backs of your relaxed hands.

THE FINGER-PALM—I

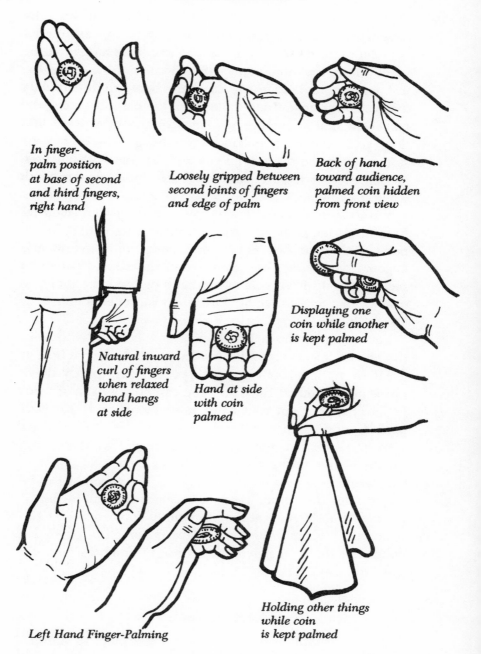

In finger-
palm position
at base of second
and third fingers,
right hand

Loosely gripped between
second joints of fingers
and edge of palm

Back of hand
toward audience,
palmed coin hidden
from front view

Natural inward
curl of fingers
when relaxed
hand hangs
at side

Hand at side
with coin
palmed

Displaying one
coin while another
is kept palmed

Left Hand Finger-Palming

Holding other things
while coin
is kept palmed

Now bring your right hand up in front of you, with the fingers still loosely cupped, and hold it palm upward. Rest a coin flat on the bases of your second and third fingers, at the place where they join your palm. Close your hand slightly, just enough to hold the coin there between the middle joints of those fingers and the edge of the palm. Keeping the coin held that way, turn your hand palm downward and drop your arm so your hand again hangs loosely at your side. Look in the mirror and you will see that with the coin hidden in your fingers, your hand still looks as natural as when it was empty.

With a coin finger-palmed, you can bring your hand up in front of you, palm toward you, and gesture with it freely, point with your first finger, even snap your thumb and fingers if you wish. You can use your thumb and fingers to pick things up from your other hand or from the table, to display another coin, to hold up a handkerchief, a pencil, or an envelope.

You can pick up a small glass and hold it with your thumb and fingers around the sides, or hold a bag, a box, or a hat by its top rear edge with your fingers partly down inside and thumb at the back. You can hold a pack of cards in your hand, or put your hand on someone's arm, pat your pockets, and reach into them. What you *can't* do is open your hand out flat and spread your fingers wide, but you usually would have no reason to do that.

A single coin or several of them stacked together can be finger-palmed in either hand, or various coins can be finger-palmed in both hands at the same time. You can also finger-palm such things as a bottle cap, poker chip, or folded dollar bill that you may want to use in combination with coins for some particular trick.

Pick-up Vanish

This is a simple way of using the finger-palm to vanish a coin, but as simple as it is, it can be effective if done quickly

THE FINGER-PALM—II

GESTURING

*Pointing finger
with coin palmed*

*Pointing with
palm downward*

PICK-UP VANISH

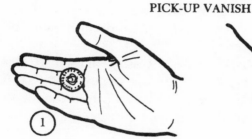

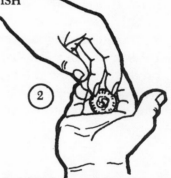

*Displaying coin to audience
in position for palming*

*Left hand pretends to take coin
from cupped right hand,
which keeps it palmed*

DROP VANISH

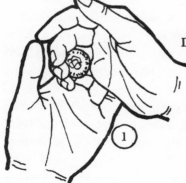

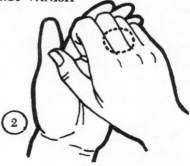

*Right hand comes inside
cupped left fingers and
pretends to drop coin . . .*

*but keeps it palmed
as hands draw apart*

and boldly. The way it looks is that you show a coin resting on the fingers of your right hand. You pick it up with your other hand and throw it high into the air, and it vanishes.

Place the coin on your right hand, at the base of the two middle fingers in a position to finger-palm it, and lower that hand a little to display it there. Bring your left hand down from above, fingertips downward, as if to pick up the coin between the thumb and fingers.

Pass the left-hand fingers across the coin, pinching thumb and fingers together as though taking it, and lift your left hand straight up. As you do that, turn your right hand slightly toward you and immediately let it drop to your side with the coin finger-palmed.

Look at your left hand, make a tossing motion as you pretend to throw the coin high into the air, open the hand wide so it is seen to be empty, and look up into the air as though following the flight of the coin as it vanishes.

Drop Vanish

Like many moves with coins, this finger-palm vanish is based on the notion that to an audience an upside-down hand is an empty hand. Watchers see your right hand turn over as it apparently drops a coin into your left hand, which closes around it, but when the left hand opens a moment later the coin is gone.

Start by showing the coin lying on your right hand. Bounce it flat once or twice so it slides to rest over the base of your two middle fingers in a position for finger-palming it.

Hold out your left hand, fingertips toward the audience and cupped upward slightly. Turn your right hand over toward you, finger-palming the coin as you bring the hand palm downward inside the cupped fingers of the left hand as if to drop the coin into it. Without pausing, draw your hands apart, closing the left fingers as if they held the coin.

Lift that hand a little as you look at it and point to it with the first finger of your palm-downward right hand.

This should all be done casually, as though you merely showed a coin with one hand, dropped it into the other, and closed that hand around it. Thrust the closed left hand forward slightly and let your right hand fall loosely to your side. Slowly open your left hand and show that the coin has vanished.

THE THUMB-PALM

The purpose

Thumb-palming is secretly holding a coin in the crotch of the thumb so that the coin is hidden from view when the back of the hand is toward those who are watching. The coin is clipped flat under the thumb below the base of the first finger and is held there at the extreme edge of the palm by the pressure of the side of the thumb.

The thumb-palm is most often used for the production or vanish of a coin at the fingertips, for quickly palming a coin while pretending to throw it into the other hand, or for palming it while seeming to drop it into something such as a hat, a bag, or a box. The fingers are free and can even be spread apart, and the hand looks from the back as though it couldn't be holding anything.

The thumb-palm is not difficult but requires some practice to do casually and naturally and to avoid rapid jerking movements of the hand while getting the coin back and forth from the fingers into the crotch of the thumb.

The handling

To understand where the coin is held when it is in thumb-palm position, first try this: Hold your right hand palm upward in front of you, fingertips toward the front and thumb toward the right. Lift your thumb up and a little to the right, to get it out of the way for a moment.

Lay a coin flat on the extreme right edge of the hand,

THE THUMB-PALM—I

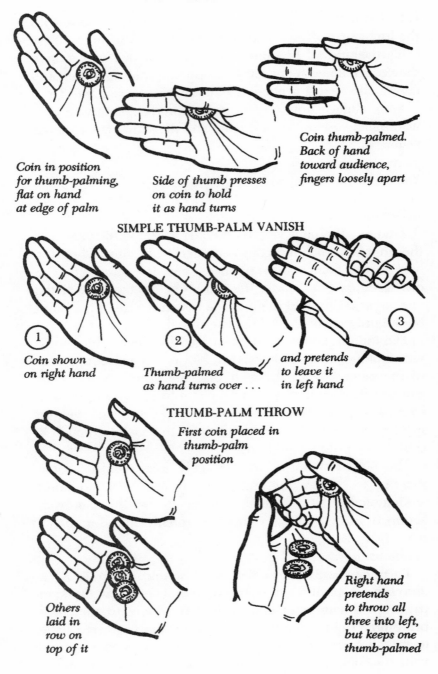

Coin in position
for thumb-palming,
flat on hand
at edge of palm

Side of thumb presses
on coin to hold
it as hand turns

Coin thumb-palmed.
Back of hand
toward audience,
fingers loosely apart

SIMPLE THUMB-PALM VANISH

(1) Coin shown
on right hand

(2) Thumb-palmed
as hand turns over . . .

(3) and pretends
to leave it
in left hand

THUMB-PALM THROW

First coin placed in
thumb-palm
position

Others
laid in
row on
top of it

Right hand
pretends
to throw all
three into left,
but keeps one
thumb-palmed

below your lifted thumb, so it rests on the hand between the fork of the thumb and the base of the first finger. Now bring the side of the thumb down against the right half of the coin and press against it to hold the coin between the thumb and the edge of the hand.

Keep your thumb and fingers as they are and turn your whole hand so the palm is toward you, thumb at the top, fingertips pointing to the left. The coin is now thumb-palmed, hidden from front view by the back of the hand. You can bring the hand palm downward to your other hand or to a table, drop the hand loosely to your side, point with it, or move it around freely, as long as you don't turn it with the palm directly toward the audience. Coins can be thumb-palmed with either hand.

A common mistake in thumb-palming is to hold the hand out stiffly, with the back of it flat and the fingers spread wide apart. There is a temptation to do that to "prove" you have nothing in your fingers, but it looks awkward and unnatural. Just hold the hand in a normally relaxed way, with the fingers slightly apart, so there is a natural curving of the back of the hand and the fingers. The tip of the thumb and part of the side of it should show above the top of the hand, but the coin should be well within the hand so none of it shows.

Simple Thumb-Palm Vanish

Show a coin with your left hand and place it on your upturned right hand so that it rests near the edge of the hand beneath the base of the first finger. Display it there and hold out your left hand, palm upward.

Turn your right hand over, palm downward, to bring it above the left hand, and as you do that just press the side of the right thumb against the coin to hold it. Continue to bring your right hand down into the left, as if dropping the coin, and start to close your left fingers loosely up around your right fingers as you draw your hands apart.

Lift your closed left hand a little, as though taking the dropped coin, and let your right hand fall to your side with the coin thumb-palmed. Look at your closed left hand, slowly open the fingers, and show that the coin has vanished.

Thumb-Palm Throw

In much the same way as the vanish, you can show several coins in one hand and pretend to throw them all together into the other hand, but really hold back one of them by keeping it thumb-palmed. This throw can be used in various ways, such as pretending to make one of several coins fly invisibly from hand to hand.

Show three coins, for example, and lay them in a row across the palm of your right hand so that one of the three is at the edge of the hand in a position for thumb-palming it. Hold out your left hand and turn your right hand palm downward over it to throw the coins from hand to hand, but squeeze the side of your right thumb to the coin positioned under it and keep that one thumb-palmed as the others fall into your left hand.

Immediately close your left hand around the coins it catches and jingle them in that hand as you drop your right hand to your side. The sound of the two coins clinking together in your left hand is deceptive and adds to the illusion that you threw all three from hand to hand.

To make a simple trick of it, pretend to throw the three from your right hand to your left, but keep one thumb-palmed and drop your right hand to your side. Hold out your closed left hand, which supposedly contains all three. Now bring up your right hand with its back toward the audience, turn it palm downward, and slowly close the fingers. Hold both closed hands in front of you and command one coin to fly invisibly from your left hand to your right. Open the left hand and drop its two coins on the table, showing that the hand is otherwise empty. Then open your right hand and drop out the coin that was thumb-palmed.

Fingertip Vanish

If you want to use the thumb-palm to make a coin held by the fingertips visibly seem to vanish, you have to secretly move it from the fingers into the crotch of the thumb to grip it there. This is done by quickly closing the hand and opening it out again. Here is how to position the coin in the fingers to do that:

Hold your right hand in front of you, palm toward you, thumb at the top and fingers pointed toward the left. Turn a coin so that its face and back are horizontal. Now hold it clipped flat between the sides of your first and second fingers, near the tips of them. As much of the coin as possible should be visible beyond the tips of the fingers, but with enough kept between the fingers to grip it securely.

That is how you display the coin at your fingertips before thumb-palming it. When performing, you can first display it in another position and then move it into the finger clip to hold it in view, or else show it first with the other hand and quickly clip it between your fingertips to show it.

To thumb-palm it so as to make it seem to vanish from your fingertips as you throw it into the air, start by showing it clipped between your fingers, with the back of your hand toward the audience. With a slight wave of your hand, pretend to throw the coin out to the left. As you make the throwing motion, close your hand so the fingers curl inward to bring the coin back into the crotch of your thumb. Press your thumb against it to hold it in the regular thumb-palm position. When it is securely held by your thumb, straighten out your fingers again.

With a little practice, this can be done quite rapidly, but more important, it should be done smoothly. The rapid closing and opening of the fingers while the hand is moving seems a natural part of the throwing motion and won't be

THE THUMB-PALM—II

FINGERTIP VANISHES AND PRODUCTIONS

VANISH

 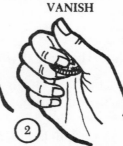 

1 Coin displayed, flat between sides of first and second fingers

2 Fingers close quickly to bring coin into crotch of thumb

3 Thumb holds it. As fingers quickly open out again, coin vanishes

PRODUCTION

1 Thumb-palmed coin hidden from front view

2 Fingers quickly curl in to take it from crotch of thumb . . .

3 and open out to produce it at fingertips

THUMB-PALM DROP

Fingers show coin and pretend to put it into a hat

With hand partly inside, fingers curl to grip coin in crotch of thumb

Hand brought out with back to audience. Seems to have left coin in hat

noticed if you do it without hesitating. All the audience really sees is that one moment the coin was at your fingertips and now they are empty.

Fingertip Production

To produce a coin at the fingertips, you use the same handling as for vanishing it, but in reverse. Instead of secretly moving the coin into the crotch of your thumb, you take it from there.

Start with a coin palmed in the crotch of your thumb in the regular thumb-palm position. Hold up your hand with its back to the audience to show the fingers empty. With a little waving motion, reach out toward the left as if to catch an invisible coin from the air. As you do that, quickly close the hand, curl the fingers inward to the crotch of the thumb, grip the coin so it is clipped between your first and second fingers, and open out your hand to show it at your fingertips.

The production and vanish are often combined, as in the classic trick of magically producing a number of coins from the air and collecting them in a hat or metal bucket. A full routine for that is explained in the section *"Catching Coins from the Air"* in chapter 4 of this book.

Thumb-Palm Drop

You can thumb-palm a coin while seeming to drop it from your right-hand fingers into a hat, a bag, a handkerchief, or something else that is being held by your left hand. For example, hold out a hat by its brim with your left hand, and display the coin as before at the fingertips of your right hand. Pretend to drop the coin into the hat with a slight throwing motion as you put your hand a little way down inside the hat. Quickly close your fingers to thumb-palm the coin, and immediately open them out and remove your hand, apparently having left the coin in the hat.

PUSHES, PIVOTS, AND DROPS

The purpose

These are ways of holding a coin to display it at your fingertips so that you can then secretly push it, pivot it, or let it drop out of sight behind your fingers. They are usually used to vanish a coin, to pretend to take it from one hand with the other, or for switching coins, substituting one for another.

The handling

Each of these pushes, pivots, and drops is handled in a slightly different way, but most of them start with the coin displayed in much the same way at the fingertips.

To understand the basic positioning, start by bringing your right hand up in front of you, with the fingertips pointing straight up toward the ceiling, palm toward you, back of the hand toward the audience, and all four fingers held together. Place the bottom edge of a coin flat against the inside tips of your first and second fingers and press the tip of your thumb against the back of the coin to hold it so that most of the coin shows from the front above the tips of the fingers.

That is how it is first displayed to the audience. But with the coin that way at the fingertips, you can turn the hand itself in other directions. For some of these moves, you won't want to keep your hand with the fingers pointed upward. You may hold it with the fingers pointed toward the left or down to the floor. In any case, and with either hand, the coin is held in view between the tips of the fingers at the front and the thumb at the back.

You may pick the coin up from the table between your thumb and fingertips to show it, take it from your pocket or your other hand to hold it that way, or first show it lying on the palm of your hand and push it to your fingertips with your thumb to display it.

PUSHES, PIVOTS, AND DROPS—I

Displaying coin between thumb and fingertips.
Hand turned in various directions

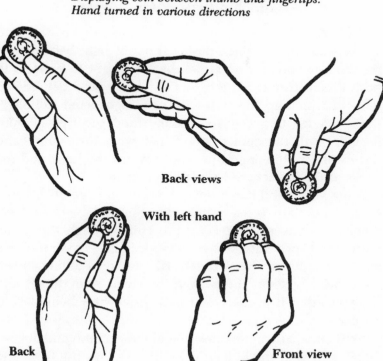

Back views

With left hand

Back

Front view

THE FINGERTIP PUSH

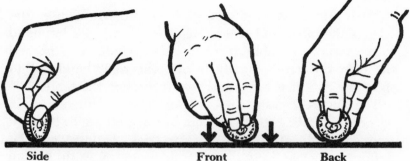

Side **Front** **Back**

Fingertip Push

With this, you simply press the visible edge of the coin against something, which pushes it out of sight behind your fingers. Let's say, for example, that you want to pretend to push a coin through the top of a table. Stand behind the table and pick up the coin with your right hand to hold it near its edge between your thumb and the tips of your fingers. With the coin gripped that way, turn your hand downward, so the fingertips point toward the table and the backs of the fingers are toward the audience.

Bring your hand down until the bottom edge of the coin touches the table top and hold the coin in view there for a moment. Then, as if pushing the coin through the table, push your hand straight down so your fingers cover the coin and the tips of them touch the table. Pushing down automatically slides the coin up between your thumb and fingers so that it is concealed from front view behind your fingers.

Without changing the position of your thumb and fingers, which still hold the hidden coin, lift your hand a little and quickly move it 6 to 8 inches to the right. Hold it there an instant, to create the illusion that since the coin is no longer visible at your fingertips it must have been pushed into the table.

Then draw that hand straight back and down under the edge of the table, and at the same time bring your left hand to the top of the table to rub the spot where you "pushed the coin through." Finally bring your right hand out to show the coin that apparently went through the table.

The fingertip push is not a trick in itself, but merely a way of pretending to push a coin into something or through some solid object as part of some trick that you may be performing. You might use it to seem to push a coin through your leg, arm, head, the back of your other hand, or the side or bottom of a box or cup in which you have a duplicate coin hidden.

The Push Vanish

This is an easy way of vanishing a coin by using the fingertip push. What you seem to do is show a coin at the fingertips of one hand and put it into the palm of the other hand, which closes around it and turns over as though holding the coin. When you open that hand a moment later, the coin is gone.

What you really do is push the bottom edge of the coin against the palm of your other hand so it slides up behind your fingers and is hidden. The closing and turning of your other hand helps draw attention away from the hand hiding the coin.

Start by holding up a coin to show it between the thumb and fingertips of the right hand. Bring your left hand palm upward in front of you, with the tips of its fingers toward the audience, and turn your right hand palm downward so the coin it is holding is directly above the left hand.

Now bring your right hand down to your left until the bottom edge of the coin is touching your left palm and hold it there a moment so the coin is clearly seen. Begin to close your left-hand fingers, and as you do, press the edge of the coin against your palm so it slides up into your right-hand fingers and is hidden behind them. As you continue to close your left hand into a fist as though holding the coin, lift your right hand away and out a few inches to the right so the audience can see that the coin is no longer at your fingertips. Immediately turn your left fist over, thumb downward, with a little forward thrust of that hand, and at the same time let your right hand drop to your side with the coin concealed.

In all of this, the position of your right thumb and fingers doesn't change at all. You just push the edge of the coin

PUSHES, PIVOTS, AND DROPS—II

THE PUSH VANISH—Side views

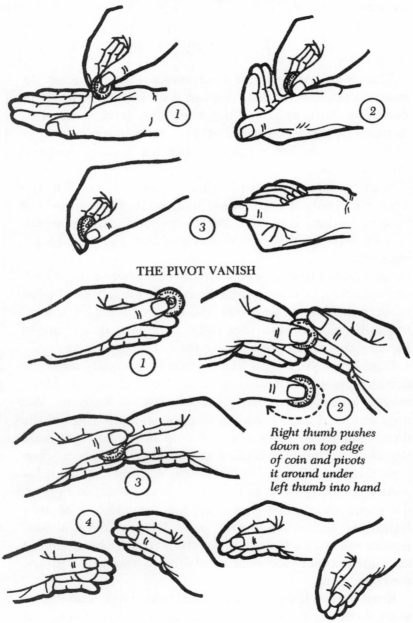

THE PIVOT VANISH

*Right thumb pushes
down on top edge
of coin and pivots
it around under
left thumb into hand*

against your left palm, keep your thumb and fingers in the same position as you lift your hand away, hold it out to the right a moment, and then let that hand drop to your side, while the left hand keeps moving and turning to attract attention.

Finally look at your closed left fist as you hold it out in front of you. Slowly open your left hand, turn it upward to show that the coin has vanished, and let that hand drop to its side.

The Pivot Vanish

In this method of pretending to take a coin from one hand with the other to vanish it, the hand displaying the coin at its fingertips does almost nothing at all. Its thumb merely acts as a pivot so that when the thumb of the other hand touches the edge of the coin it gives it a tiny downward turn that hides it from view. The whole thing is quick, natural-looking, and easy to do.

Pick up a coin and hold it at its edge between the thumb and the tips of the first two fingers of the left hand, with that hand in front of you so the fingers are toward the right and the back of the hand is toward the audience. Reach over with the right hand, palm toward you, as if to take the coin between its thumb and fingers. Bring the hands together so the right-hand fingers go to the front with their tips close to the knuckles of the left hand. This brings your right thumb to the top edge of the coin.

As your right thumb touches the top of the coin just push down on it gently so it pivots around under the tip of your left thumb and down behind the left fingers. The left hand doesn't move at all and the only movement of your right hand is the tiny downward push of the thumb as it touches the top edge of the coin.

Keep your left hand as it is and draw your right hand away to the right as though taking the coin. The backs of both hands are still toward the audience. It should look as though you just showed the coin at the fingertips of your left hand and casually took it with your right hand.

As you lift your right hand a little, let your left hand drop naturally to your side. Then open your right hand and show that the coin has vanished. While you do that, your left thumb can easily slide the hidden coin into a finger-palm position inside the left hand, so that you can then use that hand more freely with the coin concealed.

Fingertip Drop

This is still another way of secretly keeping a coin in one hand while pretending to take it with the other. Again the hand displaying the coin seems not to move at all, and in this trick the coin really hides itself. Under the cover of your other hand, it drops from your fingertips because of its own weight and slides right down into position for finger-palming it.

Start by holding up the coin to show it between the thumb and fingertips of the left hand, with that hand held upright so the fingers point toward the ceiling and the back of it is toward the audience. The hand should be held at about waist level.

With the right hand, reach over as if to take the coin, bringing the tips of the right fingers in front of the upright fingertips of the left hand and the right thumb just in back of the coin.

As your right hand screens the coin from front view for an instant, lift your left thumb to release the coin and let it slide down from your fingertips. It will drop by its own weight and slide down against the inside of your fingers to the base of them in finger-palm position.

Keeping your left hand as it is, take your right hand away as if holding the coin and close the fingers into a loose fist as though the coin were in it. As you look at your lifting right hand, let your left hand drop to your side with the finger-palmed coin. With a little rubbing motion of your right-

FINGERTIP DROP

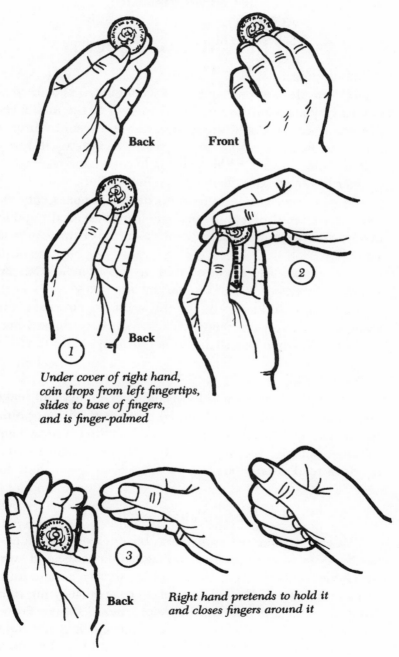

Back   Front

*Under cover of right hand,
coin drops from left fingertips,
slides to base of fingers,
and is finger-palmed*

*Right hand pretends to hold it
and closes fingers around it*

hand fingers, pretend to vanish the coin, and then open the right hand to show that it has disappeared.

SWITCHES AND FALSE COUNTS

The purpose

Switches are ways of secretly exchanging a coin that is hidden in your hand for one that is shown to the audience. For example, you might show a quarter and seem to drop it from one hand into the other, really switching it for a hidden coin, so that when you open your hand again the quarter has magically changed to a half-dollar.

You might switch a coin for a bottle cap, a poker chip, or some other small object. There are also tricks that depend upon switching a duplicate coin for one borrowed from a spectator.

False counts usually are used to transfer a counted number of coins from hand to hand while you secretly keep an extra coin hidden. You might want to convince the audience that you are doing a trick with only three coins, for instance, when you really have four.

The handling

The simple switches and false counts given here all make use of moves previously explained, such as the finger-palm, thumb-palm, and fingertip drop. The handling is somewhat different because you will have two or more coins in your hands instead of only one.

Finger-Palm Switch

This can be done with any coins, but for explanation let's say that you want to pretend to magically change a quarter into a half-dollar by secretly switching them.

You start with a half-dollar finger-palmed in your right hand. The back of that hand is kept toward the audience, fingers pointed toward the left and curling naturally inward, with the concealed half-dollar held in the usual

SWITCHES AND FALSE COUNTS—I

FINGER-PALM SWITCH

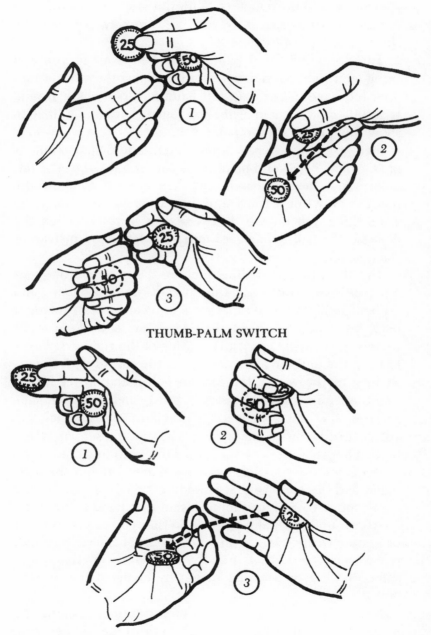

THUMB-PALM SWITCH

finger-palm position between the middle joints and base of the second and third fingers. With the same right hand, you openly show the quarter by holding it in view between the thumb and tips of the first two fingers.

Turn your left hand palm upward in front of you and bring your right hand down over it and toss the quarter into your left hand. Close your left-hand fingers quickly around it and then open them again and lower that hand a little to show the quarter on the palm of it.

Pick up the quarter with the thumb and first two fingers of the right hand, and once more toss it back into the left hand, close the left hand, and then open it to show the quarter. Now for a third time you seem to do exactly the same thing, but on the third toss you secretly switch the coins so the half-dollar goes into your left hand instead of the quarter.

This third time, as before, pick up the quarter from your left hand with your right thumb and first two fingers, and without hesitating make the same movement of throwing it back into your left hand. But this time slide your right thumb back a little against the inside of the right first finger to keep the quarter there, and open the rest of your fingers slightly to throw out the hidden half-dollar instead. The slight opening of your second, third, and fourth fingers releases the finger-palmed half-dollar and also almost automatically hides the quarter behind those partly extended fingers so it is no longer visible from in front.

Quickly close your left hand again as it catches the half-dollar and this time keep it closed. As you draw your hands apart, move your right thumb inside that hand to slide the quarter into finger-palm position so that you can then point or gesture freely. Only a tiny movement of the right thumb is necessary to do that. Finally, open your left hand and show that the quarter has magically changed into a half-dollar.

The switch really amounts to no more than opening the fingers of your right hand enough to drop the hidden coin, but the moves should all blend into one simple action of seeming to toss a coin from one hand to the other. What takes a little practice is the timing, so that you don't do it too slowly or too quickly, but with the same even speed each time. The movement should look the same no matter which coin is thrown.

Thumb-Palm Switch

This serves the same purpose of showing one coin and secretly switching it for another. Let's suppose again that you wish to show a quarter and secretly switch it for a half-dollar.

Start with the half-dollar finger-palmed in your right hand. With that hand, openly display the quarter and then hold it clipped flat between the sides of your first and second fingers, just as you would if you were about to vanish the quarter from your fingertips by thumb-palming it.

Turn your left hand palm upward in front of you and bring your right hand palm downward to it, as if to drop the quarter into your left hand. But what you really do is thumb-palm the quarter with your right hand. As you bring your right hand down, quickly close its fingers so as to curl them in and leave the quarter in the crotch of your thumb, and then quickly open your fingers out again. The opening out of your fingers releases the half-dollar so that it drops into your left hand instead of the quarter.

You simply thumb-palm the quarter as if you had no half-dollar finger-palmed in that hand, and the half-dollar will drop out by itself as you reopen your fingers.

Shut your left-hand fingers around the half-dollar and take your right hand away. The quarter is now safely thumb-palmed in your right hand, which looks empty from the back, since you can hold it naturally with the fingers slightly apart. When you are ready to reveal the change, open your left hand and show that the half-dollar is there instead of the quarter.

The Glass Switch

This is almost the same as the thumb-palm switch, but instead of dropping the switched coin into your left hand, you drop it into a drinking glass. You can use this technique to switch a duplicate coin for one you borrow from someone in the audience, so that you seem to leave the borrowed coin in full view in the glass that you put on your table. That gives you secret possession of the borrowed coin for use in whatever trick you may be doing.

You will need an ordinary drinking glass and a coin of the same denomination as the one you intend to borrow. A quarter is probably better to use than a half-dollar, because people are more likely to have quarters with them.

Have your own quarter finger-palmed in your right hand, which hangs naturally at your side, and have the glass on your table. Ask if one of the spectators will let you borrow a quarter. When one is offered, ask the person to please look at it and read the date aloud so everyone will remember it.

While he is doing that, pick up the glass near the bottom of it with your right hand, between the thumb and first two fingers, and with the back of the hand toward those who are watching. Holding the glass in that hand for a moment gives the impression that the hand is otherwise empty and helps to conceal the finger-palmed coin.

As you step toward the spectator, transfer the glass to your left hand. Reach out with your palm-downward right hand and take the offered quarter between your thumb and first two fingers.

Hold the coin in view clipped between your first two fingers in a position for thumb-palming it. Immediately bring your right hand to the top of the glass as if to drop the borrowed quarter into it, but quickly close and then reopen your fingers to thumb-palm the borrowed one and let your own quarter fall into the glass instead. Shake the glass with your left hand to rattle the coin inside it and let your right hand drop to your side.

SWITCHES AND FALSE COUNTS—II

THE GLASS SWITCH

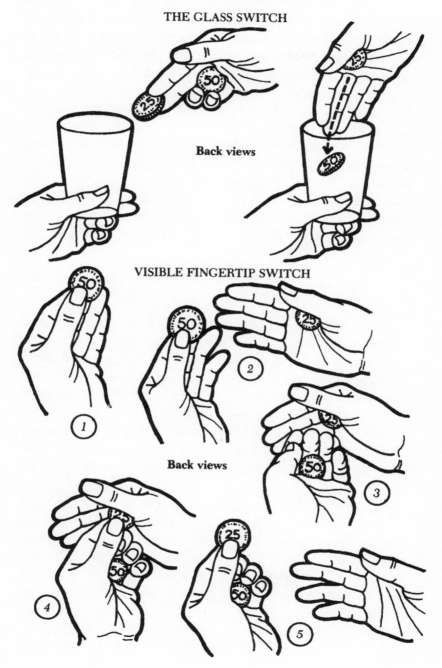

Back views

VISIBLE FINGERTIP SWITCH

Back views

With the glass still in your left hand, hold it high and rattle the coin in it again as you turn slightly toward the left and step back to your table. Keep the glass in full view, put it on the table, and leave it there. As far as the audience knows, the borrowed quarter remains in the glass, but you have it thumb-palmed in your right hand to make use of it as you wish.

After you have secretly planted the borrowed coin somewhere else, you can pick up the glass, pour out the duplicate that the audience assumes is still the borrowed one, and vanish it. Then you can seem to make it reappear wherever you have hidden the borrowed one and have the date on it called out to verify that it is the same one the spectator gave you.

Visible Fingertip Switch

What seems to happen is that you show a coin at your fingertips and pass your other hand in front of it, and it visibly changes to a different coin. As you touch it for a moment with your other hand, a half-dollar at your fingertips might change to a quarter, to a red poker chip, or from silver to a foreign coin of copper.

There is no intricate manipulation. It is based on the simple fingertip drop. For explanation, we'll suppose that you want to show a half-dollar and visibly "shrink" it to a quarter.

Start with both coins in your otherwise empty right-hand pocket. With that hand, reach into your pocket and get the quarter thumb-palmed by pushing it up into the crotch of your thumb. Take the half-dollar so it is clipped between the sides of your first two fingers and bring it out of the pocket to show it, with the back of the hand toward the audience.

Hold out your left hand, drop the half-dollar on the palm of it, and let your right hand fall to your side for a moment.

Lower the left hand a little to display the coin, and let the coin slide out to the fingers so the thumb can push it into position for the fingertip drop. Lift that hand with its back toward the audience so the fingertips point upward and the half-dollar is held in view between the fingertips at the front and thumb at the back.

Bring your right hand up with its fingertips toward the left so it goes horizontally across in front of your upright left-hand fingers, touching against the outside tips of them. As your right hand screens the left for a moment, let the half-dollar drop and slide down into the base of your left-hand fingers, ready for finger-palming.

Continue to move your right hand across horizontally until the thumb-palmed quarter comes into your left thumb and fingertips. Close your left thumb on the bottom edge of the quarter to hold it between thumb and fingertips just as the half-dollar was held. Then lower your right hand to reveal the change. The half-dollar that was displayed at your left fingertips magically has changed to a quarter.

The whole thing really amounts to letting the half-dollar slide down into your left-hand fingers as your right hand moves across in front of them to leave the thumb-palmed quarter in place of it. The passing across and lowering of the right hand should be done in one continuous motion, with the left hand not changing position at all.

Hold the quarter as it is for a moment, so everyone can see the change that has taken place. Then casually show your right hand empty, take the quarter with it, and let your left hand fall to your side, finger-palming the half-dollar.

Thumb-Palm False Count

This is a way of using the previously explained thumb-palm throw to convince spectators you have only two coins when you really have three, or three when you really have four. It is a move that serves many purposes. The counted-out coins are fairly shown, first in one hand and then the other, yet you are able to keep an extra coin hidden.

Let's say that you want to show only two half-dollars and that you have reached the point in some trick where you have a third half-dollar thumb-palmed in your right hand. Place the two that you want the audience to see on the palm of your left hand, spread out so one of them is close to the edge of that palm, in position for thumb-palming.

Lower your left hand a little and hold it slightly toward the left to show the two coins to the spectators at that side. Then, with a slight inward swing toward the right, turn your left hand palm downward as if to drop the two coins into your right hand, which turns upward to take them. But as you turn your left hand over, close the side of that thumb on the coin beneath it so that only one of the coins you have just shown falls into your right hand when the hands touch together.

Lift your right thumb to release the extra coin it was holding and move your right hand out toward the right, to show the spectators at that side the two coins that are now lying on your right hand. You are really showing them the one coin that fell from your left hand and the one that was already in your right hand. It looks as though you are showing the same two after having dropped them from one hand to the other, but you now have an extra coin thumb-palmed in your left hand.

This should be done in a natural, unhurried way, by bringing the left hand down over the right as if to casually transfer the two coins from hand to hand so as to show them clearly, first to the spectators at one side and then to those at the other side.

The moves can be made in reverse, of course, by starting with an extra coin thumb-palmed in your left hand and finishing with one hidden in your right hand, if some particular trick requires that. The handling is the same if you want to show three coins when you really have four.

SWITCHES AND FALSE COUNTS—III

THUMB-PALM FALSE COUNT

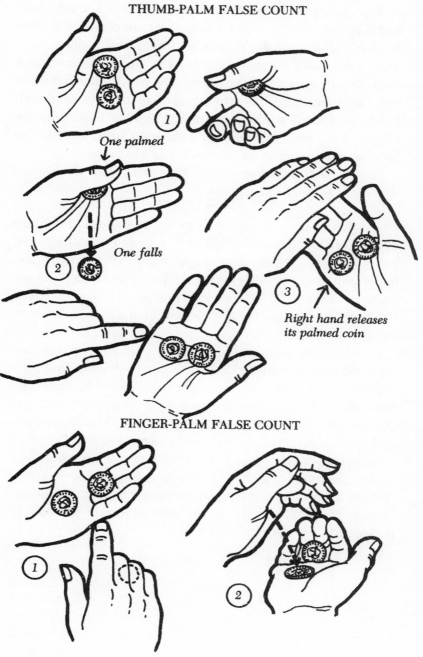

One palmed

One falls

*Right hand releases
its palmed coin*

FINGER-PALM FALSE COUNT

This also can be used to show that you have a quarter and a half-dollar, while you keep a duplicate of one or the other hidden. Or you can do it with a copper and a silver coin, with a coin and a bottle cap, or with a coin and a poker chip. It permits you to show any two small objects, first in one hand and then the other, and also to show that both hands appear to be otherwise empty, and leaves a duplicate of one of the objects hidden in whichever hand you plan to have it in, depending on the trick you are doing.

Finger-Palm False Count

This is the same thing, done by finger-palming the coins instead of thumb-palming them. To show two coins when you really have three, you might start with an extra one finger-palmed in your right hand. The other two are shown spread out on your left hand, with one of them resting at the base of the two middle fingers in position for finger-palming.

As you turn your left hand over, you finger-palm that coin and keep it, while seeming to drop both coins into your right hand. Then you hold out your right hand to show two coins—the one that was dropped from your left hand and the one that was already in your right hand. That leaves you with the extra coin finger-palmed in your left hand.

Which of the two false-count methods you use is a matter of personal preference. But it is a good idea to learn various ways of accomplishing the same magical results, so you can choose the moves that seem most natural for you in performing a particular trick.

2

DO-ANYWHERE TRICKS WITH COINS AND BILLS

UP ONE SLEEVE AND DOWN THE OTHER

How it looks

"Magicians are always being accused of making things go up their sleeves," you say to the audience, "and that's exactly what I'm going to do." You show a coin, put it into your left hand, and close that hand around it.

Pointing to your left arm with your other hand, you explain, "I'm going to make it go up this sleeve, across my back, down my other sleeve, and then flip over twice so it will land right inside my pocket." You pull out the right-hand pocket of your slacks to show it empty and then push it back in again. "I'll bet you don't believe I can do that, do you? Neither do I. But let's try."

You jerk back your closed left hand as if shooting the coin from that hand up your sleeve, open your hand and show it empty, wiggle your shoulders as if the coin were passing across your back, and shake your right arm as though it were coming down your other sleeve.

"Did you see it flip over twice and land right in my pocket?" you ask. "Well, it did." Showing your right hand empty, you put it into what was the empty pocket and take out the coin. "That always surprises me," you say. "I've never figured out how I do it."

What you need
All you need is a half-dollar or quarter in the otherwise empty right-hand pocket of your slacks.

What you do
Reach into the pocket with your right hand, bring out the coin between your thumb and fingers, hold it up to show it, and let it drop from your fingertips to the palm of that hand. Lower the right hand to display the coin and bounce it flat so it slides to the base of the two middle fingers in position for finger-palming.

Hold out your left hand, fingertips toward the audience and cupped upward slightly. Turn your right hand over toward you and bring it down inside your partly cupped left-hand fingers as if to drop the coin, but keep it finger-palmed in your right hand. As you draw your hands apart, close the left fingers as though holding the coin, and keep that closed left hand held out in front of you.

Without hesitating, immediately touch the tip of your right first finger against your left sleeve as you point to it and say, "I'm going to make it go up this sleeve. . . ." Run the tip of your pointing finger up along the sleeve toward your shoulder.

In a continuing motion, with the finger pointing up toward the ceiling, turn the right hand with its palm toward the audience and move it out away from you and across from left to right, making a sweeping outward half-circle at chest level, as you say, "Across my back. . . ."

UP ONE SLEEVE AND DOWN THE OTHER

Audience views

Pointing finger moves
up along left sleeve,
coin finger-palmed

"Up this sleeve . . ."

Finger points
up palm to
audience, coin
still hidden

"Across my back . . ."

"Down my other sleeve . . ."

"And right inside my pocket."

Pocket pulled inside out,
coin stays finger-palmed

This gives the audience a brief glimpse of the palm side of your right hand, helping to create the impression that it is empty and that the coin must be in the closed left hand still held out in front of you. But the finger-palmed coin remains concealed by your loosely curled right-hand fingers as the first finger points upward and your hand moves across. You simply turn your hand outward and sweep it across from left to right without changing the position of your fingers. "Down the other sleeve. . . ."

As you look down at your right sleeve, drop that hand to your side and tap the still-extended first finger against the outside of your pocket. "And then flip over twice and land right inside my pocket." Put your hand into the pocket, keep the coin finger-palmed, and grip the bottom of the pocket lining between your thumb and first finger.

Pull your hand out, to pull the lining inside out, and hold the lining out with your thumb and finger still gripping it. Hold it that way long enough for everyone to see that the pocket is empty. Then push the lining back in and leave the finger-palmed coin inside the pocket as you immediately take your hand out again.

All of your explanation about what you intend to do takes only a moment. The coin the audience thinks you are still holding in your closed left hand is now secretly tucked away inside your presumably empty pocket, and both hands are really empty. But as far as the audience knows, the trick hasn't started yet. All the rest is acting.

"I'll bet you don't believe I can do that. . . . Neither do I!" you say. "But let's try." Hold out your closed left hand, jerk it back as if shooting the coin from it up your sleeve, and open the hand to show that the coin is gone. Wiggle your shoulders slightly as if the coin were passing across your back. Then shake your right arm down at your side. Tap your finger to the outside of your pocket as before, and ask, "Did you see it flip over twice and land right inside my pocket? Well, it did."

Hold up your right hand to show it empty and put it into your pocket. Get the coin between your finger and thumb and bring it out to hold it up and show it as you say, "That always surprises me. I've never figured out how I do it."

CASH OFFER

How it looks
You take a facial tissue from your pocket, shake it open to show clearly that there is nothing in it, and roll it into a small ball in your hands. Holding it up, you ask, "If I offered to sell you this for a dime, would you buy it?"

Without waiting for an answer, you snap your fingers over the ball of tissue, tear it open, and remove a shining half-dollar from inside it. As you show the half-dollar, you say, "For a dime, you should have bought it!"

What you need
A standard-size facial tissue
A shiny new half-dollar

How you fix it
Open out the facial tissue, stuff it loosely into the otherwise empty right-hand pocket of your jacket, and put the half-dollar into the pocket with it.

What you do
Reach into your pocket, get the half-dollar finger-palmed in your right hand, grip part of the tissue between your thumb and first finger, and take it from your pocket with your other fingers loosely curled inward to hide the coin.

Bring both hands in front of you, their backs toward the audience, and open out the tissue so as to hold it up by one top corner between your right thumb and first finger and the opposite corner between your left thumb and finger.

CASH OFFER

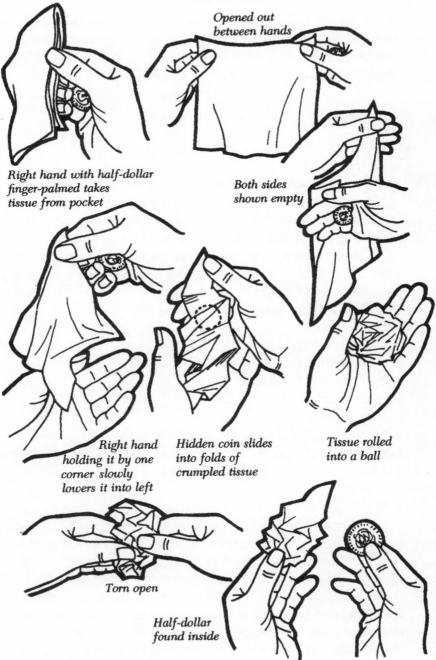

Right hand with half-dollar finger-palmed takes tissue from pocket

Opened out between hands

Both sides shown empty

Right hand holding it by one corner slowly lowers it into left

Hidden coin slides into folds of crumpled tissue

Tissue rolled into a ball

Torn open

Half-dollar found inside

Shake it out to show it is empty, move your left hand forward and all the way over to the right to show the other side of the tissue, and bring both hands back as they were with the tissue stretched between them.

Drop the left corner from your left hand so the tissue hangs down from your right hand. Shake it again with your right hand and show your left hand empty. Cup your left hand in front of you, fingers toward the front, and bring your right hand above it so the botton corner of the tissue touches the left palm.

Slowly lower your right hand so the tissue loosely folds itself down into your cupped left hand. As your hands touch together, with your right hand inside the folds of the partly crumpled tissue, let the finger-palmed coin slide into it. Keeping your hands together, fold the tissue up around the coin and quickly roll it into a ball. Hold it on your left palm, with that thumb resting lightly on top of it to keep it from unrolling, and take your right hand away.

Display the ball of tissue on your outstretched left palm and ask, "If I offered to sell you this for a dime, would you buy it?" Show your right hand empty and snap your fingers over the tissue. Take it with both hands, slowly tear it open, and bring the half-dollar into view. Throw the tissue aside, hold up the half-dollar, and say, "For a dime, you should have bought it!"

BREAKING A HALF INTO QUARTERS

How it looks

"There are people who claim the strange psychic ability to bend keys and spoons and other things made of solid metal with the power of the mind," you say with mock seriousness as you begin this magical spoof. "I can't do that, but sometimes I can break a half-dollar in half."

You take a half-dollar from your pocket, hold it at the fingertips of your upright left hand, and start squeezing it with your right hand, as you explain with a smile, "I don't use mind power . . . just brute strength."

As you lift your right hand away, you ask, "And what do you get when you break a half in half?" Fanned out at your left fingertips, in place of the half-dollar that was there, you show two 25-cent pieces. You drop them singly from your left fingertips into your right hand and say, "Why, two quarters, of course."

What you need

A half-dollar and two quarters, which you have in an empty right-hand pocket at the start

What you do

Reach into your pocket, stack the two quarters, and push them up into the crotch of your right thumb to hold them thumb-palmed together. Get the half-dollar clipped by its sides between your first two fingers and bring it out to show it with the back of your hand toward the spectators. (Your remarks about the psychic power to bend keys and spoons will give you time to position the coins in your hand inside your pocket without rushing it, as if you were searching among the change in your pocket to find the half-dollar.)

Hold your left hand outstretched, drop the half-dollar into it from your right hand, and let your right hand fall to your side. Display the coin on your left palm and tilt your hand so as to slide it forward. Hold it by its edge between your thumb and fingertips as you raise your hand into position for the fingertip drop, with the back of the hand toward the spectators, fingers pointing upward, and the half-dollar visible from in front at your fingertips.

As you say, "I don't use mind power . . . just brute strength," bring your right hand up, fingertips toward the left, so it goes horizontally across in front of your upright left fingers, screening the half-dollar from front view. Let the half-dollar secretly drop from your left fingertips and slide down into that hand in finger-palm position. With

BREAKING A HALF INTO QUARTERS

(1) *Half-dollar taken from pocket, two quarters thumb-palmed*

(2) *Half-dollar dropped into left hand*

(3) *Pushed up to fingertips*

(4) *Right hand comes to squeeze half-dollar*

(5) *It slides down into left hand and is finger-palmed*

(6) *Left thumb and fingers take the two quarters*

(7) *Quarters fanned out at left fingertips*

(8) *Half-dollar shown "broken" into quarters*

(9) *Quarters dropped singly into empty right hand*

your left thumb and fingers, take the two thumb-palmed quarters from the right hand. Slide them slightly apart to fan them, and close your right hand around them as if squeezing the half-dollar the audience thinks is still at your fingertips.

There is no need to hurry. You can take your time switching and positioning the coins while you keep your two hands together, pretending to squeeze and break the half-dollar. If necessary, you can even push your right thumb down inside your left hand to make sure the half-dollar is properly finger-palmed there. Then you ask, "And what do you get when you break a half in half?"

Keep your left hand as it is and take your right hand away to reveal the two quarters fanned at your left fingertips in place of the half-dollar. Hold them that way a moment. Let it be seen that your right hand is empty and turn it palm upward about six inches below your left hand. Turn your left hand over, left to right so the fingers are pointing down, and drop the quarters singly into your right hand as you say, "Why, two quarters, of course."

Let your left hand fall to your side and jingle the quarters on your right palm to show them. Finally bring your left hand up, pick up the two quarters with your thumb and fingertips, and put them away in your left-hand pocket, leaving the finger-palmed half-dollar in the pocket with them.

THE FLIP SIDE

How it looks

You show a quarter, flip it into the air, catch it, and slap it down on the back of your other hand, in the usual way of tossing a coin. "Which is it," you ask someone, "heads or tails?" Whatever his guess, you lift your fingers, show him the coin, and pick it up as you say, "Let's try again."

But as you seem to flip it into the air a second time, the

THE FLIP SIDE

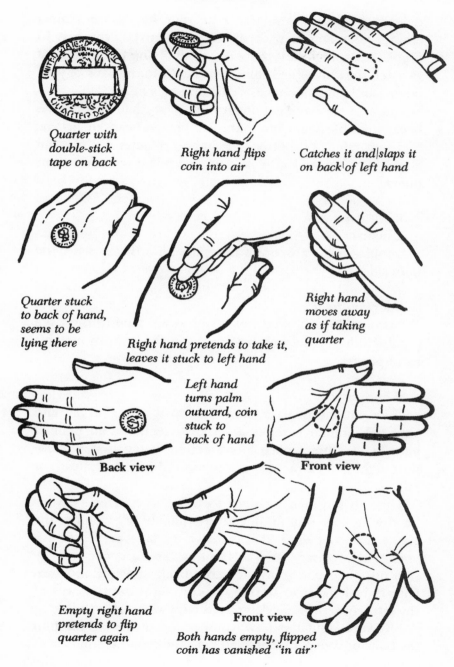

Quarter with double-stick tape on back

Right hand flips coin into air

Catches it and/slaps it on back of left hand

Quarter stuck to back of hand, seems to be lying there

Right hand pretends to take it, leaves it stuck to left hand

Right hand moves away as if taking quarter

Left hand turns palm outward, coin stuck to back of hand

Back view

Front view

Empty right hand pretends to flip quarter again

Front view

Both hands empty, flipped coin has vanished "in air"

quarter suddenly vanishes. Both your hands are plainly empty, your fingers wide apart. "I'm sorry," you say. "I flipped it too high. But there it is again." You reach out as if to catch the "invisible" coin, then slap it to the back of your other hand and announce, "This time, it's heads."

You lift your covering fingers and show that the coin has become visible again and that it has landed heads up, as you said it would. "I'd better quit before it fades out of sight again," you say as you pick it up and put it back into your pocket.

What you need
A quarter
Double-stick transparent tape, the kind that is sticky on both sides

How you fix it
Fasten a ¾-inch length of double-stick tape to the back ("tails" side) of the quarter and have the coin in a right-hand pocket.

What you do
Take out the quarter, show it, flip it into the air with your right thumb, catch it, and show it again on the palm of your hand. Flip it once more, catch it, and loosely close your right hand around it as you ask, "Which is it, heads or tails?"

That gives you a moment to feel the coin inside your hand with your thumb, so you can quickly tell whether the sticky side is upward. If it is, leave it that way; if not, tilt your partly closed hand so the quarter turns over, sticky side up. Hold out your left hand, back upward, and turn your right hand over to slap the coin down on the back of the left hand, pressing down so the quarter sticks to it.

Lift your right hand away, show the quarter resting on the back of your left hand, and hold it close to the person as you point to it and either congratulate him for guessing correctly or tell him that he missed. Whatever his guess, you say, "Let's try again."

Move your left hand back a little and turn your body slightly to the left. Cover the coin with your right fingers just as if you were picking it up with those fingers and thumb. Sweep your fingers lightly across it, as if taking it, and at the same time turn your left hand palm outward, with its fingers spread widely apart. The quarter is now stuck to the back of your left hand, with the empty palm of that hand toward the spectator so it appears that you must have taken the coin with your right hand.

Without hesitating, continue to bring your right hand to the right as though it had the coin. Go through the motions of pretending to flip it into the air with your thumb. Look upward as though watching the coin. Open your right hand wide, fingers spread apart so it can be seen that both hands are empty, and say, "I'm sorry. I flipped it too high." Reach out with your right hand as though to catch it from the air. "But there it is again."

Immediately slap your right hand to the top of your left hand. Announce, "This time, it's heads." As your right fingers cover your left hand, turn your left hand palm downward, which brings the coin under your right fingers. Lift your right hand away and show the quarter visibly resting on the back of your left hand again. Hold it close to the spectator and point to it so that he can see it is "heads up" as you said it would be. Then pick it up from the back of your left hand and put it away in your pocket.

(Note: The tape must be really sticky to hold the quarter to the back of your hand, so replace it after you have used it a few times. Just peel the old strip off with your thumbnail and apply a fresh one.)

ONE HUNDRED AND TWO

FOLDING THE DOLLAR BILL

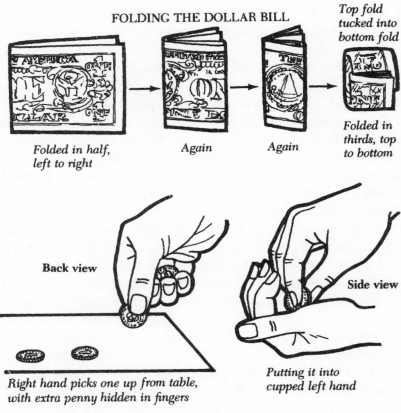

Top fold tucked into bottom fold

Folded in half, left to right

Again

Again

Folded in thirds, top to bottom

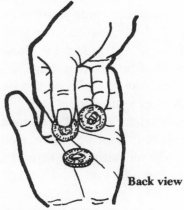

Back view

Right hand picks one up from table, with extra penny hidden in fingers

Side view

Putting it into cupped left hand

Back view

"Two in the hand . . ."
Dropping hidden penny with it

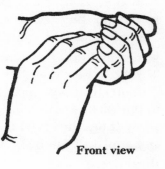

Front view

ONE HUNDRED AND TWO

How it looks

"This is a little test of your powers of observation," you say as you take three pennies from your pocket and put them out on a table. Picking them up one at a time, you put two of them into your other hand and the third one into your pocket. "How many are in my hand?" you ask. The answer will be two, but you open your hand to show that all three pennies are in it.

You repeat the same thing, singly putting two into your hand and the third into your pocket, and again open your hand and drop out three. "I'll do it one last time," you say. "One cent in my hand . . . two cents in my hand . . . and the third one goes into my pocket. How many are in my hand?"

Whatever the answer, you say, "I'm sorry. You weren't watching closely. I have in my hand . . . exactly one hundred and two." You turn your hand over and drop out two. "One cent . . . two cents." Then you reach into your hand and produce a one-dollar bill as you say, "And that's exactly one hundred more."

What you need

A dollar bill

Four pennies, either all new or all old, so they look somewhat alike

How you fix it

Put the dollar bill on a table so its long edges are at the top and bottom. Fold it in half from left to right, in half the same way again, and then once more. Now fold the top third down, vertically from top to center, and the bottom third up, from bottom to center. Finally, tuck the top fold inside the bottom fold and crease the folds so it all stays together in a compact little package. Folded that way, the bill is not much bigger than a penny.

Have the folded bill and four pennies in the right-hand pocket of your jacket.

What you do

Reach into your pocket with your right hand. Gather up the pennies, making sure you have all four, and close your fingers loosely around them. Bring your hand out and hold it a little above the top of the table. With your thumb, push off three of the pennies, one at a time, dropping them on the table. Leave the fourth one in your hand, hidden by your partly closed fingers. There is no need to palm it; just keep your three lower fingers closed enough to hold it.

Hold your left hand palm upward, fingers toward the front. Pick up one of the coins from the table with your right thumb and first finger and put it into your left hand, closing it as you say, "One cent in my hand."

Pick up another with your right hand and open your cupped left hand enough so your right hand can go down into it. As you leave the second penny, let the hidden one secretly drop from your right hand with it, so the two go together into your left hand. There are now three in your hand, but you say, "Two cents in my hand."

Pick up the last penny from the table with your right hand and say, "And the third one goes into my pocket." Show it and put your hand into your pocket as if to leave it there. But just keep it hidden in your fingers instead of leaving it in your pocket and immediately bring your hand out again and let it fall to your side for a moment.

Ask, "How many are in my hand?" The spectators should say there are two. Turn your left hand over, drop the three pennies from it to the table, one at a time, and then turn that hand palm upward and say, "I'll do it again."

Pick up one from the table with your right hand and put it into your left. "One in my hand." Pick up another and put that into your cupped left hand, letting the penny in your right hand secretly drop with it. "Two in my hand." Pick up the third one and say, as before, "And the third one goes into my pocket."

Show it and put your hand into your pocket. But this time, really drop the penny into your pocket, leave it there, and scoop up the folded dollar bill so it is hidden in your fingers. Immediately bring your hand out again and let it fall to your side. Just keep your fingers loosely closed around the folded bill, the same way as you hid the penny before.

Once more ask, "How many in my hand?" Some spectators may say there are two and some may say three. Whatever the answer, open your left hand and drop out the three pennies. Say, "I'll do it one last time."

Pick up one penny and put it into your left hand. "One cent in my hand." Pick up the second and put that into the left hand, secretly leaving the dollar bill with it. "Two cents in my hand." Pick up the last penny, show it, put it into your pocket, and leave it there as you say, "And the third one goes into my pocket. . . . How many are in my hand?"

Finally say, "I have in my hand exactly one hundred and two." Turn your left hand over, fingers downward and count out two pennies on the table, but still keep that hand partly closed. "One cent . . . two cents." Show your right hand empty, reach up into your left hand, and with the help of both hands quickly open out the dollar bill to show it as you say, "And that's exactly one hundred more."

THE STRAPHANGER

How it looks

You take a nickel from your pocket, hold it at your fingertips, and transfer it from hand to hand, showing your hands otherwise empty. A touch of your fingers instantly changes the nickel to a half-dollar, and you again show your hands empty before you put it away in your pocket.

THE STRAPHANGER

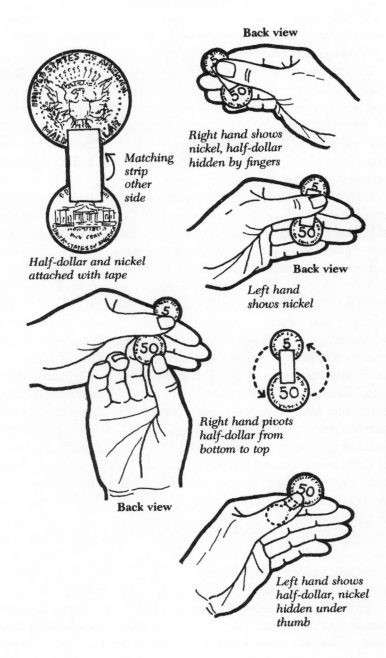

Matching strip other side

Half-dollar and nickel attached with tape

Back view

Right hand shows nickel, half-dollar hidden by fingers

Back view

Left hand shows nickel

Right hand pivots half-dollar from bottom to top

Back view

Left hand shows half-dollar, nickel hidden under thumb

What you need
A nickel
A half-dollar
Transparent tape

How you fix it
The instant change from nickel to half-dollar is accomplished with a simply made trick coin. Put the half-dollar on a table and the nickel ½ inch below it. Leaving that space between them, fasten a strip of transparent tape from one to the other. Turn over the attached coins and fasten a matching strip of tape at the back, sticking the tapes together where they meet between the coins. The result is that if you hold up one coin, the other will hang directly beneath it at the end of the attached tape.

Have the trick coin in an empty right-hand pocket.

What you do
Reach into the pocket with your right hand and take the nickel between your thumb and first finger so the tips of them hold the very edge of it and the attached half-dollar lies inside your fingers. Bring your hand out with the back of it toward the audience, fingers pointed toward the left, and hold up the nickel to show it. The half-dollar hangs behind your fingers, which hide it from front view.

Show your left hand empty and then take the nickel with that hand by bringing your left fingers over in front of the right fingers, backs of both hands toward the audience, and gripping the bottom edge of the nickel between your left thumb and first finger. Draw your right hand down and away from your left. This leaves the nickel displayed by your left hand as it previously was by your right hand. The half-dollar hangs hidden behind your left fingers.

The sudden change is now made by one quick continuous movement of the right hand, with the left thumb acting as a pivot. The left thumb doesn't move; it rests as it is, lightly against the tape between the two coins. Just bring your right hand up from beneath into the palm of the left hand, grip the hanging half-dollar with your right thumb and fingers, and swing it out to the right and on up to the top.

This swings the whole tape around from bottom to top in a counterclockwise circular motion, like a spindle on a dial, bringing the half-dollar up to where your thumb can hold it, and at the same time bringing the nickel down under your left thumb.

Immediately take your right hand away, show it empty, and display the half-dollar at your left fingertips in place of the nickel that was there. Shake your left hand a little to wiggle the half-dollar at your fingertips so viewers are fully aware of the sudden change. Press your left thumb against the tape and hidden nickel and turn your left hand outward to the left, palm toward the audience, to show both sides of the half-dollar. Then put it away in a left-hand pocket and leave it there.

MONEY IN MIND

How it looks

"I'd like to try a little experiment in mind control," you say. "I know I have no power to control your minds, so I'm going to ask one of you to try to control *my* mind." You choose one of the persons watching. "You impress me as someone with a strong mind. Just for fun, would you like to try it?"

You take a handful of change from your pocket, pick out a quarter, a nickel, a penny, and a dime, and put the four coins on a table. "I want you to think of any one of those four coins," you say. "Don't tell me which one. But once you have decided, please don't change your mind. Just keep thinking about that one coin."

From your pocket, you remove four little manila envelopes. You drop one coin into each envelope, close the

MONEY IN MIND

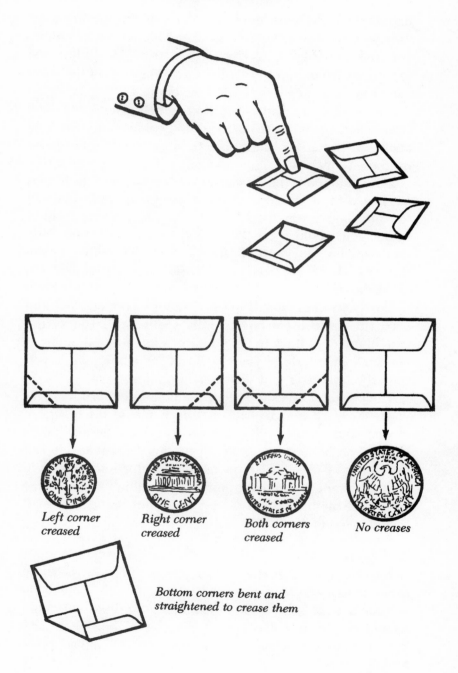

Left corner creased

Right corner creased

Both corners creased

No creases

Bottom corners bent and straightened to crease them

flaps, and spread the envelopes face down on the table. "Please mix these all up so they are in no particular order," you tell the person, as you demonstrate by sliding the envelopes around on the table. "Mix them so neither of us can guess which coin is in what envelope."

You turn your head while that is being done. "Now I want you to spell out the name of the coin you are thinking about, one letter at a time, each time I tap my finger on one of these envelopes," you explain. "Don't say anything aloud. Just spell the name in your own mind. If you happened to be thinking of the dime, for instance, when I tap my finger, you would spell 'D.' Then when I tap it again, you would spell 'I' ... and so on. And when you finish spelling to yourself the name of the coin you are thinking about, just put your hand over mine. Do you understand?"

Slowly you tap your finger to various envelopes, pausing each time as the person mentally spells one letter of the coin in mind. "I'll try to get an impression of the thought as you spell each letter," you say. "And remember, when you spell the last letter, put your hand on mine."

The person finishes the silent spelling and puts a hand on yours. You ask him to call out the name of his mentally chosen coin. "Now will you open the envelope our hands happen to be resting upon," you say. "Let's see if the experiment worked." He opens the envelope and inside it finds the one coin he had in mind. "You didn't know it was there and neither did I," you say, "but somehow your thoughts led me to it."

What you need

A handful of small change, including a dime, a penny, a nickel, and a quarter

Four 2 × 2 inch manila envelopes, the kind coin collectors use, with a flap that opens at the top. These are available in most variety stores at counters that sell supplies for collectors.

How you fix it

The secret depends in part on the fact that when the coins are considered in order according to their size, the name of each coin has one more letter than the coin before it: *dime* has four letters, *penny,* five letters, *nickel,* six, and *quarter,* seven. Actually, you don't know until the very end of the trick which coin the person has in mind, but because of the successive spelling the last one you touch is always the mentally chosen one.

That much of the trick works automatically, as will be explained, and is nothing you have to think about while performing it. But since the coins are inside envelopes and you can't see them to tell which ones to touch in order, the envelopes must be secretly "marked" so that you know where each coin is after the envelopes have been mixed up on the table. They are "marked" by creasing the bottom corners.

Hold one of the envelopes so its flap end is at the top. At the *bottom* of that envelope, fold up the tip of the *left* corner and crease it firmly, then fold the same corner to the back, crease it again, and finally straighten it out, leaving the crease mark. In the same way, crease the *right* bottom corner of a second envelope. Crease *both* bottom corners, left and right, of a third envelope. Leave the fourth envelope plain and *uncreased.*

Make sure the corner crease marks are clearly visible, so you can identify each envelope at a glance. These crease marks may seem obvious to you, because you know where to look for them, but to the spectators they will appear to be creases made accidentally while carrying the envelopes around in your pocket and handling them. Even if they were noticed, which isn't likely, the mental spelling out of the name of the coin, which leads your finger right to it, would remain a puzzle.

The coins are *always* put into the envelopes according to size order, from small to large. The dime goes into the envelope with its left corner creased, the penny into the one with its right corner creased, the nickel into the envelope with both corners creased, and the quarter into the uncreased envelope. When the coins are in their proper envelopes, all you have to remember is: left, right, both, none.

Have the coins in the pocket in which you usually carry your change and the four empty envelopes, in any order, in one of your other pockets.

What you do

Take out the handful of change, pick out the four coins, and spread them across the table in any order. Ask the person to think of any one of the coins, but not to say which one. Take out the little envelopes and drop those on the table.

Pick up any envelope, glance at its corners, and then pick up the coin that belongs in that envelope. (If you happened to pick up the envelope with its right corner creased, for instance, you would know the penny belonged in that one.) Drop it into the envelope, close the flap, and put it flap upward on the table. Continue until all four coins are in their proper envelopes.

Explain to the person that you want the envelopes mixed up, and demonstrate by sliding them around on the table to mix them. Then turn your head away while the person mixes them, "so that neither of us can guess which coin is in what envelope."

Now it is necessary to give very clear instructions about the mental spelling out of the name of the coin the person has in mind. Follow the patter as given, explaining that one letter is to be spelled silently each time you tap your finger, and that when the spelling is finished the person is to put his hand over yours. This is important so that he will stop you when he has finished mentally spelling out his chosen coin. After you start the tapping, remind him again by saying, "And remember, when you spell the last letter, put your hand on mine."

Tap your finger on any envelope and wait a moment, as if you were trying to get a "mental impression" of the first letter the person silently spelled. Then tap any other, wait, and then tap a third one. The first three times, it makes no difference what envelopes you tap. But starting with the fourth one, you must tap each in order, wherever that particular envelope happens to be on the table.

Forget about the coins inside the envelopes. Just think: left, right, both, none. When you come to the fourth tap, simply look for the envelope with its left corner creased. Put your finger on that and wait a moment. If the person mentally chose the dime, he will put his hand on yours (because it takes four letters, four taps, to spell out the word *dime*.) If he doesn't stop you, then look for the envelope with its right corner creased and tap your finger on that. Again, wait a second; if he doesn't stop you, next tap the one with both corners creased. Finally, if you are still not stopped, tap the one with no corners creased.

With the envelopes mixed up on the table the flaps may be in various positions, not always directly facing you at the top. Always glance first at the flap, then at the creased corners in relation to the way the flap may be turned. The presentation allows you plenty of time between each tap of your finger to make sure which envelope should be next.

When the person puts his hand on yours, ask him to call out the name of the coin he had in mind. Have him open the envelope and show the coin to everybody, and say, "You didn't know it was there and neither did I, but somehow your thoughts led me to it."

ONE AND ONE MAKE THREE

How it looks

"The hand is never quicker than the eye," you say as you take a dollar bill from your pocket, unfold it, and show both sides of it. "Scientists will tell you that old saying about the

ONE AND ONE MAKE THREE

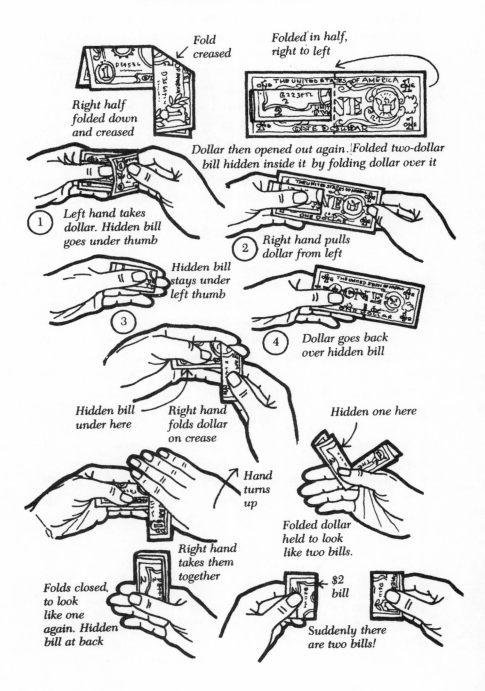

Fold creased

Right half folded down and creased

Folded in half, right to left

Dollar then opened out again. Folded two-dollar bill hidden inside it by folding dollar over it

1. Left hand takes dollar. Hidden bill goes under thumb

2. Right hand pulls dollar from left

3. Hidden bill stays under left thumb

4. Dollar goes back over hidden bill

Hidden bill under here

Right hand folds dollar on crease

Hand turns up

Hidden one here

Folded dollar held to look like two bills.

Right hand takes them together

Folds closed, to look like one again. Hidden bill at back

$2 bill

Suddenly there are two bills!

swiftness of the hand just isn't true. But sometimes the eyes can be fooled by a very simple optical illusion that makes people think the hand is quicker. If I fold this dollar bill so the two ends are held out separately . . . it looks like two dollars instead of just one, doesn't it?"

You fold the bill and hold it so that the two separate ends sticking up out of your hand look like two bills, and carefully show that your hands are otherwise empty. "If I had it secretly folded like that and just showed it to you that way, you might believe I had two," you say. You straighten the two ends so they are together. "I mean, if you didn't know I had only one."

Suddenly you draw your hands apart and there *are* two folded bills, one in each hand. "Of course, it's only an optical illusion." You unfold one of the bills and drop it open on the table. "Because I really have three dollars . . . not two." You point to the one on the table. "That's one. . . ." Quickly you unfold the other one and show that it is a two-dollar bill, and drop that on top of the first one as you joke, "And here's *two*."

What you need
A one-dollar bill
A two-dollar bill

How you fix it
Place the one-dollar bill back upward on a table, long edges top and bottom, and fold it in half, top to bottom. Now fold the right half over and down toward you, folding it upon the bill diagonally at the center to bring that end down until it points directly toward the rear edge of the table. The right half should now be vertical, the left half horizontal. Crease the diagonal fold with your thumbnail. Then open out the bill again.

Put the two-dollar bill back upward on the table, long edges top and bottom, and fold it in half, top to bottom.

Fold it in half again from right to left, and crease the folds so it will lie flat. Place the folded two-dollar bill, with its open edges toward the left, on the left side of the one-dollar bill.

Fold the one-dollar bill in half from right to left so the folded two-dollar bill is hidden inside it. Turn them so the center fold of the outer bill is toward the bottom, and have them that way in the otherwise empty left-hand pocket of your slacks.

What you do

As you talk about the quickness of the hand and simple optical illusions that can fool the eye, take out the folded bill, hold it pressed together, and show both sides of it. Transfer it to your right hand, which takes the center folded edge between thumb and fingers. Casually show your left hand empty and then bring that hand in front of you, palm cupped toward you, back of the hand toward the audience.

Bring your right hand over to return the bill to your left hand, open edges of the bill toward the left. As you take it with your left hand, push your left thumb inside the bill, under the top fold, so the two-dollar bill concealed within it comes into the crotch of the thumb and the thumb lies across it. Pushing your thumb into the outer bill partly opens its top fold. With your right hand, take that right edge of the outer bill and open it out all the way.

This should look as though you merely put the folded bill into your left hand to hold it and pushed it partly open with your left thumb so your right hand could unfold it. At this point, the left edges of the folded two-dollar bill are in the crotch of your left thumb, which lies across it behind the opened dollar bill. The dollar bill is stretched between your hands, with your right thumb and fingers holding the right edge of it.

Press your left thumb on the concealed two-dollar bill. With your right hand, pull the dollar bill away from your left hand, keeping the hidden bill under your left thumb. Shake open the dollar bill with your right hand to show it. Then put it back into your left hand so the edge slides back under your left thumb, on top of the hidden bill. The lower-left part of the open dollar bill should now be exactly on top of the folded two-dollar bill, with your left thumb holding both.

Turn your left hand out to the left, palm outward, to show the open dollar, which covers the hidden bill, and then bring your left palm toward you again. With your right hand, fold the dollar in half from top to bottom against your left palm. Then fold the right half of it over and down toward you, folding it diagonally at the center. (This is the way you first folded it on the table when you were preparing the bill for the trick, so it is already well creased and will fold easily.)

The horizontal left half of the diagonally folded bill now lies directly over the folded two-dollar bill. Square them together at the left and bottom edges with your right hand as it finishes folding the dollar bill. From now on, keep them exactly together.

Turn your right hand palm downward and bring your right thumb *under* the folded center of both bills, so that your right first finger lies across the top corner of the diagonal fold. Hold that corner tightly between your right thumb and fingers and then turn your right hand up so the back of it is toward the audience.

The two folded halves of the dollar bill now stick up above the top of your right hand, separated so that from the front they look somewhat like two bills. Say, "If I fold this dollar so the two ends are held out separately, it looks like two dollars instead of just one, doesn't it?" The two-dollar bill remains hidden behind the upright left half of the dollar, squared evenly with it and folded the same way so the whole thing looks like one of the folds of the dollar. Keep them as they are in your right hand and show your left hand empty as you say, "If I had it secretly folded like that and just showed it to you that way, you might believe I had two."

Bring your left hand, palm toward you, in front of your right hand. Close the right fold of the displayed dollar toward the left so that the two separate folds are brought together, as if closing a fan. Lift your left hand away and show what appears to be the single folded dollar sticking up from your right hand, and say, "I mean, if you didn't know I had only one."

Again bring your empty left hand over in front of your right hand. Grip the folded two-dollar bill between your left thumb and fingers, and suddenly pull your hands wide apart, holding a folded bill in each hand, to show there are really two instead of one.

Open out the bill in your right hand with the fingers of that hand, show it, and drop it on the table as you say, "Of course, it's only an optical illusion. . . . Because I really have three dollars, not two." Point to the dollar bill on the table. "That's one. . . ." Quickly unfold the two-dollar bill with your left hand, show it fully opened, and drop it on top of the first one. "And here's *two*."

WINNER TAKE ALL

How it looks

You take an envelope from your pocket, remove a poker chip and a quarter from it, and drop the empty envelope on the table. You pick up the poker chip and put it into the envelope, then pick up the quarter and put that into your pocket. "What's in the envelope?" you ask someone who is watching. He answers that the poker chip is in the envelope. "So far, you're absolutely right," you say. "I'll bet you've played this game before. Let's try it again."

Once more, you put the poker chip into the envelope and

WINNER TAKE ALL

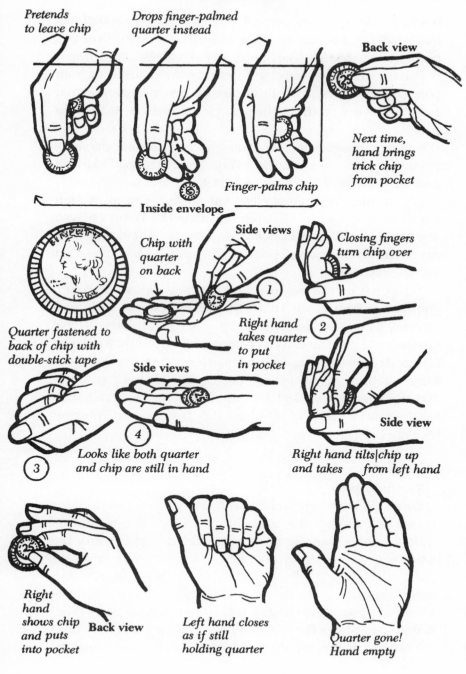

*Pretends
to leave chip*

*Drops finger-palmed
quarter instead*

Back view

Finger-palms chip

*Next time,
hand brings
trick chip
from pocket*

← ———— **Inside envelope** ———— →

*Quarter fastened to
back of chip with
double-stick tape*

*Chip with
quarter
on back*

Side views

*Closing fingers
turn chip over*

①

②

*Right hand
takes quarter
to put
in pocket*

Side views

④

*Looks like both quarter
and chip are still in hand*

Side view

*Right hand tilts|chip up
and takes   from left hand*

③

*Right
hand
shows chip
and puts
into pocket* **Back view**

*Left hand closes
as if still
holding quarter*

*Quarter gone!
Hand empty*

the coin into your pocket and ask what's in the envelope, but when he answers that the chip is, you say, "No, this time you've missed. They've changed places." You dump the quarter from the envelope and take the poker chip from your pocket. "I think it's the envelope that's confusing you. Let's make the game a little simpler. I'll do it out in the open."

You lay the poker chip and the quarter on the out-stretched palm of your left hand. Then you pick up the quarter from your hand, close that hand around the poker chip, and put the quarter into your pocket. You ask which one is in your hand. When he says that the poker chip is, you say, "No, I'm afraid you missed again. They're *both* in my hand." You open your left hand and show both the chip and the quarter.

"Maybe it will be easier if I do it the other way around," you say, as you close your left hand over the chip and quarter. You take the chip from your hand, leaving the quarter, and put the chip into your pocket. "Now what's in my hand?" He answers that the quarter is, but you say, "No, there's nothing in my hand." You open your hand to show that the quarter has vanished, and brush your empty hands together as you say, "That's how the game is won. Winner take all."

What you need
An envelope
Three quarters that look alike
Two poker chips that look alike
Double-stick transparent tape, the kind that is sticky on both sides

How you fix it
One of the quarters is attached to the back of one of the chips, so that from the front it looks like only a poker chip, but when it is turned over and lying flat on your hand it

looks like a chip with a quarter on top of it. The quarter is fastened to the chip off-center, so the edge of the coin is close to the edge of the chip, which looks more natural than if it were right at the center.

Put one of the chips on a table. Take a strip of double-stick tape and cut it to a ¾-inch length. Fasten that strip vertically to the chip, starting just below the chip's top edge. Run another strip the same length horizontally across the middle of the first one. Then attach two cross-strips the same length to the back of the quarter. Stick the tapes on the quarter to the tapes on the chip and press the two together firmly with your thumb. (You can glue the quarter to the chip, if you prefer, but if they are taped as explained they will hold together tight with no edges of tape showing.)

Inside the right-hand pocket of most men's jackets there is a little "ticket pocket." Women can have one sewn into blazer or suit jacket pockets. Put the tricked chip in that, so the side with the attached quarter is toward your body. Put one of the other quarters into the bottom of that jacket pocket. Put the remaining chip and quarter into the envelope, close the flap, fold the envelope in half, and have that in the same pocket.

What you do

Take the envelope from your pocket, open it, and slide the chip and quarter out of it onto the table. Show the envelope empty and drop that on the table. "This is a little game with a poker chip and a quarter," you say, as you turn over each of them to show both sides and also to let it be seen that your hands are empty.

With your left hand, pick up the envelope to hold it at the top by its open flap, with the back of the envelope toward you. Take the poker chip with your right hand and put it into the envelope, then pick up the quarter and put that into your right-hand jacket pocket.

Ask what is in the envelope, and when the person answers that the chip is, say, "So far, you're absolutely right." Slide the chip out of the envelope onto the table and put down the envelope. Say, "And, of course, the quarter is in my pocket." Reach into your pocket with your right hand, get one of the quarters finger-palmed, and take the other quarter between your thumb and first finger to bring it out and show it. Then put that quarter on the table next to the chip as you say, "I'll bet you've played this game before. Let's try again."

Pick up the envelope with your left hand to hold it as before. With your right hand, pick up the chip and put your hand into the envelope. Drop the hidden quarter from your fingers into the envelope and with your thumb slide the chip up into your fingers and finger-palm it. Take your hand out of the envelope as though you have left the chip there. Pick up the quarter from the table, show it, put it into your pocket, and leave both the quarter and finger-palmed chip in your pocket as you bring your hand out again.

Ask what's in the envelope and when the answer is that the chip is there, say, "No, this time you've missed. They've changed places." Tip the quarter out of the envelope and put the envelope aside. With your right hand, reach into your pocket and take the chip with the attached quarter from the little "ticket pocket." Keep the back of it toward you as you bring it out and hold it up to show it as though it were the same chip you had been using before.

"I think it's the envelope that's confusing you," you say. "Let's make the game a little simpler. I'll do it out in the open." Hold your left hand outstretched, palm upward, fingertips toward the front. Lay the poker chip on the fingers of that hand with the quarter side down. Then pick up the quarter from the table and lay that on your left palm in back of the chip. Show them both on your outstretched left hand.

Take away the quarter with your right hand and close

your left hand in a loose fist around the chip, closing the fingertips back against the palm. That automatically turns the chip over inside your left hand, so the side with the attached quarter is now facing upward in the closed hand. Keep the left hand closed. With your right hand, openly put the quarter into your pocket and leave it there, bringing your hand out to show it empty.

Ask whether the quarter or poker chip is in your left hand. When the person answers that the chip is, you say, "No, I'm afraid you missed again. They're *both* in my hand." Open your left hand and show the chip with the attached quarter lying on top of it.

"Maybe it will be easier if I do it the other way around," you say. Keep your left hand outstretched as it is and close the fingers of that hand loosely around the chip and attached quarter. Bring your right thumb and first finger to the side of the left hand, opening that hand enough so that they can go inside and grip the edge of the chip, but keep the left fingertips cupped upward at the front. Hold the *very edge* of the chip between your right thumb and finger, tilt the chip up so the attached quarter is hidden at the back, and take it from your left hand.

Keep your left hand closed as though it still held a quarter. Show the chip with your right hand, spreading your fingers open wide so everyone can see that you have nothing else in that hand, and put the chip into your pocket. Leave it there and bring your right hand out.

Move your closed left hand forward a little and ask, "Now what's in my hand?" When the person answers that you are holding the quarter, say, "No, there's nothing in my hand." Open your left hand slowly, show that the quarter has vanished, and brush both hands together as you say, "That's how the game is won. Winner take all."

3

NOVEL
MONEY MAGIC

TOPSY-TURVY

How it looks

"I'll show you how to train a dollar to do tricks for you,"
you say, as you take a dollar bill from your pocket, unfold it,
and hold it between your hands, so the audience can see the
full face of the bill. "If you fold it in half from left to right,
then fold it again, and open it up . . . it will stand on its
head for you—upside down."

You show that the design on the face of the bill has
turned upside down. "But if you fold it in half from right to
left, fold it again, and open it up . . . it's back on its feet—
right side up," you say, as you do that and show that the
design has righted itself again.

"Some of you probably know that little trick," you say, as
you pretend to explain. "If you turn it from right to left, it
stays head up." Without folding the bill at all, you turn it

TOPSY-TURVY

MAKING THE TOPSY-TURVY BILL

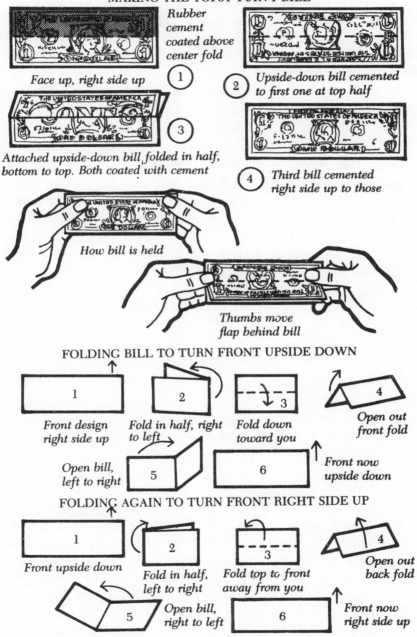

Rubber cement coated above center fold

Face up, right side up ① ② *Upside-down bill cemented to first one at top half*

③ *Attached upside-down bill folded in half, bottom to top. Both coated with cement*

④ *Third bill cemented right side up to those*

How bill is held

Thumbs move flap behind bill

FOLDING BILL TO TURN FRONT UPSIDE DOWN

1

Front design right side up

2

Fold in half, right to left

3

Fold down toward you

4

Open out front fold

5

Open bill, left to right

6

Front now upside down

FOLDING AGAIN TO TURN FRONT RIGHT SIDE UP

1

Front upside down

2

Fold in half, left to right

3

Fold top to front away from you

4

Open out back fold

5

Open bill, right to left

6

Front now right side up

from front to back a few times, showing both sides right side up. "But if you turn it from left to right, then it flips itself over—upside down." Still without folding it, you turn it again. The full back of it is now right side up, but the face of it is upside down.

You repeat that, pretending to explain once more, and again the designs on the front and back turn topsy-turvy. As you turn the whole bill from front to back in one direction, both sides are normally right side up. But as you turn it in the other direction, the back is right side up and the face upside down. "Just don't turn it from top to bottom," you say, "because that gets very confusing." You do that and now there is a face design on *both* sides of the bill, but no back design at all.

"Turn it from left to right," you say, doing that, "and it's upside down." You show that it is. "But just turn it from right to left and we're back where we started—heads up again." You show both sides of the bill are now normal and right side up once more. "If that's all clear to you. . . I hope somebody will explain it to me," you say as you fold the bill and put it back into your pocket. "Because I just don't understand it at all!"

What you need
Three play-money dollar bills
Rubber cement

How you fix it
The three bills are cemented together to look like one, forming a flap that is secretly thumbed up or down at the back to make the various changes before turning the bill around.

Put one of the bills on a table, face up, with its long edges top and bottom and with its design right side up. *Carefully* fold it in half from top to bottom, making sure both edges meet exactly, then firmly crease the center fold with your thumbnail and open out the bill again as it was at the start. Liberally coat the top half of it, the entire part above the center fold, with rubber cement.

Take a second face-up bill, turn it so its face design is *upside down,* "standing on its head," and put it squarely on top of the first one. Stick the two together, pressing down so they are tightly cemented, especially around the edges. Wait for the cement to dry. Then carefully fold that second bill from bottom to top, making sure the edges meet, and crease the fold with your thumbnail.

Leave that second one folded in half as it is. Coat the whole surface of both parts with rubber cement, everything that now shows—the folded-up part of the second bill at the top and the unfolded part of the first bill at the bottom. Place the third face-up bill, with its design *right side up,* squarely on top of those and stick them together, again making sure the edges meet exactly and are well cemented. Let the whole thing dry thoroughly before you try using it.

Now hold it up horizontally between your two hands, long edges top and bottom, the face of it toward you, and the back of it toward where the audience would be. Your hands should be at the right and left side edges, fingers in front and thumbs at the back, so the audience will see the whole bill except for the edges you are holding.

Held together that way, it looks like a single bill with front and back designs normally right side up. Still keeping it horizontal, you can turn it around end for end, transferring the right edge to your left hand and left edge to your right hand, or the other way around, to show the back or front of it.

With the face of it toward you, allow the top of it to open slightly, and with your thumbs behind the bill fold the open top part down to the bottom. The face design is now upside down, but the back design is still right side up. If you hold it together at the bottom and turn it around to show the face to the audience, the bill seems to have turned itself upside down. Now hold it with the *back* of the bill toward you and move the flap from bottom to top with your thumbs. A face of the bill shows at both sides.

The folds must be well creased in all directions for this to work easily. Fold the bill in half a dozen or so times each way, top to bottom, back and front, and also in half from left to right and right to left. You should be able to fold it and handle it like an ordinary bill.

When you want to change the face design so it is right side up or upside down, always start with the *face* of the bill toward you; when you want to make the back of it vanish so only faces show, always start with the *back* of the bill toward you.

In this routine, you always turn the bill from right to left to show the face design right side up; left to right to show it upside down. All the moves should be slow and deliberate, so the audience has a chance to take in each change before the next one is made. Doing it slowly also gives you plenty of time to secretly move the flap up or down with your thumbs behind the bill.

To set it up, turn the bill face toward you with the flaps positioned so the back and front designs are both right side up, and fold it in half from left to right. Have it that way in your shirt pocket or the right-hand pocket of your slacks.

What you do

Take the bill from your pocket, unfold it, and hold it horizontally between your hands at the side edges of it, with the face of the bill toward the audience. The first part, folding and then unfolding to turn the design upside down, is a well-known little stunt with a dollar bill. Familiar to many, it is not intended to fool anybody, but merely to build up to what is to come. Here is how it is done:

You are holding the face of the bill toward the audience with the design right side up. Fold the right half of it over to the front, from right to left. Then fold the top half toward you, down to the back. Open out the front half to bring it to the top. Unfold the bill from left to right. The face design, as the audience sees it, is now upside down.

To turn it right side up again, fold the left half of it over to the front, from left to right. Then fold the top half away from you, down to the front. Open out the back half to bring it to the top. Then unfold the bill from right to left. The front design is now right side up, as it was at the start.

"Some of you probably know that little trick," you say. "If you turn it from right to left, it stays head up." Without folding the bill, horizontally turn it around from right to left. Hold it a second and turn it again. Hold it and then turn it once more. That leaves the face of it toward you.

Snap the bill between your hands and remove your right hand for an instant to hold it only with your left hand. Bring your right thumb back to the right top edge, slide your thumb inside the flap, and take the bill again with the right fingers in front as before. Release the top left corner from your left thumb. Behind the bill, slowly turn the flap down to the bottom with your thumbs, and hold it together. The face design is now upside down, but still toward you.

"But if you turn it from left to right," you say, "then it flips itself over—upside down." Turn it horizontally left to right, hold it so the audience can see the change, and then turn it once more. The face is toward you again.

With your thumbs behind the bill, shift the flap from bottom to top, and say, "If you turn it right to left, it's right side up." Turn it and show it. Then turn it again so it faces you. Shift the flap from top to bottom. "But left to right— it's upside down." Turn it left to right and show it upside down.

The back of the bill is now toward you. "Just don't turn it from top to bottom—because that get's very confusing," you say. Behind the bill, bring your thumbs to the bottom, turn the flap to the top, and continue to turn the bill over to the front, from top to bottom, using the fingers of both hands to turn it. Grip it tightly at the bottom, snap it between your hands, and turn it over again from top to bottom, so the audience can see there are only faces on both sides and the back design has disappeared.

Behind the bill, secretly shift the flap from top to bottom. This leaves the front upside down and the back right side up. Turn the bill around horizontally from right to left to show that it has a back design again and it is right side up.

"Turn it from left to right," you say, "and it is upside down." Turn it around from left to right to show the face upside down. Now turn it right to left to show the back still right side up. Secretly shift the flap from bottom to top and say, "But just turn it from right to left and we're back where we started—heads up again." Turn it from right to left and show that the face now also is right side up.

"If that's all clear to you ... I hope somebody will explain it to me." Turn it twice more, right to left, showing that both sides of the bill are normal again, and fold it up and put it away in your pocket as you say, "Because I just don't understand it at all!"

COMEDY CUT BILL

How it looks

You cut a dollar bill in half, hold up the two pieces separately, and then put them together and trim off the cut edges. "Will you just snap your fingers?" you ask someone in the audience. When he does, you shake the bill open to show it is whole once more. "There it is. Just as good as new ..."

But something has gone wrong! The bill is together in one piece, but the two halves are reversed. Half of the back of the bill is joined to half of the face, so the two parts are in opposite directions. "Which hand did you use when you snapped your fingers?" you ask the spectator. When he answers, you say, "No wonder. That was the wrong hand."

COMEDY CUT BILL

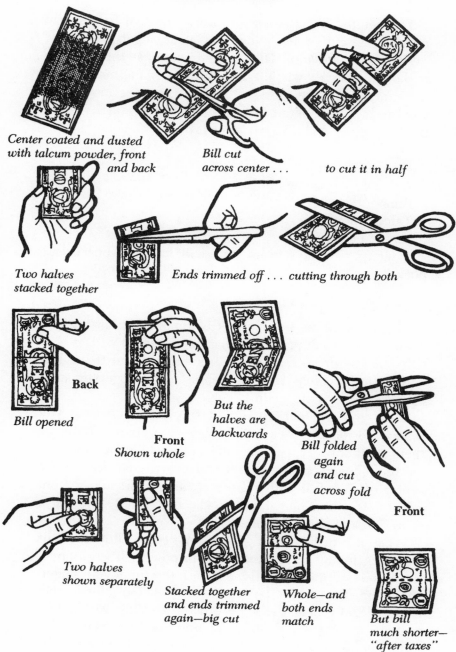

Center coated and dusted with talcum powder, front and back

Bill cut across center . . .

to cut it in half

Two halves stacked together

Ends trimmed off . . . cutting through both

Back

Bill opened

Front
Shown whole

But the halves are backwards

Bill folded again and cut across fold

Front

Two halves shown separately

Stacked together and ends trimmed again—big cut

Whole—and both ends match

But bill much shorter— "after taxes"

You cut the bill apart again, show the two halves, and trim off the cut edges. "Now snap your fingers," you say. "With the other hand." He does and you shake the bill open to show it properly whole again. But it is much smaller than it was at the start because so much has been cut away. "We seem to have lost about forty cents' worth," you say. "But that's how any dollar looks—after taxes."

What you need
A dozen play-money bills
Rubber cement
Talcum powder
An old newspaper
A sharp pair of scissors that will fit into your breast pocket

How you fix it
This is based on an old trick of repeatedly cutting and restoring a strip of paper that has been treated with rubber cement. The pressure of the scissors as they cut through it automatically sticks the cut center edges together so it appears to be whole again.

Since you will cut up one of the bills each time you practice or do the trick, it is easiest to prepare a batch of them all at once. Lay all the bills separately in face-up rows on the opened-out newspaper. Thickly coat the entire center of each bill with rubber cement, right across from side to side, brushing it out to the edges and covering a center area of about 3 inches.

When it is dry, apply a good second coat. Allow the bills to dry again and then spread talcum powder liberally over the coated sections, smoothing it with the tip of your finger. Shake off the excess powder, turn all the bills' backs upward, and repeat the same process, so they are double-coated and powdered at the center on both sides. The supply of bills can be stored in an envelope. Because of the powder, they won't stick together.

Turn one of them with its narrow edges top and bottom, and fold it exactly in half, top to bottom. Have it that way in your breast pocket with the scissors.

What you do

Take out the bill and scissors. Unfold the bill, show it, and hold it with your left hand. With the scissors in your right hand, cut across the center crease to cut the bill in two. Hold one half in each hand, show them, and bring the halves together in your left hand so that the *back* of one half lies squarely against the *face* of the other half, with the cut edges of both at the top.

Trim off the two cut edges together, cutting evenly right across through both, to cut off about ¼ inch. Let the trimmed-off scraps fall to the floor and put the scissors into your breast pocket. Bring your right hand to the bottom edges of the bill and take the outer edge between your right thumb and fingers, still holding the bill with your left hand.

Ask a spectator to snap his fingers. When he does, hold up your right hand so the bill unfolds and hangs open from that hand. Because the rubber cement holds the cut edges, the bill appears to be restored in one piece, but with the two halves reversed, so that one part of it is the face of a bill and the other part the back of a bill.

Stare at the strange-looking bill, then look at the spectator and ask, "Which hand did you use when you snapped your fingers?" Whatever he answers, say, "No wonder. That was the wrong hand."

Bring the palm of your left hand against the bottom part of the bill that is hanging from your right hand and fold the bill shut. Take the scissors from your pocket. Cut right across through both of the two edges together, again trimming away about ¼ inch. Separate the two pieces and show one in each hand.

Now bring them together into your left hand again, one atop the other, but this time so that the two pieces are *face to face* or *back to back*. You can easily arrange that as you show the pieces separately and turn them over. Hold the two together and trim about ½ inch off the already cut edges, cutting evenly through both pieces at once as before. Put the scissors away in your pocket. Holding the bill in your left hand, take the outer bottom edge of it between your right thumb and fingers.

"Now snap your fingers," you tell the spectator. "With the other hand." When he does, hold up the bill with your right hand so it unfolds and hangs open, properly restored but now so much shorter that it looks like a midget-sized bill. Say, "We seem to have lost about forty cents' worth. But that's how any dollar looks—after taxes." Fold the small bill and put it away in your pocket.

IN THE RED

How it looks

"I wonder if money will ever go out of style?" you say, as you take four bills from your pocket and transfer them one at a time from hand to hand, showing both sides of each, their designs the usual black and green. "Some people say that with all the credit cards there are—who needs money?" You hold the packet of bills stacked together. "The trouble is that if you keep buying too many things on credit—sooner or later, you're sure to wind up in the red!"

As you speak, the front bill of the packet suddenly turns red. Then you show that they have all become red, on both sides. "I've heard of dirty money," you say, as you put them back into your pocket, "but did you ever see money *blush* before?"

What you need
Eight play-money bills
A red felt-tip pen
Nonshiny transparent tape

IN THE RED

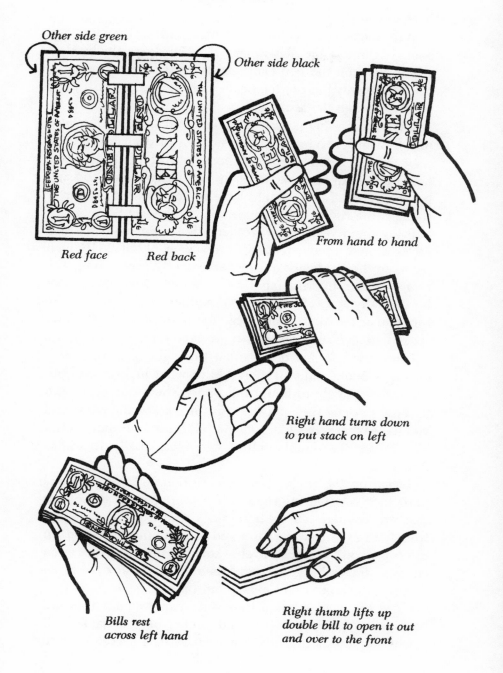

Other side green

Other side black

Red face   Red back

From hand to hand

Right hand turns down
to put stack on left

Bills rest
across left hand

Right thumb lifts up
double bill to open it out
and over to the front

How you fix it

With the red pen, color the printed parts of the faces and backs of three of the play-money bills, but leave the borders white. Just run the pen back and forth within the borders, coloring evenly but not too heavily, so the designs still show faintly through the red.

Then color *only the face* of a fourth bill and *only the back* of a fifth bill, leaving the reverse sides of each of those as they are, and again leaving the borders white. Put those two on a table with their red sides up and narrow ends top and bottom. The left one should have its top printed border to the left; the right one its top border to the right.

Bring them vertically together side by side so their long edges almost touch, leaving a space of about 1/16 inch between them. Make sure they are exactly even. Hinge the two together by running three 1½-inch lengths of tape horizontally across from one to the other, one strip near the top, one at the center, one near the bottom. Keep the tiny space between the two bills so the tape hinges won't bind.

Close the left one down upon the right one, as though closing a book, and you should have what looks from both sides like a single ordinary bill. Open them out again and fold the left one the opposite way, around to the back, and you have what looks like a single bill but red on both sides. The folder-like double bill should close easily in either direction.

To set up the trick, open out the double bill so the red parts face you. On the right half of it, place the three bills that are colored red on both sides. Close the double bill from left to right, so the three red ones are inside it, and tap the edges so they are all evenly squared up. Keep the open edges of the double bill toward the right and stack the three ordinary uncolored bills evenly on top of it.

Have them all stacked that way, narrow ends top and bottom, in the inner right-hand pocket of your jacket. (If you wish, you can have them stacked in a secretary-type wallet, the kind that holds bills full-length without folding them.)

What you do

Take the bills from your pocket, keeping them stacked as they are, and tap the edges to even them again, if necessary. Hold them vertically upright in your left hand, narrow ends top and bottom, thumb across the center, and with the back of your hand toward the audience.

Bring your right hand over, its back also to the audience, and thumb the top bill from your left hand into your right, which takes it vertically with its thumb across the center to hold it. Turn your right hand outward to the right to show the other side of the bill to the audience, and then bring it back as it was to take the second one from the left hand.

Thumb the second one off on top of the first one in your right hand, just as though you were dealing cards from the top of a pack, but keep both hands upright. Show both sides of it as before and continue in that way, taking the third on top of the second, and finally taking the double bill as if it were a fourth single one. Transferring them singly from hand to hand has now put the double one on top of the stack, facing you in your right hand.

Hold your left hand palm upward in front of you with the tips of the fingers toward the audience. Turn your right hand over toward you and bring it down to place the stack of bills *horizontally* across your outstretched left hand. The double bill is now at the bottom as they rest upon your left palm, and the open edges of that bill are toward your body. Keep your right hand as it is, with its thumb at the rear and its palm above all the bills.

With your left thumb, bend down the left corner of the bottom bill, which is the lower part of the double bill, to separate it a little from all the others above it. Slide your right thumb into the opening, so it is inside the double bill.

Now lift all the bills above your right thumb straight up

from the rear, then forward together between your thumb and fingers, and over to the front of the whole stack. That brings the stack horizontally upright, with the bottom edge of all the bills touching your left palm, and a red bill has suddenly appeared at the face of the packet.

What it really amounts to is opening up the front half of the double bill and closing it again in the opposite direction. The three all-red bills are now at the front of the stack and the three ordinary uncolored bills are now hidden within the double one, which shows both sides red instead of green and black. That has been done by simply lifting all the bills that were above your thumb and turning them over together from back to front. There is no need to hurry the move; do it openly and casually, as though merely turning over the bills on your left hand.

So far the audience has seen only the one red bill at the face of the packet. Hold them all as they are with your left hand for a moment and remove your right hand to tap the edges and square up the stack. This is important, to make sure the ordinary bills are well concealed within the double red one, so it can be handled again as if it were a single bill.

When they are squared up, hold them with your left hand as you did at the start, vertically upright with their narrow ends top and bottom. Transfer them one at a time from hand to hand as at the beginning, thumbing them off from the left hand into the right. Show the front and back of each bill as you take it, so the audience discovers they have all turned red on both sides, and finally put your "blushing money" back into your pocket.

THE TRAVELING MILLIONAIRE

How it looks
"How would you like to travel all over the country like a millionaire and never have to think about money?" you ask, as you take some strips of newspaper from your pocket,

open them out, and count them from hand to hand, showing both sides. "No credit cards. No travelers' checks. Just a few scraps of paper ... and right away, you've got instant money!"

As you speak, you slap the newspaper strips against your other hand and they instantly change to dollar bills, which you show singly, front and back. "Money for plane tickets ... for hotels ... for meals ... for sightseeing ... for souvenirs."

Gathering them together, you say, "I wish I could really do that. But they *are* just scraps of paper." You slap your other hand with them again and the bills suddenly change back into strips of newspaper. Once more, you show them from hand to hand. "I wish somehow, in some way, I could turn them all into money." You shake your head and tuck the paper strips back into your pocket. "But to *really* do that—I'd have to be a magician."

What you need
Six play-money bills
An old newspaper
Liquid adhesive such as white craft glue
A pencil, a ruler, and scissors

How you fix it
You will need six pieces of newspaper, each cut to the *exact* size of one of the bills. Because the dimensions have to be precise, measure one of the bills you have and then use the ruler and pencil to mark out guidelines for cutting the paper strips to that size.

Stack the six newspaper strips evenly together on a table with their narrow ends top and bottom. Measure 1 inch down from the top and at that point draw a very light horizontal pencil line across the first strip of the stack. Fold all six strips together up from the bottom to that line, crease the fold with your thumbnail, and then erase the pencil mark.

THE TRAVELING MILLIONAIRE—I

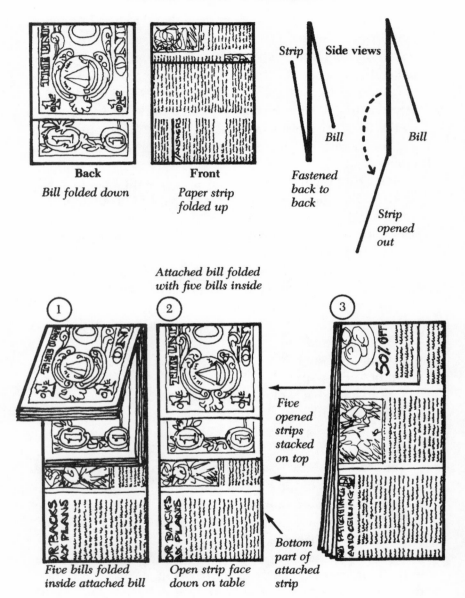

Back

Bill folded down

Front

Paper strip folded up

Strip **Side views**

Bill

Bill

Fastened back to back

Strip opened out

Attached bill folded with five bills inside

① ② ③

Five opened strips stacked on top

Five bills folded inside attached bill

Open strip face down on table

Bottom part of attached strip

THE TRAVELING MILLIONAIRE–II

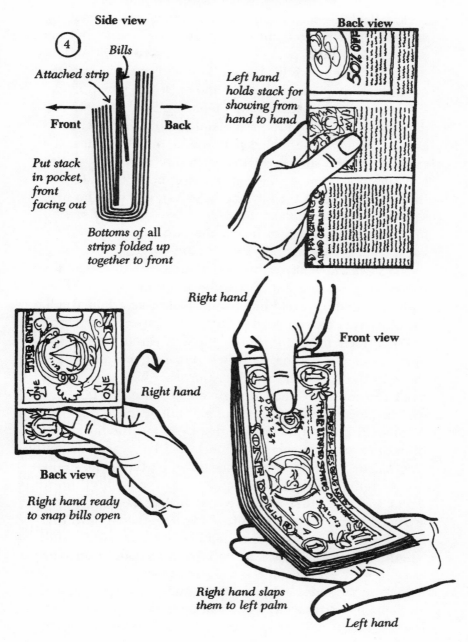

Side view

④

Bills

Attached strip

← Front

Back →

Put stack in pocket, front facing out

Bottoms of all strips folded up together to front

Back view

Left hand holds stack for showing from hand to hand

Right hand

Front view

Right hand

Back view

Right hand ready to snap bills open

Right hand slaps them to left palm

Left hand

Now stack the six bills squarely together, narrow ends top and bottom. This time, measure 1 inch up from the bottom edge, draw a faint pencil line across the first bill at that point, and carefully fold all the bills together *down from the top* to that line. Crease the fold and erase the pencil line.

Put five of the bills aside for a moment. Fold the sixth one down from the top on its crease and turn the bill over to its opposite side, so the folded part is underneath, against the table. Coat the surface of the part that now shows with adhesive. Take one of the paper strips, hold it so the part that is folded up at the bottom faces you, and put the strip squarely upon the adhesive-coated bill so all edges exactly match. Press it down to fasten the two together back-to-back, making sure the edges are secure.

You should now have a bill on one side with its top folded down attached to a paper strip on the other side with its bottom folded up. Held one way it looks like a folded bill, the other way like a folded strip of newspaper.

When the adhesive is thoroughly dry, carefully trim any uneven edges with the scissors so none of the newspaper shows at the side with the bill or the other way around. But don't trim off more than tiny slivers because this fake one still has to cover the other strips and bills.

To set it up for the routine, first open out the bottom of the paper strip attached to the bill, so the strip is full length. Turn that open strip face down on the table, so the side with the bill is face up.

Put the five other bills face up inside the fold of the attached one. Fold all the bills down together. Leave that face down as it is. Now open out the five paper strips full length and lay them face down on top of that. Make sure the edges are all even at the top and sides.

Pick up the stack, hold it upright, and fold the bottoms of all the paper strips away from you, up to the front together. Have it that way in your shirt pocket or the breast pocket of your jacket.

What you do

Take it from your pocket with your right hand and hold it vertically in front of you. With your left hand, open out the strips full length. Put your left fingers around the stack at the center and hold it with that hand, with the back of the hand toward the audience and thumb to the rear. Adjust the stack with your right hand to square it up and make sure the bills are covered. Casually turn your left hand out to the left to show the back of the stack and then bring that hand in front of you again.

You now transfer the strips singly from hand to hand to show both sides of them. Bring your right fingers to the top of the stack and separate the first strip at the back, making sure you have only one. Take it with your right hand, show the face of it, turn that hand out to the right to show the back of the strip, and then put it at the *front* of the entire stack and leave it there.

Continue to show each of the others the same way, returning each to the front of the stack your left hand is holding. This moves all the separate strips from the back of the stack to the front of it.

Once or twice, while you are showing a strip with your right hand, let your left hand swing out to the left at the same time, so the audience sees the back of the stack. When you have shown five strips and replaced each at the front, the next one will be the one with the folded bills attached. Leave that on the stack as it is, without removing it. Keep the stack upright and close to you so nobody catches a glimpse of the folded bills at the back.

You are now about to make the bills suddenly appear. Bring your right hand to the stack that your left hand is holding. Fold the bottoms of all the strips up together against the face of the stack. Hold it between your right fingers at the front and thumb at the back, with the thumb just beneath the bottom edge of the folded bills. Bring your left hand in front of your waist, palm up, and swing your right hand over and down to slap the stack against your outstretched left palm. That snaps the bills open so they suddenly unfold full length and come into view.

Immediately take the stack with your left hand, by turning that hand palm downward across the face of the bills, thumb underneath, and lift it to hold the stack vertically upright in front of you. Bring both hands together and spread the bills out in a fan between them, like a fan of playing cards you might be holding in a card game.

With the bills spread out, take the five separate ones with your left hand, put them all *behind* the one remaining in your right hand, and square up the stack. Keep the stack with your left hand, fingers across the front and thumb at the back, and remove your right hand.

You are now set to show the bills one at a time, just as you showed the paper strips at the start. With your right hand, separate one of the bills from the back of the stack, show the bill back and front, and replace it at the *front* of the entire stack. Continue as before until you have shown five of the bills. That leaves the stack ready to change the bills back into paper strips.

You do it exactly the way you first changed the strips into bills. First fold the bottoms of all the bills up together against the face of the stack. Hold the stack with your right-hand fingers at the front and your thumb just beneath the bottom edge of the folded strips at the back. With your right hand, slap the stack down against your outstretched left palm. The strips suddenly snap open full length, so it seems to the audience that the bills visibly change back to strips of paper.

Again take the stack with your left hand down across the face of it, bring it vertically upright in front of you, and spread the strips into a fan between both hands. But this last time keep all the strips as they are at the face of the stack. Square it up, separate one strip from the *front*, show both sides, and put it at the *back* of the stack.

Continue showing the strips singly as you put them from the face to the back, and also occasionally show the back of the stack, until you have shown five of the strips. Then fold the bottoms of all the strips up to the front, put the stack away in your pocket, and say, "But to *really* do that—I'd have to be a magician."

(The routine ends with the stack in its original order, so you won't have to set it all up again for the next time you want to do the trick.)

THE MONEY SPELL

Here is another trick that uses the same basic method as The Traveling Millionaire, but with an entirely different presentation. It is especially effective as a quick opening trick, but is one that can be carried in your pocket, ready to perform at any time.

How it looks
"I'm about to cast a spell," you say as you show some cards with letters of the alphabet on them. Each card has one letter on the front and another on the back, and you spell them aloud as you show the letters, one at a time: "M-A-G-I-C . . . M-O-N-E-Y." Holding the cards stacked together in your hand, you say, "That spells 'magic money' . . . and here it is!"

You swing the stack of alphabet cards down to tap them against the palm of your other hand and suddenly the cards all change into dollar bills. As you count the bills from hand to hand, showing both sides of them, you say, "M-A-G-I-C . . . and that spells 'magic'!"

What you need
Six play-money bills

Two 5 x 8 inch unlined office file cards or other thin cardboard

THE MONEY SPELL

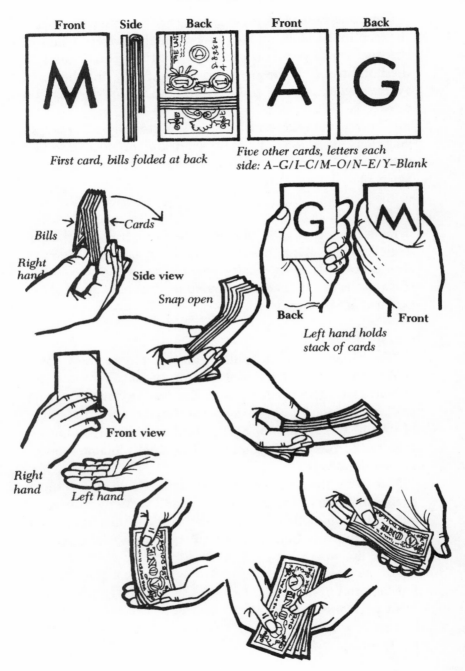

Front   **Side**   **Back**   **Front**   **Back**

First card, bills folded at back

Five other cards, letters each side: A–G/I–C/M–O/N–E/Y–Blank

Cards

Bills

Right hand

Side view

Snap open

Front view

Right hand

Left hand

Back

Front

G

M

Left hand holds stack of cards

Adhesive such as white craft glue
A rubber band
A black felt-tip pen, a pencil, a ruler, and scissors

How you fix it
The two file cards provide the cardboard for making six small cards, each the *exact* width of the bills and 3¾ inches long. It is easiest to cut one of the small cards first and use that as a pattern for marking out and cutting the others. Since play-money bills vary somewhat in width according to their manufacture, measure the exact width of the bills you are using. Then take one of the file cards and with the pencil and ruler mark off a section exactly that wide and 3¾ inches long. Cut out that small card and use it to mark around so you can cut five more small cards the same size.

Turn one of the bills face down with its narrow edges top and bottom. Coat the face of one of the small cards with white craft glue and fasten that card to the bottom part of the bill so that their edges match squarely at the bottom and both sides.

When the adhesive is dry, turn the bill face up, with the attached card now underneath, against the table. Trim off any tiny edges of the card that may show beyond the edges of the bill. Fold the unfastened top part of the bill down against the face of it, toward the bottom, and crease the fold so the bill is flat.

Now turn the card side of it face up. With the felt-tip pen, print a big block letter "M" on it, filling the face of the card. (You may prefer to use a stencil or stick-on self-adhesive letters.) Take a second card and print a big "A" on its face and a "G" on its back. Print "I" on the face of a third one and "C" on its back. On the opposite sides of a fourth, print "M" and "O," and on a fifth, "N" and "E." Print a "Y" on the face of the last one and leave the back blank.

Turn the card with the attached bill so the bill is facing

you and open out the top fold. Lay the five other bills evenly face up on that one, with all edges matched, and fold them all down from the top together, inside the fold of the attached one. Again crease the fold.

Stack the cards on top in this order, from the bottom up as the letters face you: first the bills, next the blank face, then E, O, C, and G. You may want to pencil small numbers lightly at the upper corners so you will be able to stack them quickly again for later performances.

Square them up, snap the rubber band around them, and have them in the otherwise empty left-hand pocket of your slacks.

What you do

As you say you are about to "cast a spell," take out the cards, remove and discard the rubber band, and hold the stack at its top edge between your right thumb and fingers so the face of the first card can be seen. Show the M at the face of it to the audience, and start spelling aloud, "M . . ."

Leave that card where it is. Bring the palm of your left hand against the face of the stack to hold the cards with that hand, fingers across the front and thumb at the back. With your right hand, take the first card from the *back* of the stack. Hold that one up, long enough for the audience to see the face of it, and spell aloud, "A." Turn that card around to show the back of it and spell, "G."

Now put that card at the *front* of the whole stack in your left hand and leave it there. Take the next one from the back, hold it up and slowly show the letters, first one side and then the other, and spell, "I . . . C." Return that to the front of the others, keeping them all squared up in your left hand as you go along.

Pause a moment and then in the same way—taking each card from the back, holding it up to show one side and then the other, and returning it to the front of the stack—spell out, "M-O-N-E-Y." With the last card, you show the Y at the face of it, turn it around to show that the back of it is blank, and return that to the front of the stack with its blank side still facing the audience.

The folded bills are now at the rear of the stack your left hand is holding. Bring your right hand to the bottom of the stack and take it with that hand, with your four fingers up in front of the bottom edge and thumb at the rear just *below* the edge of the folded-down bills. Hold the stack firmly and keep it upright so nobody glimpses the bills at the back.

Lower your left hand to a level below your waist, turn it palm upward, and hold it outstretched in front of you. Say, "That spells 'magic money' . . . and here it is!" Bring your right hand straight down to the front so the stack lightly slaps against the palm of your left hand and the folded bills snap open. Close your left thumb across the top of the bills and fingers around the side edges to hold the bills and keep them fully opened out. Keep the cards squared in the palm of that hand beneath the bills, which now hide the cards from view, and tilt the hand forward so the front edges of the bills slant slightly toward the floor.

Your left hand is now holding the stack and both hands are still in front of you, down below your waist. With your right hand, separate the first bill from the top of the stack, making sure you have only one. Hold it up, show the audience the front and back of it, and say, "M . . ." Put that back under all the cards and bills in your left hand, sliding it in at the bottom of them, and leave it there. Separate the next bill from the top of the stack, hold it up to show both sides, and say, "A . . ." Return that to the bottom of all the others.

Continue in that way, taking a bill from the top, showing it, saying aloud the next letter, and returning it to the bottom of the stack, just as you naturally would if you were counting a stack of bills. But instead of counting, you spell aloud, "M-A-G-I-C."

(Actually, you count only five bills from hand to hand, leaving the sixth one, which had the card glued to it, on top of the stack at the end. But the spelling aloud of the five-letter word *magic,* while showing a bill for each letter, leads the audience to believe you have shown both sides of all of them. It also leaves the hidden cards sandwiched between the bills, so they are now covered, top and bottom.)

The spelling and counting off of the bills should be done quickly. As you finish the spelling, casually show both sides of the stack of bills in your left hand, and as you fold down the tops of them to put them back into your pocket, say, "And that spells 'magic'!"

HOW TO STRETCH A DOLLAR

How it looks

"I'm going to show you how to double your money," you say as you open out a small piece of cardboard, folded across the center, and show that it is empty. You place a dollar bill against the cardboard, fold the cardboard shut, and then open it to bring out the folded bill, and say, "Already, we've doubled our money."

All you have done is to fold the bill by closing the cardboard with the bill inside it. Continuing to joke about "doubling" the money by folding it, you put the half-folded bill into the cardboard, fold it shut on the bill again, and then take the bill out to show that it has been folded in quarters, and say, "We've doubled it again." You run your fingers along the creased edges of the bill and say, "And if I *crease* it here . . . and *crease* it there . . . you can see the money *increases.*"

The idea has been to lead the audience to think it is just a gag, which makes the magic that is about to happen a more sudden surprise. Twice you have shown the cardboard empty except for the single bill, and your hands also are obviously empty. Closing the cardboard again, you tuck the

HOW TO STRETCH A DOLLAR

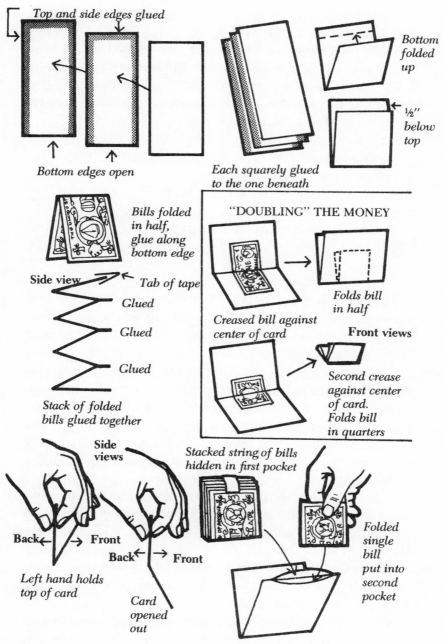

Top and side edges glued

Bottom edges open

Bottom folded up

½" below top

Each squarely glued to the one beneath

Bills folded in half, glue along bottom edge

Side view — Tab of tape

Glued

Glued

Glued

Stack of folded bills glued together

"DOUBLING" THE MONEY

Creased bill against center of card

Folds bill in half

Front views

Second crease against center of card. Folds bill in quarters

Side views

Back ← → Front

Back ← → Front

Left hand holds top of card

Card opened out

Stacked string of bills hidden in first pocket

Folded single bill put into second pocket

folded bill down inside it. "But if you really want to stretch a dollar," you say, "try this!"

Suddenly you pull a long string of attached dollar bills from the cardboard folder, so they tumble down from your hand like a paper streamer, and you again show the cardboard empty. The single bill apparently has changed into a garland of money.

What you need
Thirteen play-money bills
Three unruled 5 x 8 inch office index file cards
White craft glue
Scissors, a pencil, a ruler, transparent tape, and a rubber band

How you fix it
Put one of the file cards on a table, narrow ends top and bottom, and coat the left, right, and top edges with white glue. Lay a second card squarely on top of the first one and fasten the two together at both sides and the top, leaving the bottom edges open. Coat the two side edges and top edge of the second card in the same way, and fasten the third card on top of the second. Press them all firmly together, and when the glue is dry trim off any tiny edges that may overlap. This gives you what should look like a single card, with two separate compartments open at the bottom edge.

With the ruler, measure ½ inch down from the top and draw a light pencil line across. Fold the bottom edge up to that line, firmly crease the card across the fold, and erase the pencil line. The part folded up at the back is now ½ inch shorter than the part at the front, so when you later put your fingers down into the openings they will be concealed from direct front view.

Put all the bills face up, narrow edges top and bottom. Separately fold each of them in half from top to bottom, horizontally across the center, and crease the folds. Fold *one* of the bills again from top to bottom so it is folded in quarters, crease that fold, and then open out the bill and put it aside. Leave the rest as they are, folded only in half.

Take the first of the remaining twelve folded bills and apply white glue right across its bottom edge, covering an area about ½ inch wide. Put a second folded bill evenly on top of the first one and firmly stick them together, back to back, along the bottom edges. Continue in that way, gluing each folded bill to the one beneath it as you stack them evenly one atop another, until all twelve are attached. As you go along, wipe away any excess glue that may squeeze out from the edges, to keep the free parts of the bills from accidentally sticking together.

Allow the glue to dry thoroughly. Then take a 2-inch length of transparent tape and attach one end of it vertically to the bottom edge of the bill that is at the top of the stack. Fold the tape and attach the other end of it to the underside at that edge, to form a small tab of tape. The tab will help you to find that bill quickly, without fumbling, when you later produce the bills.

The result should be an accordion-like string of bills. If you take the tab of the top one with your right hand and lift your arm as high as you can, the rest will unfold to hang down in a string. Put the palm of your left hand beneath the bottom bill of the string and slowly bring your hands together, and they will all fold together again into a stack.

To set things up for the trick, first turn the stack of bills so that all the folds are at the bottom and the bill with the tab is facing you, tab at the top. Hold the folded card upright, with the shorter part to the rear and open edges at the top. Open out the *front* compartment and slide the stack of bills all the way down into it so they are hidden inside, tab still at the top and toward the back.

Open out the card and put the separate unfolded bill in it, so it lies horizontally across the inside center of the card, with the two ends of the bill sticking out from the sides. Close the card, snap the rubber band vertically around it, and have it on your table with the open edges toward the back and the shorter part at the bottom.

What you do

Hold the card upright with your right hand and bring your left hand over to take it at the top. Put your left thumb at the back, first finger down inside the center and other fingers at the front. Press your thumb and first finger together to keep the top opening of the shorter part shut. Your left hand will hold the card at the top that way until the end of the trick.

With your right hand, remove the rubber band and put it on the table. Then take the edge of the bill with that hand, draw it out, and open the card as your left fingers release the front part so it can be opened. With your left hand, casually turn the card to show the front and back of it. Tell the audience, "I'm going to show you how to double your money."

Hold the bill vertically against the face of the card, so the bill's center crease is at the card's center fold. Close up the front of the card, which folds the bill in half; then open the card again and take out the folded bill to show it as you joke, "Already, we've doubled our money." Put the second crease of the bill against the card's center, close the card and open it, and show the now doubly folded bill. "We've doubled it again."

Close up the front of the card and keep it closed with your left hand. Holding the twice-folded bill with your right hand, touch your finger to its edges as you joke, "And if I *crease* it here and *crease* it there . . . you can see the money *increases.*"

Bring the folded bill to the top of the card. With your right fingers, pull open the *back* compartment of the card. Slide the folded bill into it and push it down until it is hidden inside. You can do this quite deliberately, with no need to hurry, since the top openings are hidden from front view by the longer part of the card that is folded up at the front. It looks as if you are merely pulling open the folded card at the top so as to slide the bill down into the center of it.

"But if you really want to stretch a dollar," you say, "try this!" Reach down into the *front* compartment, grip the tape tab firmly between your right thumb and first finger, and lift your arm straight up into the air, pulling the whole stack of bills out of the card so they fall open and hang down from your right hand.

Display the string of bills for a moment. Then open out the card with your left hand to show that it is empty and bring it beneath the bottom bill of the string, so that bill rests upon the card. Slowly lower your right hand to let the bills fold again into a stack as your hands come together. Close the card with the stack of bills inside it, pick up the rubber band from the table, snap it around the card, and put it away in the inside pocket of your jacket.

4

SHOWTIME TRICKS
WITH MONEY

PENETRATING COINS AND PURSE

How it looks

You take a small change purse from your pocket, casually
show both sides of it, open the purse, and tip four half-
dollars out into your hand. One at a time, you put the coins
back into the purse and show that both hands are otherwise
empty.

Taking the purse in one hand, you pick up a glass from
the table with your other hand. You strike the top of the
glass sharply with the purse, and one of the coins seems to
pass right through the closed purse to fall with a clink into
the glass. When you open the purse and pour the coins from
it, there are only three. One by one, you pass the remaining
coins from the purse into the glass in the same way.

What you need

A small imitation leather change purse, about 2½ inches

PENETRATING COINS AND PURSE

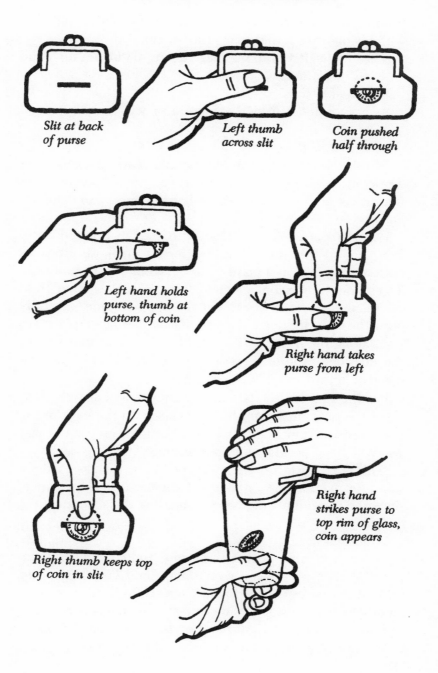

Slit at back
of purse

Left thumb
across slit

Coin pushed
half through

Left hand holds
purse, thumb at
bottom of coin

Right hand takes
purse from left

Right thumb keeps top
of coin in slit

Right hand
strikes purse to
top rim of glass,
coin appears

from top to bottom and 4 inches across the center, the kind with a single clasp that snaps shut at the top

A straight-sided drinking glass, about 4½ inches high and 3 inches in diameter across the top

Four half-dollars

A sharp-pointed pair of scissors, a pencil, and a ruler

How you fix it

In this trick, what seems to happen really does happen. The coins actually do pass through the purse, because there is a slit cut across the back of it—but the purse and coins are handled so as to hide that.

Lay the purse on the table with its top pointed away from you. With the ruler, measure 1 inch up from its bottom edge, and at a point centered from the left and right edges draw a horizontal pencil line 1½ inches long. Hold the purse open so as not to cut the opposite side, carefully push through the point of the scissors, and cut a clean slit right along the penciled line. (In the directions that follow, the slit side of the purse will be called the "back" and the uncut side the "front.")

Put the four half-dollars into the purse and snap it shut. Have the purse in a right-hand pocket with the back of the purse toward your body, and have the glass on a table that you will stand beside while performing.

(This is a "platform" trick, planned to be used as part of a stand-up magic show; it is not for close-up performance, since the purse must not be examined by the spectators.)

What you do

Reach into your pocket with your right hand, grip the purse at its top between your thumb and first finger, and bring it out with its back toward you. Hold it up to show it and shake it from side to side to rattle the coins inside it.

Take it from your right hand by bringing your left hand to the side of it to hold it between your fingers at the front and your thumb just beneath the slit at the back. With your right hand, unsnap the purse and open it wide, then bring that hand down cupped beneath it.

Tip the purse over from left to right with your left hand, still keeping the slit side toward you, and shake the coins out into your cupped right hand. Turn your left hand over from right to left to bring the purse upright again and hold it that way.

Count out the coins from your right hand by dropping them, one at a time, flat onto the table. Then pick one up, hold it between your thumb and first finger, and put it into the purse in your left hand. As you put the coin down inside, push the bottom edge of it through the slit so that part of the coin comes out at the back under your left thumb, which holds it there against the back of the purse.

With your right hand, pick up another coin from the table, show it, and put that into the bottom of the purse. Continue until all four are in the purse and then snap it shut.

Show your right hand empty and bring it down over the top of the purse that is still in your left hand. With your right thumb and fingertips pointed downward, take hold of the top of the purse between them, fingers at the front and thumb at the back. The tip of your right thumb should be just *above* the slit. Press your thumb against the purse there to keep the coin in the slit from falling all the way out, and take your left hand away from the purse.

You are now holding the purse with your right hand at the top. At the back of the purse there is a coin halfway through the slit, with the top half of that coin still inside the purse, kept there by the pressure of your thumb.

Take the glass from the table with your left hand around the back of it near the bottom and hold it firmly out in front of you at waist level.

With your right hand, bring the purse down quickly against the top rim of the glass, rather flat and with the back of the purse at a downward angle. Release the pressure of your right thumb on the coin and it will fly from the slit to strike the inside of the glass and clink down into it.

Hold up the glass, rattle the coin inside it, and put the glass on the table. Transfer the purse to your left hand, which takes it by the side, fingers in front and thumb against the slit at the back. Open the top clasp with your right hand and then hold that hand cupped beneath.

With your left hand, tip the purse from left to right, still keeping the back of it toward you, and pour the coins from it into your cupped right hand. Drop them one at a time onto the table to show there were only three left in the purse.

All of this takes only a few moments, and with the purse in your left hand and three coins on the table you are now ready to repeat it again, by singly putting the three coins into the purse, striking the glass, and passing another one through. Then you put two coins into the purse and pass one of them into the glass. Each time you do it, the coin that falls into the glass is left there.

Finally, you put the fourth coin into the purse and pass that into the glass. When you reach that point, transfer the purse from your right hand to your left, taking it with your left hand at the side of it, fingers in front and thumb against the slit at the back. With your right hand, unsnap it and open the top wide. Turn your left hand over from left to right to tip the purse upside down, shake it to show it is empty, and turn your hand right to left to bring the purse upright again.

Take the glass with your right hand and spill the four coins out flat onto the table. Gather them up, bring that hand above the mouth of the purse, and drop them down into it one at a time. Snap it shut, rattle the coins in it with your left hand, and put the purse away in your left-hand pocket.

THE CONTRARY COINS

How it looks

"Four silver coins," you say as you point to a row of coins displayed on a small cardboard stand. You show your hands empty and gather up the coins. "For this trick, it is very important to have exactly four." You start counting them aloud, from hand to hand: "One, two, three, four . . . *five?*"

You pretend to be surprised to discover that you suddenly have a fifth coin. "That's funny—where did that come from?" You toss the extra coin aside on the table and put the other four back in a row on the stand. "I'm sorry. I'll try that again. . . . Exactly four silver coins." Gathering them up, you count them from hand to hand, and discover that this time you have two extra coins: "One, two, three, four . . . *five, six?*"

You throw the extra two on the table, put four back on the stand, gather them up, count them from hand to hand, and discover that you have seven: "One, two, three, four . . . *five, six . . . seven?*"

With mock annoyance, you toss all the coins onto the table, brush your hands together, and say, "Forget it! The more money I throw away, the more I've got. . . . If I keep this up, I'll turn into a millionaire!"

What you need

Ten half-dollars

A piece of white poster board, cut to a size of 5½ × 10 inches

White plastic adhesive tape, ¾ inch wide

Two white envelopes, each 4⅛ × 9½ inches (standard business-letter size)

A ruler, a pencil, and scissors

THE CONTRARY COINS

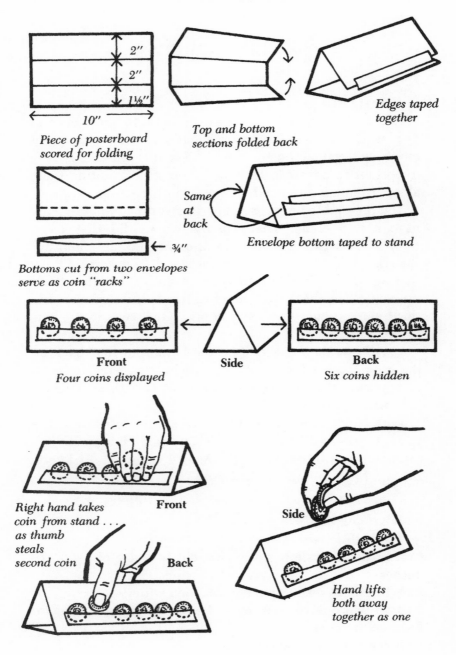

2"
2"
1½"
10"

Piece of posterboard
scored for folding

Top and bottom
sections folded back

Edges taped
together

Same
at
back

Envelope bottom taped to stand

← ¾"

Bottoms cut from two envelopes
serve as coin "racks"

Front
Four coins displayed

Side

Back
Six coins hidden

Right hand takes
coin from stand . . .
as thumb
steals
second coin

Front

Back

Side

Hand lifts
both away
together as one

How you fix it

The secret is in the coin stand, which is easily made by forming the poster board into a long triangle. Simple in appearance, it has the advantage of not looking like a "tricky" prop, but extra coins can be hidden along the back of it so you can secretly add them to those that your hand openly takes from the front.

To make the stand, first turn the piece of poster board lengthwise, long edges top and bottom. Measure 1½ inches up from the bottom edge and draw a pencil line across from one side to the other. Now measure 2 inches up from the line you have just drawn and pencil another line straight across. Hold the ruler in place and run the point of the scissors along each line to score them for easy folding.

Fold the top and bottom sections back away from you along the scored lines, crease the folds with your thumb and fingers, and form the board into a long upright triangle. Cut a 10-inch length of white plastic adhesive tape and fasten the two open edges of the triangle together where they meet, running the tape along so its width overlaps to bind them securely. The result should be a triangular stand 10 inches long that will rest by itself on its 1½-inch base, with slanted 2-inch panels at the front and back.

Two long and narrow envelope-like pockets serve as "racks" to hold the coins on the stand. They are made from the bottoms of the two envelopes. Turn both envelopes lengthwise and measure ¾ inch up from the bottom of each and draw a line across. Cut off those bottom sections and discard the remainder of the envelopes.

Very lightly pencil a guideline across the front panel of the stand, ½ inch up from its bottom edge. Take one of the cut-off envelope bottoms, open it out a little, and fasten a 9-inch length of white plastic tape along its entire top *inside* edge so that half the width of the tape sticks to the inside. Position the envelope piece with its bottom edge along the penciled guideline, center it from the sides, and fasten it to the front of the stand by pressing the tape firmly into place. Attach the second envelope piece to the back panel of the stand in a similar way, again with its bottom edge ½ inch up from the bottom of the stand.

Put four coins along the front of the stand, spaced out in a row to display them. The bottom edges of the coins rest in the envelope "rack" so that the coins lean back flat against the stand, with most of each coin in full view. Space out the six other coins in a row at the back of the stand where they will be hidden from front view. Have the stand that way on your table.

What you do

Position yourself at the back and slightly to the right of the table. Point to the coins displayed on the stand, and say, "Four silver coins."

Show both hands empty and then bring your right hand down over the top of the stand to start gathering up the coins. With the back of that hand toward the audience, fingertips pointing downward and thumb to the rear, place your fingers over the first coin in the row at the front, and draw it up and away from the stand between your fingers and thumb. Keeping that coin, move your hand along to the next coin in the front row, bringing your hand down over the stand with your fingers in front and thumb at the rear as before.

You will find that as your fingers come over the coin at the front, your thumb comes against a coin at the back of the stand. This is almost automatic because of the way the front and back of the triangular stand slant toward each other. If you pinch your thumb and fingers together as you draw your hand upward, the coin from the front of the stand and the coin at the back will slide up together so you can take them both as one.

It looks as if you are just taking the coin from the front, but you secretly steal the extra coin from the back at the same time. You now really have three coins in your hand instead of the two the audience has seen you take from the front of the stand. Without pausing, move your hand along to take the third visible coin from the row at the front, and then along again to take the fourth one.

"For this trick, it is very important to have exactly four," you now say, and you start counting them aloud as you drop them one at a time from your right hand into your unturned left hand. "One, two, three, four . . ." Pretending surprise, you discover you have a fifth coin and raise your voice questioningly as you say, "*Five?*" Hold that one up between your right first finger and thumb, stare at it, and say, "That's funny. Where did that come from?"

With a shrug, toss it aside flatly onto the table, and then dump the others from your left hand into your right. Put the four out along the front of the stand again, spaced so they are opposite coins hidden at the back. "I'm sorry. I'll try that again," you say, pointing to the coins on the stand. "Exactly four silver coins."

Show your hands empty and bring your right hand down over the stand as before and take the first one from the front. Move your hand along to take the second, but as you take it, steal a coin from the back with your thumb. Take a third coin from the front and steal another along with it from the back. Without hesitating, gather up the fourth from the front. Apparently you have just gathered up the four from the front, but you actually have six.

Again count them aloud as you drop them singly from your right hand into your left: "One, two, three, four . . ." Discover that you have another. "*Five?*" Hold it up as you stare at it. Drop it flat onto the table. Then discover that you have still another. "*Six?*" Shake your head and drop that one flat onto the table.

Now quicken the pace. Drop the remaining four coins from your left hand into your right. With your right hand, put them in a row on the stand so that three of them are opposite the three coins still hidden at the back. One coin at the front will have no coin directly behind it. This is the one you take first as you gather them up again. Then move your right hand to the right side of the stand to take the second coin and also steal the one behind it, lifting both together. Move your hand along to take the third and fourth ones from the front, each time also taking one from behind.

Count them from hand to hand: "One, two, three, four ..." Raise your voice as you discover you have more, and throw those forcefully one at a time into your other hand. *"Five ... six ... seven?"* Spill them all out flat across the table from your left hand and brush your hands together. "Forget it! The more money I throw away, the more I've got.... If I keep this up, I'll turn into a millionaire!"

THE UNBORROWED COIN
IN THE BALL OF WOOL

A popular trick with old-time magicians was the finding of a vanished coin securely wrapped in a box inside a ball of wool. Included in beginners' sets of magic tricks and often explained in print, this classic of coin magic has been somewhat neglected in recent years because the secret use of a small metal slide to get the coin into the ball of wool became too well known. Here is a version that may fool those who know the old secret and that should amuse modern audiences, many of whom have never seen the ancient trick.

How it looks

"Have you ever learned to knit?" you ask a male spectator invited to help you. "So many men as well as women have taken up knitting as a hobby that I just wondered if you were an expert.... What I want to show you is a little trick my grandmother taught me to do with a ball of wool. She was not only a knitter.... She was also a magician."

THE UNBORROWED COIN IN THE BALL OF WOOL

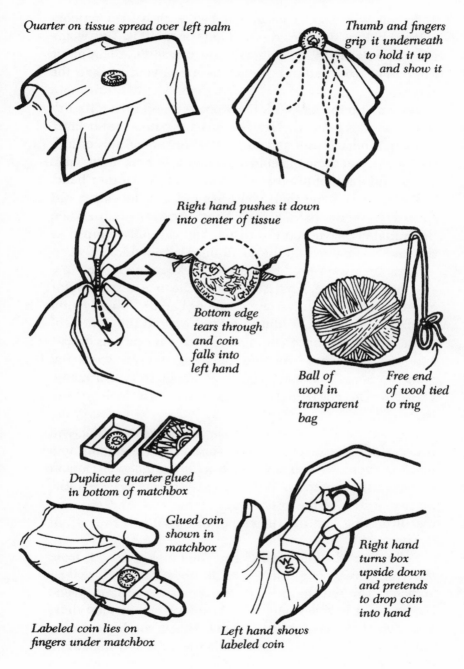

Quarter on tissue spread over left palm

Thumb and fingers grip it underneath to hold it up and show it

Right hand pushes it down into center of tissue

Bottom edge tears through and coin falls into left hand

Ball of wool in transparent bag

Free end of wool tied to ring

Duplicate quarter glued in bottom of matchbox

Glued coin shown in matchbox

Labeled coin lies on fingers under matchbox

Left hand shows labeled coin

Right hand turns box upside down and pretends to drop coin into hand

You show a small transparent bag with a little bright-colored ball of wool inside it. "Don't worry. . . . You won't have to knit anything. But will you please take charge of this ball of wool and put it away in one of your pockets for now?"

You fold up the bag with the wool in it and give it to him to put into his pocket. "Here's a quarter with a paper label stuck to the back of it so you can write your initials on it," you say, as you show the coin and hand it to him, along with a pen, and ask him to write his initials on the label.

While he is doing that, you open out a facial tissue and spread it over the palm of your hand, then ask him to place the initialed quarter on the tissue. You carefully wrap it in the tissue and give him the small bundle to hold.

"Granny always used to warn me to keep my money in a safe place. . . . She kept hers under the mattress. But for added security, we'll just use a rubber band." You give him a rubber band and ask him to snap it around the bundle of tissue. "Now you have my money, with your initials on it— and you also have my bag of wool. If you were my grandmother, I'd suspect you were about to knit a magic spell. . . . Do you mind if I have one last look at my money?"

You take back the tissue and tear it to shreds, which you toss aside. "The quarter's gone—just as I suspected," you say. "Are you sure you never met my grandmother? Do you still have the wool? . . . Will you take it from your pocket, please? Just hold the plastic bag at the top—and give me that little ring that has the end of the wool tied to it. Hold the bag tight."

Pulling out the end of the yarn, you quickly draw it from the transparent bag, gathering it up in strands, so the audience can see the ball of wool bouncing around inside the bag as it unravels. A folded envelope comes into view, wrapped at the center of the wool. When you have drawn out the last of the wool, you ask the spectator to remove the envelope from the bag and unfold it. "Is the envelope sealed?" you ask. "Here's a pair of scissors. Will you please cut open the envelope and take out whatever you find inside it?"

He finds a matchbox in the envelope. You take the matchbox, place it on the palm of your hand, and carefully remove the cover. "What do you see inside the box?" He sees a quarter. You dump it out on your hand. "And on the back of the quarter, there's a label with initials on it," you say, as you hold out the quarter to him. "Will you please say whether those initials are yours?"

The spectator confirms that the initials are his, and as you thank him, you say, "I don't know how good you are at knitting . . . but as a magician, Granny would have been proud of you."

What you need

Two quarters that look somewhat alike

A pocket-sized wooden matchbox, the kind with a drawer and sliding cover

A skein of rug yarn, red, blue, green, or some other bright color

A transparent plastic sandwich bag

An envelope

A small plastic ring, such as a curtain ring

A standard-size facial tissue

A self-adhesive paper label, cut to a size slightly smaller than a quarter

A pair of scissors small enough to fit inside your jacket pocket

Several rubber bands

A felt-tip pen

White craft glue or other strong adhesive

How you fix it

Remove the drawer from the matchbox and glue one of the quarters, *face up*, inside the bottom of the drawer, at one end of it. When the glue is thoroughly dry, slide the drawer back into its cover. Attach the self-adhesive paper label to the *back* of the other quarter and put that aside for a moment.

Put the matchbox into the envelope, seal the envelope, and fold it compactly around the matchbox. Fold it as small as you can.

Cut off a string of yarn about 7 yards long. The length doesn't have to be exact, but if you use a longer piece the later unwinding of it slows the pace of the trick and delays the climax.

Take one end of the yarn, wrap it around the folded envelope, and continue winding it, first in one direction and then another, until you form a tight ball of wool entirely covering the enveloped matchbox at its center. When you come to the end of the yarn, tie that end tightly to the plastic ring. Drop the little ball of wool into the transparent sandwich bag and pull out the free end with the ring attached so that it hangs down at the front of the bag.

Fold the tissue and put that into the right-hand pocket of your jacket. Put the pen and the quarter with the label attached into the same pocket. Have the scissors and rubber bands in the left-hand pocket. Put the bag with the ball of wool in it on the table you will use when performing.

What you do

Pick up the bag and explain that it has a ball of wool in it as you show it to the audience and to the spectator. Fold the bag around the wool and ask the spectator to put it into one of his pockets.

Take the quarter from your right-hand pocket. Hold up the coin to show it, turn it to show the paper label attached to the back of it, and hand it to the spectator. Ask him to write his initials on the label, and reach into your right-hand pocket again and take out the pen and facial tissue. Give him the pen and shake open the tissue. Bring your left palm upward in front of you and spread the opened tissue over the palm of that hand.

When he has written his initials, take back the pen with your right hand and put it away in your pocket. Ask him to place the quarter on the tissue. Grip it through the tissue from underneath, between the tip of your left thumb at the back and tips of your fingers in front, and hold the coin upright by its bottom edge. Display it that way so everybody can see it at the center of the tissue.

The bottom edge of the coin now rests in a little fold of tissue between your thumb and fingertips. Bring your right hand to the top edge of the upright coin and push it down as though pushing it into that fold. But really push it right down *through* the tissue so that the coin falls into your left hand, which is still covered by the tissue. This takes hardly any pressure, since the bottom edge of the pushed-down coin easily tears through the bottom of the tissue fold that is gripped between your thumb and fingers.

With both hands still together, fold up the tissue with your right hand as though the coin were inside it, bunching it into a wad with the torn part in the center. Close your left fingers around the coin to hide it, and take the wadded tissue with your right hand to hold it up and show it as you let your left hand fall to your side with the concealed coin.

Give the wadded tissue to the spectator. Then say that "for added security, we'll use a rubber band." Put your left hand into your left pocket. Leave the coin in the bottom of the pocket, bring out a rubber band, and give it to the spectator as you ask him to snap it around the bundled tissue.

"Now you have my money, with your initials on it—and you also have my bag of wool," you say. "If you were my grandmother, I'd suspect you were about to knit a magic spell. . . . Do you mind if I have one last look at my money?"

Take the tissue from him, remove the rubber band, and toss it aside. Hold the wadded tissue in full view, gripped between the thumbs and fingers of both hands, and suddenly pull your hands apart, tearing the tissue in two.

With repeated pulls, quickly tear it into shreds, then throw them all into the air and let them flutter down to the floor as you show both hands empty, and say, "The quarter's gone—just as I suspected."

(This convincing vanish of a coin can be used in other tricks. It provides more dramatic action, something more for the audience to see, than if you merely vanished a coin from a handkerchief or in some other standard way. Ripping the tissue to shreds also destroys the evidence that it was already torn.)

Ask the spectator to take out the bag with the little ball of wool in it, which he has had in his pocket since the start of the trick. Have him unfold the bag and hold it open by its top edge so the bag hangs down from his hand. Make sure he holds it tight. Take the plastic ring that is tied to the end of the yarn, draw it *up* and step back a few feet, so the audience has a clear view of the bag.

Hold your right hand high and pull the wool *up* out of the bag, using your other hand to quickly gather it as the ball unravels and the envelope at its center comes into view inside the bag. Put the gathered wool aside on the table, have him remove the envelope, and take the empty bag from him and put that aside.

Ask him if the envelope is sealed and say you will give him a pair of scissors to cut it open. Reach into your pocket with your left hand. Get the coin into your fingers and feel it to make sure the side with the paper label faces *upward*. Finger-palm it that way, or simply close your lower three fingers loosely around it to hide the coin. Take the scissors between your thumb and first finger and bring them out of your pocket. Transfer the scissors to your right hand and let your left hand, with the coin hidden in it, fall to your side.

Hand him the scissors and ask him to cut open the envelope. Take back the scissors with your right hand and put them on the table. After he has removed the matchbox from the envelope, take it from him with your right hand

and hold it up to show it, fingers wide apart so it can be seen that there is nothing else in your hand.

Bring your left hand up in front of you, slightly cupped toward you and with the back of it to the audience. Put the matchbox into your left hand, right on top of the hidden coin so it covers it, and hold your left hand out flat to show the matchbox resting on it. With your right first finger, push the drawer of the matchbox open a little. Slide back the cover, remove it, and keep it in your right hand. This leaves the drawer of the matchbox lying on your left fingers, hiding the coin beneath it. Inside the drawer is the face-up duplicate coin that was glued there.

Hold out your left hand and ask the spectator what he sees in the box. When he answers that there is a quarter in it, say, "And on the back of it there's a label, with initials on it." With your right hand, turn the drawer over upside down, as if dumping the glued coin out of it into your left hand. Immediately lift the drawer away, still upside down, and show him the labeled coin on your left hand. Hold it out so he can take the coin and ask him to say whether the initials are his.

While he is doing that, casually put the matchbox and cover away in your right-hand pocket. When he has confirmed the initials, thank him and say, "I don't know how good you are at knitting . . . but as a magician, Granny would have been proud of you."

CATCHING COINS FROM THE AIR

Few classics of coin magic have more audience appeal than the catching of coins from the air, which combines sight, sound, and action with the magical wish fulfillment of seeming to produce money from nowhere. Here is a short, direct version with an updated plot, and a simple device that converts an ordinary metal can into a self-contained prop for delivering coins as you need them.

CATCHING COINS FROM THE AIR

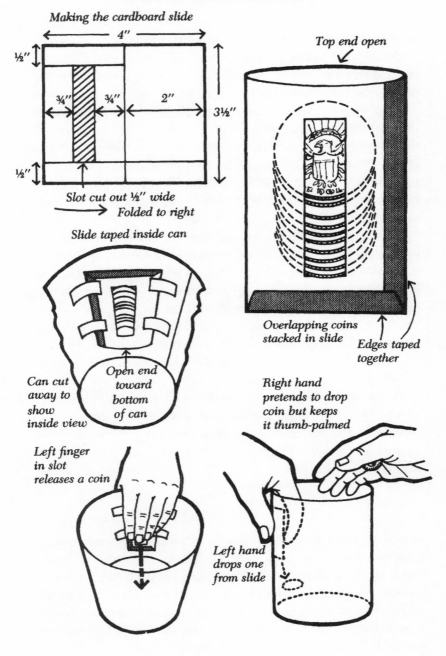

Making the cardboard slide

4"

½"

¾"   ¾"   2"

3½"

½"

Slot cut out ½" wide

Folded to right

Top end open

Slide taped inside can

Overlapping coins
stacked in slide

Edges taped
together

Can cut
away to
show
inside view

Open end
toward
bottom
of can

Right hand
pretends to drop
coin but keeps
it thumb-palmed

Left finger
in slot
releases a coin

Left hand
drops one
from slide

How it looks

"Everybody these days seems to be worrying about taxes—and with good reason," you say, as you show both hands empty and pick up a large metal can. "But I think I have a way to solve the whole problem."

You hold the can upside down to convince the audience there is nothing in it and then take it with your left hand. "All the government has to do is hire a bunch of magicians as tax collectors and put them to work in Washington, collecting the taxes by plucking the money right out of the air—in the form of cold, hard cash."

Reaching out with your right hand, you seem to catch a coin from the air, then you drop it into the can where it lands with a loud clink. You tip it out of the can into your right hand to display it and then drop it back into the can. "There's the sales tax." Another coin appears at your fingertips and you drop that into the can. "Property tax . . ."

One at a time, you produce coins from behind your knee, your ear, beneath your elbow, the heel of your shoe, dropping each into the can. "Excise tax . . . luxury tax . . . income tax . . . *thumb tacks?*"

You catch another at your fingertips as you say, "Wouldn't that be a lot easier than all the red tape we go through filling out tax forms and everything? Just reach out . . . and you've got it."

Holding that coin well above the can, you let it drop down into it, and show your hand empty. Then you sweep your hand through the air, close your fingers and catch still another, which you drop into the can. "Almost any tax collector could be taught to do it. It wouldn't take any long government training program. Anybody could learn—with the help of a little magic."

You look out toward some person in the audience. "There's one floating past you, sir. As it comes past, will you just reach out and close your hand around it? . . . Now throw it back, please." You hold up the can to "catch" the invisible coin as the person pretends to throw it, and it is heard to land inside the can. "Thank you. There's no use trying to hold out on the tax collector, you know."

Tipping the can over, you spill all the coins out into your hand, then dump them back into the can with a clatter. "As every taxpayer knows," you say, "this is called paying through the nose. . . ." You bring your hand up to your nose and a sudden shower of coins seems to pour down from your nose into the can.

You rattle the coins, put the can back on the table, and say, "Thank you all for paying your taxes so promptly. . . . I'll take this over to the tax office right after the show."

What you need
Ten half-dollars

A large fruit-juice or tomato-juice can, about 7 inches high and 4¼ inches in diameter, washed and dried, with the top cleanly removed so there are no rough edges and the label peeled off

A small piece of poster board, cut to a size of 3½ × 4 inches

Cloth or plastic adhesive tape, ¾ inch wide

A pencil, scissors, and a ruler

How you fix it
As in most versions of the coin-catching trick, this one depends upon repeatedly producing the same coin with the right hand, which only pretends to drop it into the can but really keeps it thumb-palmed so that the same coin can be made to appear at the fingertips again. Each time the right hand pretends to drop a coin, the left hand releases a coin so it clinks into the bottom of the can that hand is holding. The sound convinces the audience that the right hand has dropped its coin into the can.

When this is done entirely by sleight of hand, it requires

secretly "stealing" a stack of coins from some hiding place with the left hand and then quietly getting them into the can in position for releasing them one at a time. To eliminate the need for that, this routine uses a slotted tube-like slide, formed of the small piece of poster board, which is fastened inside the top of the can to hold ten overlapping coins.

At the start, the coin-loaded can is upside down on the table, so the interior is hidden from view even if the audience is fairly close. Both hands start completely free of any hidden coins and the inverted can may be handled casually without any worry that the coins may rattle or spill out as long as it is kept bottom up. As soon as the left hand takes the can and turns it upright, the coins are set to be released one at a time.

To make the slide, start by placing the piece of poster board lengthwise on a table. At its center, 2 inches in from each side, draw a vertical pencil line, from top to bottom. Run the point of the scissors down that line to scribe it for later folding.

On the part that is to the left of that center line, draw two horizontal lines, the first ½ inch down from the top and the second ½ inch up from the bottom. Now draw two vertical lines, one ¾ inch in from the left and the other ¾ inch in from the right. Cut out and remove the section between the two vertical lines so that you have an open slot ½ inch wide, starting ½ inch down from the top and ending ½ inch up from the bottom.

Fold the left half of the whole piece squarely down upon the right half, along the scribed center line, as if closing a book. Bind the right edges together by attaching half the width of a strip of cloth tape to the front and folding it around to the back. With another strip of tape, bind the bottom edges together, but leave the top end open.

That completes the making of the slide, but it has to be

opened out a little so the coins will slide freely. Hold its side edges between your thumb and fingers and squeeze inward so as to billow out the front and rear, flexing it until the top end remains open. It is now ready to fix into place inside the can.

Rest the can on its side on the table, mouth toward you. Lay the poster-board slide vertically inside the can, with the open end of it toward the can's bottom and the closed end about an inch down from the top rim. Fasten it securely in that position with four 2-inch lengths of tape, two at the top and two near the bottom, by sticking one end of each piece of tape to the outer edge of the slide and pressing the rest of it onto the inside of the can.

The coins now have to be loaded into the slide. With your left hand, hold the can up by its side so the mouth of it is tilted slightly toward you. Take one of the coins with your right hand and insert a side edge of it into the center slot, then slide it forward a little until you can get its opposite edge into the slot. When both edges of the coin are inside the slot, draw it back toward you to the top of the slide.

Insert the edge of a second coin into the slot, push it forward until both edges are inside, and again draw it toward you until it partly overlaps the face of the first coin. Continue to insert the rest of the coins the same way, each partly overlapping the one beneath. Adjust them with your fingertip in the slot so they overlap evenly.

This is explained in detail because the coins cannot be properly positioned by putting them in through the open end of the slide; they must be inserted singly through the center slot. After you use it a few times, the poster board will become quite flexible and you will find you can load all ten coins quickly and easily.

When the can is loaded with all ten, turn the mouth of it toward the floor. Hold it so the part with the slide is to the rear and rest it that way, bottom up, on the table you will use when performing.

What you do

Let it be seen that both hands are empty and bring your right hand over the inverted can to pick it up by the bottom rim between your fingers at the front and thumb at the back. Take it from the table, still bottom up, and let your hand fall to your side with it, which is silent "proof" to the audience that the upside down can must be empty. Step away from the table as you talk about taxes and say that you have a way to solve the problem. At this point, both hands are at your sides.

Bring the can in front of your legs to take it from your right hand with your left, by turning your left hand palm upward so its four fingers go up inside the can and cover the slide, with the rim of the can at the crotch of your thumb and the thumb at the outside. Press the tip of your left second finger through the slot to hold the coins in the slide, and as you take the can, let your left hand fall naturally to your side again. That automatically turns the can upright, mouth to the top.

Say that if the government hired magicians as tax collectors, they could pluck the taxes "right out of the air— in the form of cold, hard cash." Then reach out with your right hand as if to catch a coin from the air. Close your fingers around the imaginary coin, hold the can up with your left hand, and pretend to drop the coin into it from your right hand by bringing that hand into the top of the can. With your left hand, release the first coin from the slide so it falls clinking into the bottom of the can as though it were the coin your right hand dropped.

Rattle the can and then tip it over toward the right to slide that coin out into your right hand. Say, "There's the sales tax." As you hold the coin up to show it with your right hand, bring it into position for thumb-palming, clipped at your fingertips between the sides of your first and second fingers. (For a detailed explanation, see the section called "The Thumb-Palm: Fingertip Vanish" in chapter 1.)

Pretend to drop the coin back into the can, but thumb-palm it as your hand goes down inside, and with your left hand release another coin from the slide so it falls to the bottom of the can. Immediately lift your apparently empty right hand away, with its coin thumb-palmed, and let it fall to your side. With your left hand, rattle the coin in the can.

Now reach out into the air with your right hand, produce the thumb-palmed coin at your fingertips, hold it up to show it, and say, "Property tax. . . ." Pretend to drop that into the can, thumb-palming it as before while your left hand releases a coin from the slide so it sounds like the one dropped from your right hand. Remove your right hand with its thumb-palmed coin, let your hand fall to your side for a moment, then reach down behind your knee to produce the same coin again. Hold it up to show it and say, "Excise tax. . . ."

Pretend to drop it into the can, really thumb-palming it, while your left hand releases another coin from the slide. Continue in that way, seeming to take a coin from your ear, from beneath your elbow, the heel of your shoe, and so on. Don't rush the productions; pause a little before each one, holding the coin up each time so it can be clearly seen before you pretend to drop it into the can. "Luxury tax . . . income tax . . . *thumb tacks?*"

After you have produced the thumb-palmed coin five or six times, pretending each time to drop it into the can, you really do drop it in. Hold it well above the can and visibly let it fall from your right fingers down into the can. Casually show the full palm side of your hand empty, and then sweep your hand through the air as though catching still another coin, closing your fingers as if they held one. Immediately bring your hand into the top of the can, open your hand as if dropping a coin, and with your left hand release one from the slide.

Drop both hands to your sides as you say, "Anybody could learn to do it—with the help of a little magic." Look out toward some person in the audience. "There's one floating past you, sir. Will you just reach out and close your hand around it?" Hold up the can with your left hand and look directly at the person. "Now throw it back, please." Hold the can still, as though waiting to catch it, and when the person throws the imaginary coin, let one drop from the slide so it clinks loudly into the bottom of the can. "Thank you. There's no use trying to hold out on the tax collector, you know."

Loudly rattle all the coins in the can. Then tip the can to the right and hold your cupped right hand close to it as you slide them all out into your hand. With your left hand, turn the can upright again. Bring your right hand to the top as though dropping all the coins back into the can, but secretly keep about half of them in your right hand. Don't try to palm them or anything; just hold some back in your hand and then let that hand fall to your side with its fingers partly closed around them as your left hand holds up the can and loudly rattles the coins you have dropped into it.

Stop rattling the can and lower your left hand to its side. Say, "As every taxpayer knows, this is called paying through the nose." Bring your right hand, back outward, up to your nose, and bring the can a few inches beneath it with your left hand. Release the coins from the bottom of your right hand, so they shower down into the can. Slap the side of the can with your right hand, put the can on the table, and say, "Thank you all for paying your taxes so promptly. I'll take this over to the tax office right after the show!"

HUSH MONEY

How it looks

You ask to borrow a dollar bill, and when one is offered, you say, "Will you please bring it up, so everybody can help you keep an eye on your money?" Taking the bill from the spectator, you have him stand beside you. "I'll write you an I.O.U. for it," you say, writing it on a small card, and including the serial number. Then you fold his bill, cover it with a handkerchief, and have him hold it.

"Just say 'Go!' " you tell him. When he does, you suddenly pull the handkerchief from his fingers, and the bill has vanished. "You said it—I didn't," you say. "I collect more dollars that way." Putting the handkerchief away in your pocket as though the trick were finished, you pick up a pack of cards, shuffle them, and announce, "Now, for my next trick. . . ."

But then you stop, smile, and put the cards aside. "Since you still have my I.O.U., I suppose I'll have to offer you some hush money," you tell him. "I have some socked away here somewhere." Reaching around under your jacket, you pull an old sock from your hip pocket and hold it up to show it. From inside the sock, you take out a baby's bottle, sealed at the top with its cap and nipple. In the glass bottle, there is a dollar bill, and you point to it and say, "Hush money."

You unscrew the cap of the baby's bottle, remove the bill, and unfold it. "Will you look at the serial number I wrote on the I.O.U.?" You read the number on the bill aloud, while he checks the number on the I.O.U. card he has been holding. "Is that your number?" When he says that it is, you hand him the bill and say, "Then this dollar must be yours."

What you need
A dollar bill

HUSH MONEY

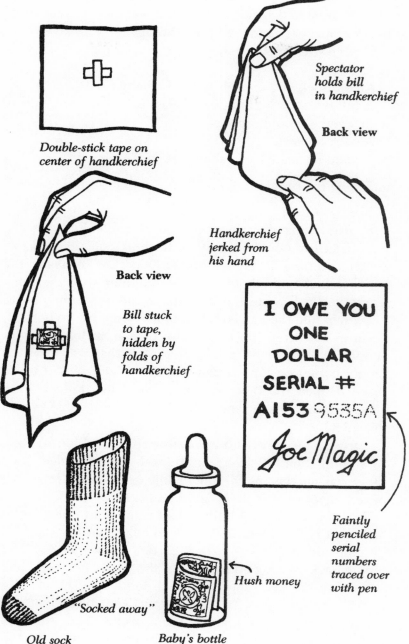

Double-stick tape on center of handkerchief

Spectator holds bill in handkerchief

Back view

Handkerchief jerked from his hand

Back view

Bill stuck to tape, hidden by folds of handkerchief

I OWE YOU ONE DOLLAR SERIAL # A153 9535A

Joe Magic

Faintly penciled serial numbers traced over with pen

"Socked away"

Old sock

Hush money

Baby's bottle

A dark-colored handkerchief or a small table napkin of heavy cloth that cannot be seen through

Double-stick transparent tape, the kind that is sticky on both sides

An old sock, big enough to hold a baby's bottle

A full-size (8 oz.) transparent glass baby's nursing bottle, with screw-cap and nipple

A pack of cards

A plain unruled 3 x 5 inch office index file card

A *broad-tipped* black felt marking pen and a pencil

How you fix it

Spread the handkerchief open on the table. Fasten a 1½-inch length of double-stick tape to the handkerchief at its center, running it across horizontally just beneath the handkerchief's middle fold. Fasten another strip the same length vertically over the first one, so the two form a cross.

Loosely fold the handkerchief in half from top to bottom, again in half from top to bottom, then from left to right, and finally from right to left. Folding it that way puts the proper corner on top, so that when you later pick it up to shake it open the tape will be at the back, hidden from view. (Fresh strips of tape should be used each time you do the trick.)

Turn the file card with its narrow edges top and bottom. At a point about 1½ inches up from the bottom edge, copy the serial number of the dollar bill on the card with the pencil, *lightly* but in fairly large numerals.

Fold the bill horizontally in half from top to bottom, in half from right to left, and again in half from left to right. Put the bill inside the baby's bottle, screw the cap and nipple back on the bottle, and put the bottle into the sock.

Put the file card into the right inside pocket of your jacket, written side of the card toward your body, and clip the broad-tipped pen into the same pocket. Stuff the sock with the bottle in it into your right hip pocket, with the top of the sock hanging out so you can reach it easily, but not so it hangs in view beneath the edge of your jacket. Have the pack of cards and the handkerchief, folded so the proper corner is on top, on the table you will use when performing.

What you do

Ask to borrow a dollar bill and invite the spectator to bring it up "so everybody can help you keep an eye on your money." Have him stand to your right, in front of the table. Take the bill from him, hold it up to show it, snap it between your fingers, and say, "This looks like a good one."

Handling the bill gives you a chance to deliberately turn it face down, so George Washington's picture and the serial numbers are facing away from you. Hold the bill that way in your right hand and say, "I'll write you an I.O.U. for it."

Turn so you are facing the spectator. With your left hand, reach into your inner jacket pocket and remove the pen and the card, keeping the card upright and with its face toward you. Hold the card against the palm of your upright left hand, thumb across it near the top, and place the bill there, to hold it at the top of the card with your thumb.

Say the words aloud as you print them on the card with the pen, "I.O.U. one dollar. Serial number . . ." Glance at the bill, "discover" that it is face down, and turn it over, face up, to hold it again under your thumb so you can read the serial numbers on it. This is an important bit of business that helps convince the spectators you are really reading the numbers from the bill as you pretend to copy them.

Look at the numbers on the bill, but ignore them, and say aloud the first few numbers that are already lightly penciled on the card as you mark right over them with the broad-tipped pen, which covers up the pencil marks, "A 153. . ." Glance up at the bill again, as if copying the numbers from that, and trace over the rest of your penciled numbers, saying, ". . . 45353 A" (or whatever your numbers happen to be). Take your time as you go along to make sure the thick pen strokes cover all the penciling. Then sign your name at the bottom of the card and hand it to the spectator. Put the pen away in your pocket.

Fold the bill from top to bottom, then right to left and left to right. Hold up the folded bill with your left hand, between your upright thumb and fingertips. With your right hand, pick up the top corner of the handkerchief that is on the table and shake the handkerchief open. Drape it over your left hand so the center of it covers your fingers and the bill.

Bring your right hand to the outside top of the handkerchief to grip the bill through the cloth. Press the center of the handkerchief to it firmly so the sticky tape underneath is fastened to the bill. Lift the handkerchief and bill away with your right hand. Show your left hand empty and, with your right hand, hold out the handkerchief to the spectator as you say, "Will you hold it, please?"

Give him the top of it so he can hold the folded bill through the handkerchief and take your hand away. Have him hold it up high and then tell him, "Just say 'Go!' "

When he does, grip a corner hanging down at the *back* of the handkerchief with your right hand, and with a sudden snap pull the handkerchief straight down out of his hand. This leaves the bill, stuck to the tape, hidden inside the folds of the handkerchief as it hangs down from your right hand. The bill seems to have vanished. Tell the spectator, "You said it—I didn't. . . . I collect more dollars that way."

Gather up the handkerchief with the bill hidden inside it, take it with your right hand, and stuff it into your right-hand jacket pocket to leave it there. As though the trick were over and you intended to keep his vanished dollar bill, pick up the pack of cards, start shuffling them, and announce, "For my next trick. . . ."

Look at the spectator, smile, shake your head and put the cards back on the table, and say, "Since you still have my I.O.U., I suppose I'll have to offer you some hush money. I have some socked away here somewhere."

Reach under your jacket and take the sock from your hip pocket. Hold it up by the top to give the audience a chance to see what it is, and laugh. Then take the baby's bottle out of it, hold that a moment, and slowly tilt the bottle back and forth so the bill can be seen inside it. Point to the bill in the bottle and say, "Hush money."

Unscrew the cap and put it on the table with the sock. Let it be seen that your hands are empty and tip the mouth of the bottle toward you so you can get your fingers into it to remove the bill. Open out the bill, hold it up and snap it between your hands, and ask the spectator, "Will you look at the serial number on the I.O.U. I gave you?"

Slowly read aloud the serial number on the bill while he checks it against the number on the card. Ask, "Is that your number?" Hand him the bill and say, "Then this dollar must be yours . . . which means I get back my I.O.U." Take the card from him, thank him, tear up the card, and drop the pieces on the table, as you say, "I'm always glad to clear up my debts."

RAINBOW REPEAT BILLS

This is a colorful new version of a trick magicians know as The Six-Bill Repeat. As it usually is shown, you count six dollar bills singly from hand to hand, discard three of them, and still have six, repeating the process several times. But in this version, although you start with six plain bills and always have six left, the ones you count off are "crazy money," with polka dots, stripes, a recipe, a health warning, and other humorous surprises, including designs in full color, and finally a rainbow.

How it looks

You take out a wallet and remove some dollar bills from it, showing each bill on both sides as you count them singly from hand to hand. "One, two, three, four, five, six dollar bills— all alike, all the same," you say. "That's the trouble

RAINBOW REPEAT BILLS

MAKING THE ENVELOPE BILLS

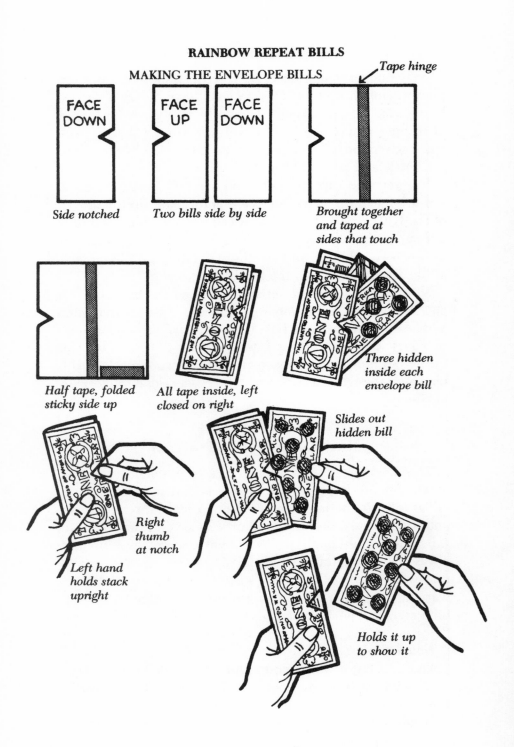

Tape hinge

FACE DOWN

FACE UP

FACE DOWN

Side notched

Two bills side by side

Brought together and taped at sides that touch

Half tape, folded sticky side up

All tape inside, left closed on right

Three hidden inside each envelope bill

Left hand holds stack upright

Right thumb at notch

Slides out hidden bill

Holds it up to show it

THE "CRAZY MONEY" BILLS

First set

1. *Both sides polka dots*
2. *Both sides stripes*
3. *Both sides arrows (other side points up)*

Second set

1. **Back** *Cooking recipe* — Clipped from magazine
2. **Back** *Advertising bill* — Ad cut from magazine / Adhesive label
3. **Back** *Health warning*

Third set

1. *Both sides red*
2. *Both sides blue*
3. *Both sides rainbow* — Various bright colors

with money. It's just plain dull. Always the same old dreary gray and green." You stack the bills together. "Don't get me wrong. I have nothing against money. I like the product—but they could use more imagination in the way they package the stuff. It hasn't changed in years. Why can't we have something different—like polka-dot bills?"

Taking one of the dollars from the top of the stack, you show that it suddenly has big black dots all over it, ten spots on each side. "At least, you could always tell a ten-spot when you had one." Discarding that by dropping it into a small basket on your table, you take another bill from the stack and show that it now has black stripes on both sides. "Or striped money?" You discard that and take a third one, which now has big arrows on each side. "Or money that would point the way—so that whenever you have to pay it out . . . you can tell somebody exactly where to go?"

As you count the remaining bills singly from hand to hand, you say, "But, no—it's always the same old dreary gray and green. . . . One, two, three, four, five, six." Stacking them together, you ask, "Why not use the backs of dollar bills to print useful information?" You take one from the stack and show that the back of it suddenly has some printing on it. "Like this recipe—for banana-lemon pie."

Discarding that, you take another and show an advertisement printed on the back. "Why doesn't the government sell the space for advertising—and use the income to cut taxes?" Taking another, you show a small label on the back of it. "Why not use it for public notices?" You read from the label: " 'Warning. . . . Unless spent properly, this product may be injurious to your health, safety, or peace of mind."

You drop that into the basket. "But, no—it's always the same old dreary gray and green," you repeat as you again count the remaining bills from hand to hand, and still have six. "Our postage stamps are different. Commemoratives for everything from forgotten vice-presidents to National

Pickle Week. All colorful and bright. Why not dollar bills in full color? Red . . . or blue . . . " You show one that is colored red on both sides, another colored blue, and then discard them. "Or a rainbow. . . . Everybody knows there's a pot of gold at the end of the rainbow." After showing a bill colored like a rainbow, you drop that into the basket.

"But I guess it won't ever happen. It's just wishful thinking. I always wind up with the same old dreary gray and green dollars I started with." You again count aloud as you drop them singly from your hand into the basket, "One, two, three, four, five, six."

What you need
Eighteen play-money bills
A secretary-type wallet or other folder in which to keep the bills flat and in order
A small basket or box, slightly longer and wider than the bills
An old magazine
A self-adhesive label, about 1 x 3 inches
Felt-tip pens, black and assorted colors
Transparent tape
Rubber cement
Scissors, a pencil, and a ruler

How you fix it
There are three envelope-like bills in which other bills are concealed. Start by putting a bill on a table, back up and narrow ends top and bottom. A triangular-shaped notch must be cut in one side to provide an opening for the tip of the thumb.

Put the ruler at the bill's right-hand margin, measure half the length of the bill from top to bottom, and make a pencil dot on the margin at that point. Make a second dot ½ inch up from that and a third dot ½ inch down from the original one. Then measure ¾ inch in from the original dot toward the center of the bill and make a dot there. Draw pencil lines from that to the upper and lower dots on the margin, and cut out the triangular piece inside the pencil lines.

Turn that bill *face up*, with the notch you just cut toward the left. Place a second bill *face down* to the right of it. Bring the two together side by side, so their inner long edges touch and the bills are exactly even at the top and bottom. Hinge them together that way by running a vertical strip of tape down the middle from top to bottom, overlapping both bills.

Attach *half the width* of another strip of tape horizontally to the bottom edge of the right-hand bill. Fold the unattached half of that strip up upon itself, sticky side up, and make sure none of it is below the bill's bottom edge.

Now close the left-hand bill down upon the right-hand one, as though closing a book, and press the taped edges together to flatten them. All the tape should be at the inside, with none showing. The result is a double bill, open at the top and right sides, with a triangular notch at the center of the right side of the upper one. From front and back, it looks like a single bill. You will need two more of those, made the same way.

Here is how the various "crazy money" bills are made:

Polka Dots: Turn a bill with its back up, narrow ends top and bottom, and pencil ten circles on it, each the size of a quarter. Space them out so they look like the two fives on a pair of dice: two dots side by side, a single one, two more side by side, and so on, so the audience will see at a glance that there are ten. Keep all the circles within the borders of the bill's printed designs, leaving the outer margins plain. Then fill in the circles with the black pen, turn the bill over face up, and make ten similar dots on that side.

Stripes: Again, keep within the borders of the bill's printed designs, leaving the margins plain. There are four slanted horizontal stripes, each about ½ inch wide, across the back of the bill, and four more across the face. Make them by ruling off parallel pairs of slanted pencil lines, and then filling them in with the black pen.

Arrows: Pencil a large vertical arrow, pointing down from top to bottom, on the back of a bill by drawing parallel lines about ½ inch apart. Draw another arrow pointing up on the face of the bill. Fill them both in with the black pen.

Recipe: Look through the old magazine and find a column of printed text that will fit vertically within the borders of the back of a bill. The audience won't be able to read it, but you want something without headlines, with solid text, that somewhat resembles a printed recipe. Cut it out and rubber-cement it to the back of a bill.

Advertising Bill: In the magazine, find an advertisement, or part of one, that has some large, simple design or illustration with a few big words. It should be something immediately recognized from a distance as an advertisement, of a size to fit within the borders of the bill, and in plain black and white so as not to spoil the later surprise of the colored bills. Clip it out and rubber-cement it vertically to the back of a bill.

Health Warning: Use a typewriter if you can, or otherwise the black pen, and type or print the following on the self-adhesive label: "Warning: Unless spent properly, this product may be injurious to your health, safety, or peace of mind." Turn a bill back upward, long edges top and bottom, and attach the label to it. Although the audience won't be able to read the words, it should look like a warning label when you show it and read it aloud.

Red and Blue Bills: With colored pens, color the face and back of one bill all red and another all blue. Color them solidly, but so that the designs of the bills faintly show through the coloring, keeping within the borders and leaving the margins plain.

Rainbow Bill: The face and back of this, within the borders, should be filled with curving bands of bright contrasting colors, arched like a rainbow. Turn a bill with its long edges top and bottom, draw curving parallel lines with a pen of each color, and then fill them in. Such colors as yellow and pink won't show up well, so use more brilliant colors: red, blue, green, orange, purple.

To set everything for the trick, place the *arrows* bill vertically face down on a table, the *stripes* on top of it, and *polka dots* on top of that. Square them up and slide the three together inside one of the face-down envelope bills. Tap the edges so the loose bills are entirely within the double one and no edges show. Put that envelope bill aside, face down on the table.

Now place the *health warning* bill face down, the *advertising* bill on top of it, and the *recipe* on top of that. Slide the three inside a second envelope bill so no edges show, and put it face down on top of the first envelope bill. Then stack the *rainbow* bill face down, the *blue* upon it, and the *red* on that, and slide them into the third envelope bill. Put that face down on top of the other two. The notched edges of all three envelope bills should be toward the right. Put three single bills face down on top of them. Then turn the *entire stack* of bills *face up*.

From the top down, the face-up bills are now stacked in this order: envelope with drawn design bills, envelope with the printed clippings, envelope with the colored bills, three single bills. Put them into the wallet that way and put the wallet into the right-hand inside pocket of your jacket. Have the small basket or box on your table.

What you do

Take out the wallet, remove the stack of face-up bills, and put the wallet aside. Square up the bills and hold them vertically in the palm of your left hand, thumb across the middle of the stack and fingers at the right edge. Deal the top bill from your left hand into the upturned palm of your right hand, as though dealing a card off the top of a pack.

Hold it with the tips of your right fingers against the left edge of the bill and thumb across the middle of it. Turn your right hand out to the right, palm toward the audience, to hold the bill vertically upright and display the face of it as you count aloud, "One . . ."

Bring your right hand back and deal the second bill from your left *on top* of the first one in your right hand. Turn your right hand palm outward as before, to display the second bill, and count aloud, "Two . . ." Continue until you have counted the six from hand to hand. "One, two, three, four, five, six dollar bills . . . all alike, all the same. That's the trouble with money. It's just plain dull. Always the same old gray and green."

You are now holding the six bills upright in your right hand. Put them back into your left hand by turning your right hand palm downward as you naturally would, which turns the entire stack *face down*. You have reversed the original order of the bills by counting them on top of one another from hand to hand. The first of the envelope bills is now on top of the face-down stack with its notched edge toward the right. Square them up and hold the stack vertically upright in your left hand.

"Don't get me wrong. I have nothing against money," you say. "I like the product—but they could use more imagination in the way they package the stuff. It hasn't changed in years."

While you are saying that, put the tip of your right thumb over the notch of the envelope bill. Press lightly on the edge of the first concealed bill, the *polka dots*, and draw it out a little, but don't yet bring it into full view. (There is no need to put your thumb inside the envelope bill; the notch is there so you can avoid doing that. Just slide the concealed bill out to the right, to take the edge of it between your thumb and fingertips.)

"Why can't we have something different—like polka-dot bills?" Hold up the spotted bill with your right hand, give the audience a moment to realize that one of the bills you previously showed plain has suddenly become spotted, and say, "At least you could always tell a ten-spot when you had one." Show it front and back and put it into the small basket on your table. Take the second concealed bill from the top of the stack in your left hand in the same way, show the stripes on the front and back, comment about it, and discard that in the basket. Finally show the bill with the arrows and put that in the basket.

That leaves an empty envelope bill on top of the stack in your left hand. Take that one with your right hand and hold it up to show it, as you say, "But, no—it's always the same old dreary gray and green." Return that one to the *front* of the stack in your left hand, under all the others. (Just remember that when an envelope bill has been emptied, you always hold it up and show it as you remark about all of them being "dreary gray and green," and then put it back under all the rest to get rid of it.)

Now deal the bills singly from your left hand into your upturned right hand, putting them face down one on top of another as you count them aloud: "One, two, three, four, five, six." Then take the whole stack with your left hand and deal them singly into your right hand again in the same way, counting them from hand to hand a second time. But the second time, do it quickly and silently, without saying anything, as if repeating the count merely to confirm that you still have six, as when you started, even though you have discarded three in the basket. When you have finished the second count, put the face-down stack back into your left hand and square up the bills.

The double counting is done to impress the audience with the fact that you have only six bills and also to restack the bills in your left hand so the second envelope bill is now on top. Hold the stack vertically upright in your left hand. With the tip of your right thumb over the notched edge as before, slide out the recipe bill. Hold it up with your right hand to show the plain face of it, then turn it to display the printed clipping attached to the back. Pretend to read from it as you comment that it is a recipe for "banana-lemon pie." Drop it into the basket.

Then bring out the *advertising* bill, show its back, comment about it, and drop that into the basket. Next show the health warning bill, displaying its label on the back and then turning it horizontally so you can read it aloud. Put that into the basket.

Again, that leaves an empty envelope bill on top of the stack, so you hold it up and say, "But, no—it's always the same old dreary gray and green," and to get rid of it you put it back under all the rest. Now count them aloud singly from your left hand to your right hand, then take the whole stack with your left hand and silently repeat the hand-to-hand count, square them up, and hold the stack vertically upright in your left hand.

The third envelope bill is now on top. Follow the routine as given and show first the red bill, then the blue, and finally the rainbow, discarding each in the basket. You are left at the end with three singles and three empty envelope bills, each of which looks like a single bill. "But I guess it won't ever happen. It's just wishful thinking," you say. "I always wind up with the same old dreary gray and green dollars I started with."

Count them slowly from hand to hand, showing both sides of each bill, and drop them singly into the basket. "One, two, three, four, five, six."

MAGIC WITH ROPE, RIBBON AND STRING

CONTENTS

INTRODUCTION

You show both hands empty, clap them together, and suddenly produce a rope, or you start to cut a rope and it mysteriously vanishes and then reappears. Instead of a rope, you magically produce a streamer of bright red ribbon from an empty hand held high above your head, or you conjure up a ribbon out of a little circle of black paper that looks far too small to have hidden it.

Those are just some of the surprises in a whole chapter of quick and unusual opening tricks this book will teach you how to do. After you have caught the attention of your audience, you may want to

show some of the tricky-knot routines, such as the
one in which you instantly tie a knot with one hand,
make it look like a pair of old-fashioned "spectacles,"
then change that knot into two others.

There are penetration tricks with fresh magical
plots, disco records, or a bar of soap; with a coffee
cup that instantly links itself to a rope, or where a
whole batch of rings falls from a ribbon at a spectator's command. You will find a variety of the ever-
popular cut and restored effects to choose from,
other tricks in which ropes and ribbons stretch, grow
long or short, or join together, or in which they seem
to defy gravity or suddenly become acrobatically
alive.

Most of the tricks are do-anywhere magic. Those
with rope or ribbon are visible enough to be shown to
almost any group, large or small, and there are other
tricks and routines with string for close-up performances. The props are inexpensive, easy to assemble
and to carry around, and ropes, ribbons, and strings
are familiar to everyone as ordinary everyday objects. Sometimes, of course, they may not be as "ordinary" as the audience assumes, since they must be
specially prepared in advance to accomplish the
magic. But all the things required for the tricks in
this book can be put together at home with commonly available materials.

What Rope to Use

The rope magicians use for most rope tricks is
soft white clothesline. Dealers in magic equipment
supply a kind specially designed for magical uses,
since most clothesline, as it comes from the factory,
is too hard and stiff to use. But there are types of

ordinary clothesline and sash cord, generally available at hardware and variety stores, that will serve just as well if the inner core is removed to make them soft, pliable, and easy to cut through.

What is needed is one of the many brands manufactured with a "braided jacket," usually identified on the label as such. The best for magical purposes are those with what is called a "solid braided cotton jacket," but others with braided plastic jackets also can be used.

The braided jacket is an outer tube-like shell. Inside it, running through the whole length of the rope, is a core of several strands of string or twisted plastic fiber. Removing the core is simply a matter of pulling out the center strings, so that you are left with the braided outer jacket to use for rope tricks. The stripping process is not difficult.

How to Remove the Core

Cut a piece of braided-jacket clothesline to the desired length. Take one end of the line in your left hand, and use your right fingers to pull apart the braiding of the outer jacket at that end until about an inch of the inner core is exposed. Close your left hand around the jacket just beneath the same end and grip the core strings tightly with your right fingers. Now pull the strings up with your right hand as you slide the jacket down with your left hand.

After you have pulled out a few inches of the core, you will find that the jacket bunches so it is hard to pull out any more. When that happens, move your left hand to grip the jacket just below where it has bunched. Pull your left hand down along the whole length of the rope, to draw the bunched jacket down toward the bottom end so part of the jacket gradually becomes an empty tube at the bottom.

Continue in this manner, pulling out a few inches of the core, smoothing the jacket down toward the bottom, and then pulling out a few more inches of the core, until the entire outer jacket has been stripped free of the core. Trim off the two ends and your rope is ready to use.

Binding the Ends

If you plan to use the same length of rope repeatedly for a particular trick, you may want to bind the ends to keep them from fraying. The easiest way is simply to wrap a short strip of white cloth adhesive tape horizontally around each end. The ends also can be bound by coiling white cotton thread tightly around them and tying it off with small knots, or by stitching the ends with needle and thread.

Another way to bind the ends is to treat each of the ends with white craft glue, working it in well with your fingers, then rolling the ends to reshape them. Allow the white glue to dry and harden thoroughly before the rope is used.

Whether the ends are bound or not, there is a limit to how often the same piece of rope can be used before it becomes soiled and ragged-looking. Old rope should be kept for practice, but reasonably fresh and clean rope should be used for public performances.

Colored Ropes and Cords

For tricks requiring colored ropes, an easy and practical way to color short lengths of cotton-jacket clothesline is with felt-tip marking pens. Longer lengths can be colored with fabric paints, available at craft and hobby shops.

There are a variety of braided colored cords manufactured for upholstery and drapery uses that will serve many magical purposes. They can be bought in different thicknesses and textures, some hard-finished and others soft and loosely braided. Another substitute for colored rope is the thick rope-like yarn made in many colors for needlework projects and as ties for gift packages.

Ribbons

Silk ribbon, traditionally used by magicians for ribbon tricks, is no longer available in most shopping areas and, if it can be found, it is quite expensive. A serviceable substitute for use in "silk ribbon" tricks is polyester satin ribbon. While it lacks some of the springy compressibility of real silk, polyester satin ribbon is brightly colored, has a silky-smooth finish, and can be bought by the yard or in pre-packaged lengths and widths at almost any variety store.

If ribbon with a less slippery finish is needed, you may prefer to use grosgrain ribbon, which has a cross-ribbed surface, or sturdy cotton or rayon binding tape.

Magic Strings

Venetian blind cord makes an excellent "string" for most string tricks. The most common variety, which is best for magic, has an outer braided cotton jacket similar to cotton-jacketed clothesline. For most magic purposes this cord can be used as packaged, but if you wish an even softer and more pliable "string," the core can be removed in the same way as from rope. Venetian blind cord is white, provides good visibility, is strong, smooth to handle, and doesn't kink or ravel as many loose-stranded strings do.

There is also a variety of small-diameter upholstery cords available in many colors and finishes. As a general rule, it is probably better to use some form of braided cord for string tricks rather than strand-twisted string or twine, unless there is a specific reason for using the latter. If twine is to be used, jute may be best. Sisal twine should be avoided because of its splintery rough finish and entangling ragged strands.

1

SUDDENLY
A ROPE

The following tricks are for "openers." They are
surprising or amusing ways to introduce a routine of
rope or ribbon magic. Most of them are over in a minute, but in that minute they should help you to catch
the attention of your audience and to make them
want to see more.

CLAP HANDS!

How it looks

You hold both hands out at your sides to show

CLAP HANDS!

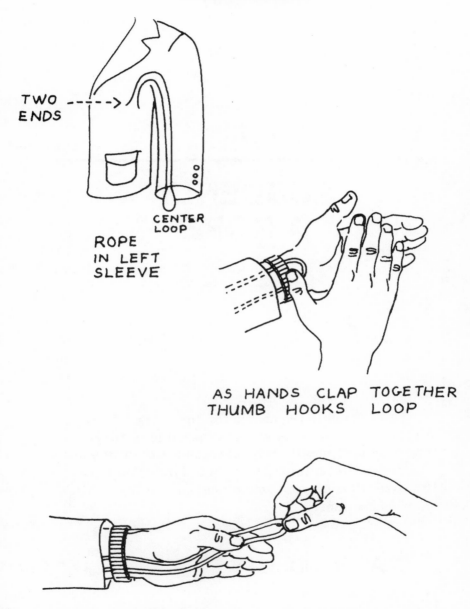

TWO ENDS

CENTER LOOP

ROPE IN LEFT SLEEVE

AS HANDS CLAP TOGETHER THUMB HOOKS LOOP

RIGHT HAND DRAWS ROPE UP THROUGH LEFT

that they're empty, clap them together in front of you, then draw them apart to produce a rope between them.

What you need

A 3½-foot length of soft rope.
You will also need to wear a wristwatch on your left wrist.

The secret

The rope is hidden up your sleeve, fixed so you can catch a loop of it with your thumb to draw it out through your hand and bring it suddenly into view. As simple as the method is, the effect is quite surprising.

Double the rope to bring its two ends together, then take the *center loop* and feed it down the left sleeve of your jacket from the inside armhole. Reach up into your sleeve and draw the center loop down until you can slide it beneath the band of your wristwatch, so the loop lies against the inside of your left wrist and extends about an inch beyond the watchband.

Hold the loop in place against your left wrist with your right thumb and stretch your left arm out full-length in front of you. Remove your right thumb from the loop and let your left arm drop to your side.

Inside, under your jacket, the two ends of rope should now hang a few inches over the armhole and down your left side. With the rope fixed that way, you can wear it safely until you are ready to do the trick, with no fear that it will fall down out of your sleeve.

What you do

Stand facing the audience with both hands naturally at your sides. Lift both hands *slightly* to show them empty by turning the palms outward. Turn your body a little to the right as you continue to raise your hands to waist level, so the back of your left hand is toward the audience.

Clapping your hands together is what puts them in position for secretly catching hold of the rope. The tip of your left thumb should point up toward the ceiling, the tips of the fingers toward the right. Bring your right palm against the left so the right fingers are vertical and the tip of the right thumb extends to the inside of your left wrist.

Clap your hands together twice, loudly, as if applauding. As you clap them the second time, catch the tip of your right thumb in the loop and draw the rope up through your left hand and out to the right, to bring it suddenly into view.

All the movements should blend together without any pause. There is nothing difficult about it, but it takes a little practice to do smoothly.

OVERHEAD RIBBON PRODUCTION

How it looks

Hold your left hand high above your head, palm toward the audience, fingers straight up and opened wide. Bringing your right hand up to it, tap a pointing finger against your left palm, quickly close your left hand, and instantly produce a long red ribbon.

What you need

A 3½-foot length of red satin ribbon, ½ inch wide.

A piece of thin cardboard cut from an index card to a size of 2½ by 3½ inches.

Transparent tape.

The secret

The cardboard is made into a small tube, shut at one end, which fits tightly on the tip of the second finger of your right hand. The ribbon is hidden in the tube, and your finger secretly snaps the tube into the left palm in the instant you bring your hands together above your head to produce the ribbon. The magical surprise of this quick opening trick depends on the unusual overhead position of your hands and the speed with which it is performed.

To make the tube, turn your right palm toward you and place one of the narrow ends of the cardboard against the inside of your second finger, with the left edge of the cardboard at the finger's middle joint. Wrap the cardboard into a tube around the finger as *tightly* as you can. Fasten it with a strip of tape and remove the tube from your finger. Pinch the left end of the tube flat and tape that end shut. Fasten another strip of tape horizontally along the seam of the tube.

Start with one end of the ribbon and pack it into the tube in little accordion folds, pushing them well down into the bottom with the tip of the little finger. When you come to the other end of the ribbon, leave an inch of that sticking up out of the tube.

OVERHEAD RIBBON PRODUCTION

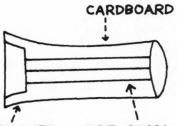

CARDBOARD

END PINCHED
FLAT _ TAPED
SHUT

SIDE SEAM
TAPED

FITS TIGHTLY ON TIP
OF RIGHT SECOND FINGER

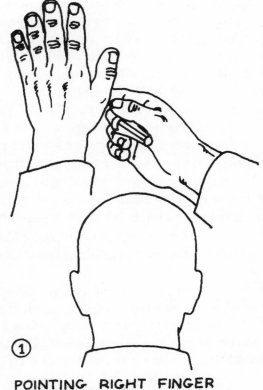

①

POINTING RIGHT FINGER
TAPS RAISED LEFT PALM

LEFT HAND
TILTS
FORWARD
AND DOWN

②

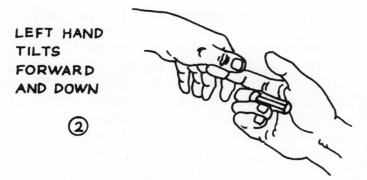

SECOND
FINGER
PUTS TUBE
INTO LEFT
PALM

③

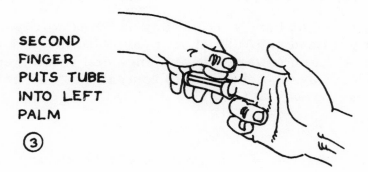

LEFT HAND
CLOSES AROUND
TUBE _ RIGHT
PULLS OUT
RIBBON

④

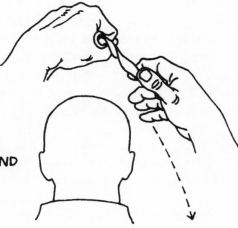

Now, if you jam the second finger of your right hand down into the tube as far as it will go, the tube should fit on that fingertip like a big tight thimble. The top end of the ribbon is between the finger and the inside of the tube, so that when you pull out your finger, the end of the ribbon is drawn out with it.

You can carry the ribbon-loaded tube in the right-hand pocket of your jacket or slacks, or you can have the tube on your table hidden behind some other prop. Just before you are ready to perform the trick, secretly fix the tube in position on the tip of your right hand's second finger. Stand with your right hand naturally at your side, with the back of that hand toward the audience and the fingers closed against the palm to conceal the tube from front view.

What you do

Raise your left hand straight up above your head, palm to the audience, thumb to the right, fingers toward the ceiling and spread open wide. Bring your right hand, with its back to the audience, up from your right side, up in front of your body, and up to the left hand raised above your head. Point with your right hand's first finger, keeping the other fingers closed back against the palm to conceal the tube. Tap your pointing first finger against your left palm just below the crotch of the left thumb.

The following moves should all blend together, quickly and smoothly, without any pause. Keep the tip of your right first finger touching your left palm near the crotch of the left thumb and tilt your left hand forward and down until its fingertips point to the floor. Straighten out your right second finger to bring the hidden tube up against the left palm. Close the left fingers into a fist around the tube and pull your right second finger from the tube, drawing out the end of the ribbon to grip it between that finger and the right thumb.

With your right hand, continue to pull the ribbon straight down from your raised and fisted left hand, until the full length of it is stretched downward between both hands. Hold it that way a moment, then drop the end of it from your left hand and let that hand fall to your side as your right hand holds up the suddenly produced ribbon.

You can get rid of the little tube that is hidden in your left hand by reaching into the left pocket of your jacket to bring out a ring, a pair of scissors, or whatever small prop you may be about to use in your ribbon routine, leaving the tube behind in the pocket. If you are not planning to use the produced ribbon in another trick, simply gather it up into your left hand, put it away in your left pocket, and leave the tube there with it.

SIGNS OF MAGIC

How it looks

You open out a small folded cardboard sign and hold it up with both hands so the audience can read it, and also so they can see there is nothing else in the folded sign as you show first the front and then the back. On the front, the sign reads: IT HAPPENS, and on the back: LIKE MAGIC! You close the folder, reach into it, and magically produce a rope.

What you need

An 8- by 14-inch piece of white poster board or other white cardboard.

A second piece of cardboard, 2½ by 5 inches.

A 3½-foot length of soft braided clothesline with its core removed.

Scissors or a sharp-pointed knife.

A paper stapler.

A pencil, ruler, black crayon or marking pen, and dull-finish transparent tape.

The secret

The folded rope is held in a small tube-like container which is stapled to the bottom front of the sign where your covering fingers hide it as they hold up the sign.

Place the cardboard on a table with its long edges top and bottom. Measure 7 inches in from the left side and draw a faint vertical pencil line down that center. Run the point of the scissors or knife down that line from top to bottom to score it. Fold the cardboard in half from left to right, press the fold flat, and open it out again. Reinforce the center fold, front and back, with vertical hinge-like strips of tape.

Turn the cardboard to its original position on the table. On the left half, measure 4 inches down from the top edge and draw a faint horizontal pencil line across. The base of the printed letters should be at that line. Because of the length of some of the

SIGNS OF MAGIC

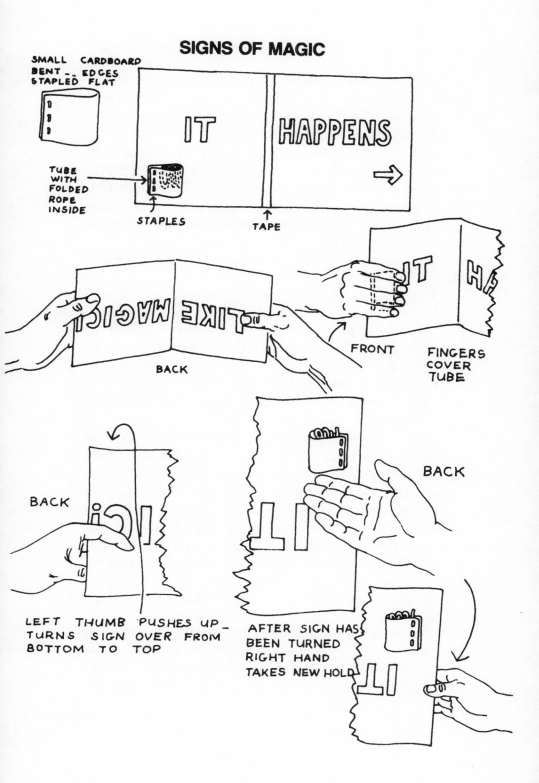

SMALL CARDBOARD
BENT — EDGES
STAPLED FLAT

IT HAPPENS →

TUBE WITH FOLDED ROPE INSIDE

STAPLES

TAPE

LIKE MAGIC!

BACK

FRONT

FINGERS COVER TUBE

BACK

LEFT THUMB PUSHES UP — TURNS SIGN OVER FROM BOTTOM TO TOP

BACK

AFTER SIGN HAS BEEN TURNED RIGHT HAND TAKES NEW HOLD

words, the lettering should be kept tall and thin, but large enough for the audience to read it at a glance. Block out the letters with pencil and fill them in with black crayon or marking pen.

On the left side, print: IT. On the right side print: HAPPENS. Beneath the word HAPPENS, draw an arrow pointing to the right. Turn the cardboard over from *top to bottom*. (This is so the printing on the back will be right side up when you later turn the card while performing.) On the left half of the back, print: LIKE. On the right half, print: MAGIC!

Put the big piece of cardboard aside for a moment and turn the smaller piece so its long edges are at top and bottom. *Bend* the cardboard in half from right to left, to bring the two side edges together at the left, but *do not fold it flat.* Fasten those two edges flatly together with three vertically spaced staples. Press the center bend with your thumb to spread the sides and round it slightly.

Place the large cardboard with the word IT now facing you upright at the left. At a point ½ inch in from the left edge and an inch up from the bottom, attach the flat part of the small tube vertically to the large cardboard with three staples. Turn the cardboard over and cover the parts of the staples that have come through it with a vertical strip of tape. (This is to avoid scratching your fingers with the ends of the staples when handling the sign.) Again turn the cardboard to the side with the attached tube.

Fold the coreless clothesline back and forth upon itself in tight 2-inch accordion folds and leave the end of rope sticking up about ¼ inch above the rest of the folds. Squeeze the folds together and push the

entire folded rope down inside the tube from the top.
Close the folding sign from left to right.

If you plan to use this as an opening trick, you
can have the folder in your hands as you enter. Otherwise, rest it on the table with the open part to the
rear.

What you do

Hold the closed folder upright with your left
hand around the spine, thumb at the back, fingers in
front, and with its open edges toward the right. Put
your right hand inside, around the right edge near
the bottom, thumb at the back, and cover the tube
with your slightly arched fingers. Move your left
hand across the front of the folder, put your left fingers inside at the bottom right, and open it out between your hands to show that side of it. Hold it long
enough for the audience to read the printed words.

You are now about to turn the opened-out sign
over *forward* to show the other side. Do this by
bringing your left first finger to the back, placing
the nail of the left thumb against the front, and
pushing up with the thumb to pivot the whole thing
over from *bottom to top*. As the quick turnover is
completed, simply open your right fingers and lift
that hand away for an instant, then grip the right
edge of the sign again. Hold it between your hands
for the audience to read the printing that now faces
them.

With your left hand, shut the folder toward you
from left to right. Slide your left hand to the top
right corner. Put your left first finger between the
two edges and, with the other left-hand fingers at
the front and thumb at the back, turn the folder to

the left until its spine is toward the floor and the open edges are at the top. Hold it that way with your left hand.

Snap your right-hand fingers, show that the hand is empty, and reach inside the folder. Grip the end of the rope, pull it *down* from the tube to the inside bottom of the folder, and then draw it *slowly* out of the folder to the right.

The same folder could be used to produce yards of ribbon instead of rope, since the tube will hold much more ribbon than rope, or you might want to use it to produce several silk handkerchiefs.

INSTANT ROPE

How it looks

You take out a pair of scissors, show both hands empty, tap the top of your left fist with the scissors, and instantly produce from that hand a 4-foot length of rope.

What you need

A 4-foot length of soft clothesline with its core removed.

Scissors that will fit into a jacket pocket. The blades of the scissors should be about 3 inches long, from their tips to the screw at the center.

The secret

This trick is based on a standard method magicians use for producing a silk handkerchief with the aid of a wand. In this case, the rope is wound into a small ball around the blades of the scissors and is hidden by the natural transfer of the scissors from hand to hand as each hand is shown empty. It is very simple to perform but provides a quick surprise and a magical way of introducing the rope for a cut-and-restored rope trick.

Turn the closed scissors with the points toward the bottom and lay one end of the rope vertically on top of the blades. Wind the rope around the scissors point in flat lateral turns, making about five turns and then winding the next five flatly upon the first ones, and so on, until all of the rope is wound. Tuck the last end of the rope in under one of the wound strands to hold the ball together. Put the scissors, handle end down, into the right-hand pocket of your jacket.

What you do

Reach into your pocket with your right hand. Close your fingers loosely around the little ball of rope, and bring out the scissors with the back of your hand toward the audience. The scissors handles are at the top as you hold the scissors by their blades, and the screw at the center lies against the inside of your first finger.

What you do now should look as though you are simply transferring the scissors from hand to hand, to show first one hand and then the other empty.

Show your left hand empty and then turn its palm toward you, with its back to the audience. Bring your right hand to the left hand, right fingers inside the left. Slide the center of the scissors under your left thumb, which grips them there. Take your

INSTANT ROPE

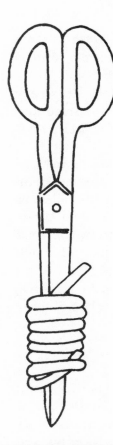

ROPE WOUND
AROUND SCISSORS

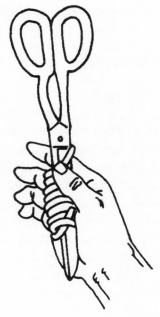

RIGHT HAND _ AFTER TAKING
SCISSORS FROM POCKET

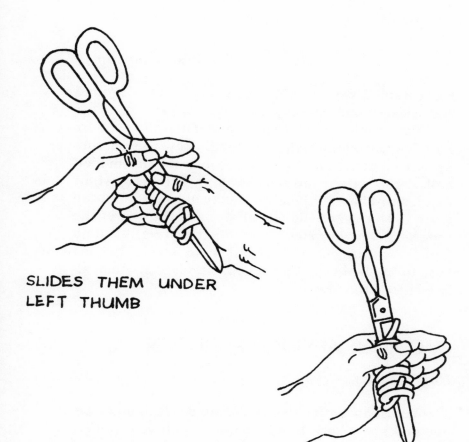

SLIDES THEM UNDER
LEFT THUMB

LEFT HAND HOLDS SCISSORS

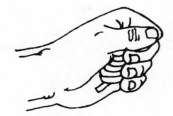

SCISSORS REMOVED _
BALL OF ROPE REMAINS IN HAND

right hand away and close your left fingers around the scissors and ball of rope.

Show your right hand empty. Take the scissors handles with your right hand and draw the scissors up out of your left fist, leaving behind the hidden ball of rope. Hold the scissors high with your right hand, snip them in the air a couple of times, then tap them to the top of your left fist. Take the end of the rope between your right first finger and right thumb and draw it up out of your left hand, stretching the rope to full length between your hands as it magically comes into view.

CIRCLE AROUND A RIBBON

How it looks

You show both sides of a small circle of black paper and show both hands empty. Then you quickly fold the circle into a cone and magically produce a long bright-colored ribbon from it.

What you need

A circle 7 inches in diameter, cut from a sheet of black construction paper.

A 3½-foot length of bright-colored satin ribbon, ½ inch wide.

Transparent tape.

The secret

The ribbon is accordion-folded and banded around with a strip of transparent tape, sticky side out, which is fastened to part of the paper circle in a position where your fingers naturally cover it while showing that side of the circle.

Fold the ribbon back and forth upon itself in flat and even 2-inch accordion folds. Turn the folded ribbon to a horizontal position. Take a 3-inch strip of transparent tape and wrap it in a flat band vertically around the ribbon, with the tape's *sticky side out.*

Fold the paper circle in half from top to bottom, then in half from left to right. Crease the folds with your thumbnail, and open the paper again. Attach the folded ribbon by its band of tape to the lower right section of the circle, centered about ¾ inch in from the circle's outer rim. Now take another short piece of tape and fasten that, *sticky side down,* exactly over the tape that bands the ribbon. (This is done so the paper won't stick together when it is folded and carried among your other props.)

Have the circle on your table, folded from top to bottom so that the ribbon is hidden inside toward the rear at the right.

What you do

Slide your right hand in under the top fold of the circle so your fingers flatly cover the ribbon. With your right thumb outside at the back, pick up the circle between thumb and fingers, hold it upright, and shake it open to show the audience the front side of it. Show your left hand empty.

Turn your right hand over toward you, turning the circle over toward you from top to bottom, and immediately take what is now the top between your left thumb and first finger. Remove your right hand as your left hand holds up the circle to show that side to the audience.

CIRCLE AROUND A RIBBON

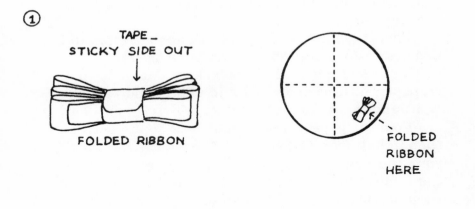

① TAPE —
STICKY SIDE OUT

FOLDED RIBBON

FOLDED RIBBON HERE

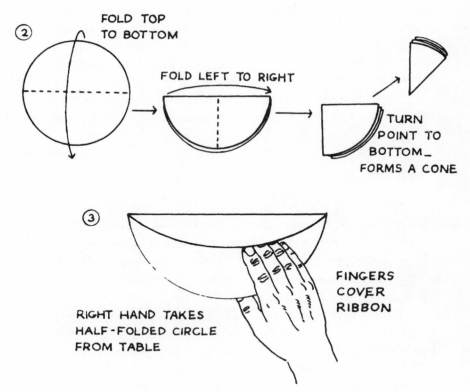

② FOLD TOP TO BOTTOM

FOLD LEFT TO RIGHT

TURN POINT TO BOTTOM —
FORMS A CONE

③ FINGERS COVER RIBBON

RIGHT HAND TAKES HALF-FOLDED CIRCLE FROM TABLE

BACK VIEWS

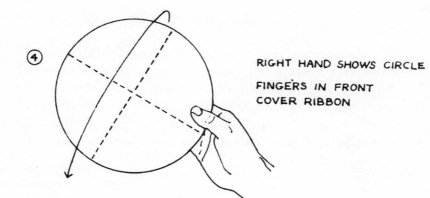

④ RIGHT HAND SHOWS CIRCLE

FINGERS IN FRONT
COVER RIBBON

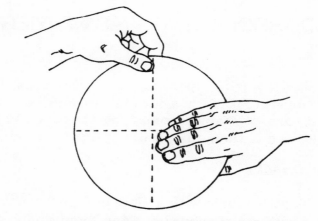

⑤ RIGHT HAND TURNS IT OVER TOWARD
YOU FROM TOP TO BOTTOM — THEN
LEFT HAND TAKES AT TOP

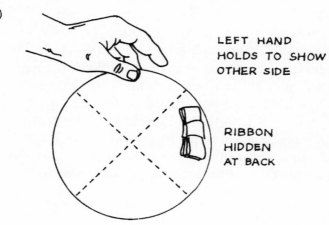

⑥ LEFT HAND
HOLDS TO SHOW
OTHER SIDE

RIBBON
HIDDEN
AT BACK

Bring your right hand to the outside center of the circle and quickly close it on its creases into the form of a cone. Hold the bottom point of the cone with your left hand, reach inside with your right hand, grasp the end of the ribbon, and pull it out to the side and then straight up to produce it from the cone.

THE ROPE THAT WASN'T THERE

This amusing opening effect starts as if you were about to perform a cut-and-restored-rope trick, but it turns to magical comedy as the rope suddenly vanishes and then, just as unexpectedly, reappears.

How it looks

"A little magic with a piece of rope," you say, as you show a rope in your left hand, "and a pair of scissors." You hold up the scissors with your right hand. "I shall now cut the rope." But as you speak, the rope instantly vanishes, leaving your left hand empty.

Pretending to be surprised, you stare at your empty hand, then look down at the floor, as though wondering where the rope went. "Well, if I *did* have a rope," you say, "I would take it by the center and cut it in half, so there would be two pieces."

You go through the motions without any rope, demonstrating in pantomime what you would do. "And then I would wrap it around my hand, say the magic words, and pull it out . . . fully restored in one piece again." Suddenly, the vanished rope reappears, stretched between your hands. "Hey, there it is!" you say. "I knew I had a rope somewhere."

What you need

Two ropes with their cores removed, each 2½ feet long.

A 3½-foot length of strong white string or cord. (Any strong string will do, but the best to use is Venetian blind cord, size 4½.)

A pipe cleaner.

A small safety pin.

Scissors that will fit in your jacket pocket.

The secret

The first rope vanishes by means of what magicians call a "pull," that is, a string that pulls it up your sleeve. The duplicate rope, rolled into a ball, is hidden under the edge of your jacket where your fingers can secretly reach it when your hand is at your side.

Take one of the ropes, double it so the two ends touch together, and tie one end of the string *tightly* to the center loop. At the other end of the string, make a large slip-knot loop (see page 26). Slide your right hand through this loop and tighten the slip-knot to fasten that end of the string to your right forearm just above the top edge of your shirt cuff. Pass the string around your back, hold the ends of the rope in your left hand, and put on your jacket.

The string, tied to the center of the rope, now passes up the inside of your left sleeve, across your back, and down the inside of your right sleeve to where the other end is fastened to your right arm.

THE ROPE THAT WASN'T THERE

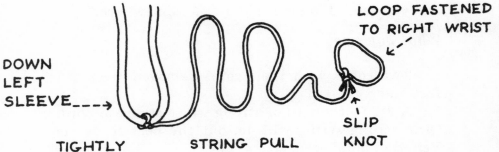

LOOP FASTENED
TO RIGHT WRIST

DOWN
LEFT
SLEEVE- - - ->

SLIP
KNOT

TIGHTLY
TIED TO
CENTER
OF ROPE

STRING PULL

①

②

BACK

STRING UP LEFT SLEEVE,
ACROSS BACK, DOWN RIGHT

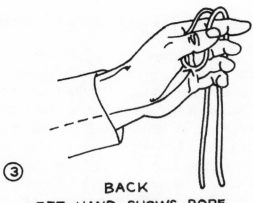

③ BACK
LEFT HAND SHOWS ROPE

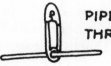

PIPE CLEANER
THROUGH HOLE

④ ENDS BENT
DOWN

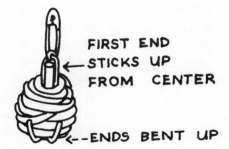

FIRST END
← STICKS UP
FROM CENTER

←--ENDS BENT UP

⑤ BALL OF ROPE ON
HOLDER UNDER
JACKET

To understand how the "pull" works, hold your left hand in front of your waist, with its palm toward you. Draw the rope and attached string through your left hand until you can grip the center of the rope between your thumb and first finger. Hold it there and suddenly swing your right hand up and out to the right. The doubled rope, pulled by the string, instantly shoots up your left sleeve out of sight. (You will have to experiment a little to decide how long the string should be, since that depends on the length of your arms. But once you have adjusted it correctly, you can use the same rope and string whenever you perform the trick.)

The duplicate rope is held under the bottom edge of your jacket by a holder made of a pipe cleaner and safety pin. Turn the safety pin so its clasp is at the top. Thread the pipe cleaner through the little hole at the bottom of the pin and bend the cleaner down until its two ends touch.

Place one end of the second rope vertically against the top of the pipe cleaner. Wind the rest of the rope into a small ball around its center, and tuck the last end of rope in under a wound strand to hold it tightly together. Bend up the two bottom ends of the pipe cleaner to keep the ball from sliding off.

Put on your jacket. Drop your two hands to your sides. Without moving your left arm, bend only your fingers up under the bottom edge of your jacket to the inside. Where your fingers touch the lining is the proper place to pin the holder with its ball of rope.

With the holder in place and the "pull" correctly adjusted, draw the rope down out of your left sleeve. Turn the palm of your left hand toward you and hold the center of the rope between your thumb and first finger, so the string runs through your partly closed hand. Since this is intended as an opening trick, you will have the rope set that way in your hand when you come out before your audience. The scissors should be in your right-hand jacket pocket.

What you do

While saying, "A little magic with a piece of rope," show the rope in your left hand and take the scissors from your pocket with your right hand. As you say, "And a pair of scissors," swing your right hand up high and out to the right to display the scissors. That pulls the string so the rope shoots up your left sleeve and vanishes. But pay no attention to your left hand. Hold it as it was and keep looking at the scissors. Snip them in the air and say, "I shall now cut the rope."

Then look at your left hand and pretend to be surprised that the rope has disappeared. Open your left hand wide, shake your head, and let your hand drop to your side. Turn your body toward the left and glance down at the floor, as though wondering if you might have dropped the rope.

As you turn your left side away from the audience for an instant, curl your left fingers up under the bottom edge of your jacket and pull the other ball of rope into your hand, closing your fingers around it. Don't move your arm—keep it at your side. Turn your body a little to the right, as you still look down at the floor as if searching for the vanished rope.

Then shrug and say, "Well, if I *did* have a rope, I would take it by the center...," bringing your closed left fist up in front of you as if it were holding an imaginary rope by the center, "... and I would cut it

Magic with Rope, Ribbon and String

in half so there would be two pieces." Clip the scissors together with your right fingers as if cutting a rope, and go through the rest of the motions.

"And then I would wrap it around my hand, say the magic words, and pull it out, fully restored and in one piece again." Reach into your left fist, grip the end of rope that sticks up out of the center of the ball, and pull the rope out of your fist, stretching it into view between your hands. "Hey, there it is! I knew I had a rope somewhere."

2

TRICKY KNOTS

BASIC TRICKY-KNOT ROUTINE

You can use rope, ribbon, or string for this do-anywhere routine of appearing and vanishing knots. It blends together seven of the standard tricky knots magicians have been using for years, in a sequence that quickly builds from one trick to the next, provides some amusing fun, and ends with a real puzzler.

The routine can be used by itself, as an introduction to rope tricks that are to follow, or it can be ex-

panded by adding some of the other tricky knots explained elsewhere in this chapter.

How it looks

You take one end of a rope in your hand, hold it
high, bring up the other end, and snap it out into the
air. "This is an angry rope," you say. "It's fit to be
tied." As you snap it into the air again, a knot suddenly appears, as if you had snapped the knot into
the end of it!

Quickly untying the knot, you bring the two
ends of the rope together, tie them, and tug at the
ends to form a tight, hard knot. Holding up the loop
to display the knot, you give the rope a quick shake.
The knot vanishes and the ends fall apart, as you
say, "But now the *tide* has gone out."

You take one end of the rope in each hand,
stretching the rope between them. "This has been
called the fastest knot in the world." Bringing your
hands together for an instant, you pull them apart
and an Overhand Knot appears at the center of the
rope. "I'll do it again," you say, as you untie the knot
and then seem to repeat exactly the same moves as
before. But this time, you instantly produce a big
Bow Knot and hold it up by its bows to show it, and
quip, "My imitation of a giant tying his shoelace."

Shaking that knot from the rope, you tie another
large Overhand Knot. The audience can see that it
seems to be a genuine knot as you pull it tight. You
drop one end of the rope to the floor and put your
foot on it so that the rope, with the knot at the center, is stretched between hand and foot. When you
snap your fingers, the knot instantly vanishes, and
you say, "A little knot ... that *is* not."

You drape the rope over the palm of your hand and lift it high, announcing, "One hand." With a quick twist and downward snap, you tie an instant One-Hand Knot.

After untying that knot, you say, "And now, here's how to tie a knot the hard way." You take one end of the rope in each hand. "If you want to have some fun when you go home, get a piece of rope such as this, or a piece of string, and try to tie a real knot in the center of it without letting go of either end . . . . It's supposed to be a physical impossibility."

You keep the ends of the rope in your hands, make some quick loops and twists, and stretch it out again between your hands to show a real knot tied at the center. "Well, they *say* it's impossible . . . Try it when you get home."

What you need

A 4½-foot length of soft white clothesline, or a similar length of string or satin ribbon.

The secret

The Snap Knot that starts the routine is really a trick rather than a tricky knot, since the knot that you seem to snap into the end of the rope has already been tied and is hidden in your hand until you switch the two rope ends. This is an ancient trick, but still a good one. Each of the other tricky knots will be explained in the order in which they are shown in the routine.

Prepare the rope by tying a large Overhand Knot (the everyday kind) about 4 inches from one end of it. Don't pull it tight; the knot should be only slightly smaller than the palm of your hand. Place the knot on the palm of your right hand, wind the rest of the rope loosely around the hand, and slip your hand out of it. Have the rope coiled that way in one of your right-hand pockets.

What you do

Put your right hand into your pocket, slide your fingers into the coil so the knot is against your palm, and bring the rope out with the back of your hand toward the audience. With your left hand, put the top end of the rope into the crotch of your right thumb to hold it so the secret knot is just beneath the thumb, hidden from front view by your hand. Uncoil the rest of the rope to let it hang down from your right hand.

The Snap Knot

Hold your right hand high to display the hanging rope. Grasp the bottom end of the rope with your left hand and bring that end up to hold it clipped between your right first and second fingers. Give your right hand a sharp downward shake and drop the end of the rope from between your fingers, as if snapping it down into the air to try to form a knot. When no knot appears the first time, you seem to do the same thing again. But what you really do the second time is switch the two ends.

Bring the hanging end up as before, with your left hand, and hold it clipped between your right fingers. Once more, give your right hand a sharp downward shake. But keep hold of the end that is between your fingers and just drop *the other end* from under

THE SNAP KNOT

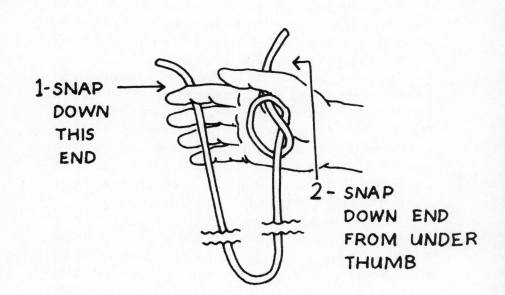

1- SNAP DOWN THIS END

2 - SNAP DOWN END FROM UNDER THUMB

your thumb, so it snaps down and the hidden knot suddenly appears. Lift the rope to show the knot and then untie it.

Fake Square Knot

You now take an end of the rope in each hand and bring the two ends together just as if you were going to tie a real Square Knot. But instead of tying the first part of a real knot by *crossing* the ends under and over, you merely hold one end straight and twist the other end a full turn *around* it. Then you tie the second part of the knot exactly as you would tie the rest of a Square Knot, by crossing the ends over and under, and pulling them as tight as you can. The fake knot looks very real and will hold its shape until the rope is given a sharp downward shake to make the knot fall apart and disappear.

Here, in detail, is how to tie it:

With both palms up, hold the rope about 4 inches from each end, and bring your hands together. Lay the left end of the rope across the right end and hold both for a moment with the tip of the left thumb. With your right hand, turn the right end of the rope around the left end and out to the left. Again, hold both ends with the left thumb. Now, just tie the two ends together in a single knot.

With the lower fingers of each hand, grip the sides of the rope beneath the knot, and with your thumbs and first fingers pull hard on the rope ends to tighten the knot. Grasp the rope just above the knot with your right hand, remove your left hand, and display the tied-together loop. Give it a hard shake and the knot vanishes as the ends fall apart.

FAKE SQUARE KNOT

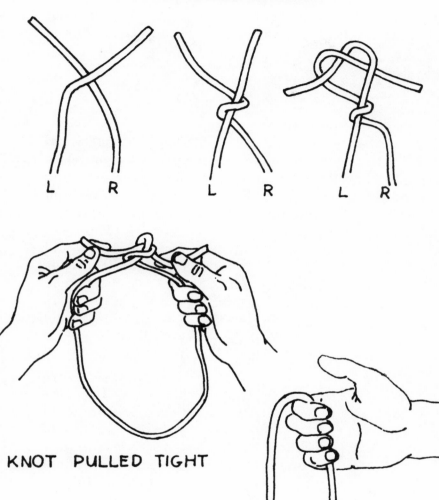

L R   L R   L R

KNOT PULLED TIGHT

SHOWING
KNOT
BEFORE
VANISH

INSTANT KNOT

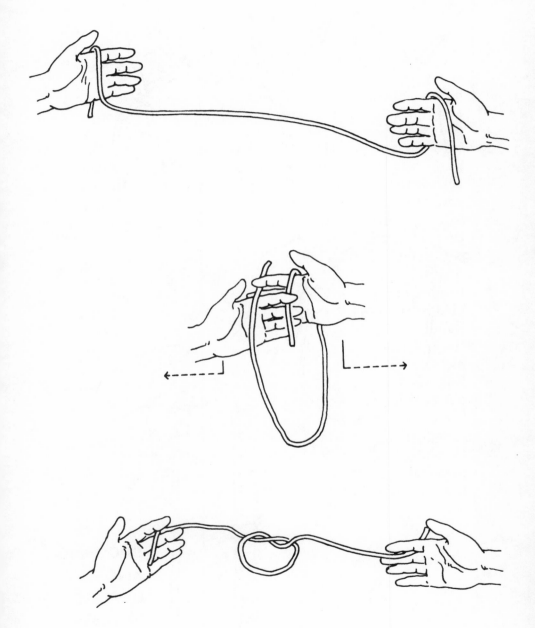

Instant Knot

This is the instant tying of an Overhand Knot as the rope is held out horizontally between your hands. With your left palm toward you, thumb up and fingertips to the right, drape one end of the rope over that hand so part of the end hangs down at the *back* of it. Take the other rope end in your right hand, but in the opposite way, so that end goes down across the *palm*. The right palm should be toward you, thumb up, and fingertips to the left. Hold the hands apart to show the rope hanging between them.

Bring your hands together, with the left hand nearest to your body, and touch the backs of the left fingertips against the palm of the right hand. This also puts the right fingertips at the back of the left hand. Tightly nip the *right* end of the rope between the *left* first and second fingers. At the same time, nip the *left* end between the *right* first and second fingers. Now, just pull your hands apart, straight out to the sides, and the Overhand Knot will form at the center of the rope.

This should all be done quickly, with your hands touching together for only an instant before they are drawn apart and the knot appears. After showing the knot, untie it.

INSTANT BOW KNOT

HANDS START
CLOSER TOGETHER

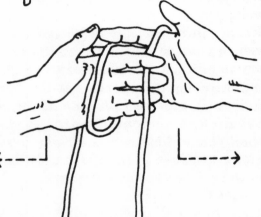

Instant Bow Knot

The instant tying of a Bow Knot is done the same way as the Overhand Knot, except that you start with your hands much closer together. Instead of holding the rope at the ends, hold it near the center so there is less than a foot of rope between your hands. The left side of the rope hangs down over the *back* of your left hand; the right side hangs down over the *palm* of your right hand.

Bring your hands together exactly as before. Grip the part of the rope that is in your *right* palm between the *left* first and second fingers. At the same time, grip the part at the back of the *left* hand between the *right* first and second fingers. Quickly draw your hands apart and you will be holding a large Bow Knot by its two big bows. (This happens because, with less rope between your hands, the two ends catch up into loops instead of passing through as when the single knot is formed.) Show the Bow Knot and then take one of the ends and shake the rope down so the knot unties.

Fake Overhand Knot

This closely imitates the tying of a genuine Overhand Knot, but one finger secretly holds back a tiny loop that converts it into a Slip Knot, which pulls apart and vanishes.

Hold your left palm toward you, back of the hand to the audience, thumb up, fingertips to the right. Hold the rope about a foot from one end and drape that part over the top edge of your left *second* finger near the tip, so the end passes between the first and second fingers and hangs down over the back of your hand. Loosely close your two lower left fingers over the part that passes down across the palm of the hand.

With your right hand, take the rope about a foot from the bottom end. Bring that end up across the other strand and under your left thumb to hold it, letting that end fall to the back of your left hand. Close your left second finger to press the tip of it against the point where the two strands cross in the form of an "X."

Reach out through the large loop with your right hand, take the end hanging at the back of the left fingers, and pull it in through the loop toward you, gradually forming a knot. As you continue to pull that end, a bight (loop) will catch around the tip of the left second finger. Slip this finger out of the bight as you finally draw the knot tight. The bight becomes caught in the tightening knot and makes it a Slip Knot.

Remove your right hand from the loop and hold the top rope end with your left hand so the rope hangs down to the floor. Step on the bottom end of

FAKE OVERHEAD KNOT

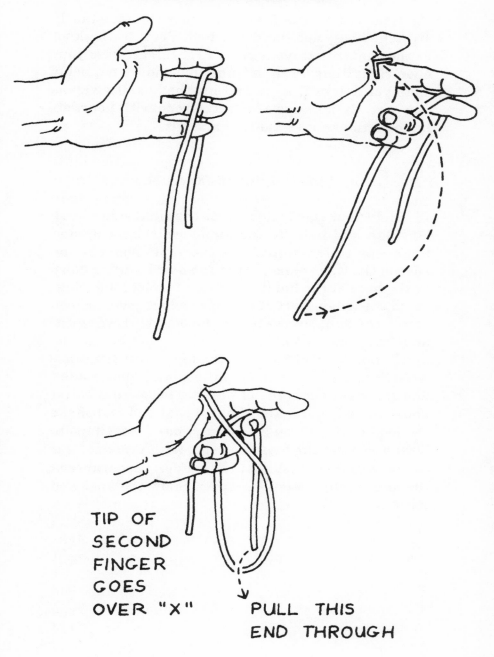

TIP OF
SECOND
FINGER
GOES
OVER "X"

PULL THIS
END THROUGH

the rope with your left foot and keep the rope tautly stretched between hand and foot. Point to the knot at the center with your right first finger. Pass your open right hand down in front of it and then quickly snap your right fingers and lift that hand away as you secretly pull upward on the rope with your left hand so the knot instantly vanishes.

Instant One-Hand Knot

Hold your right hand out to the right side, shoulder high and palm to the audience, thumb up and fingertips to the right. Lay the rope over the top edge of the right hand so that the part hanging down at the back of the hand is less than a foot long. Now, catch the longer part of the rope, which passes down across the palm, between the third and little fingers, and say, "One hand."

Bend the right hand straight down from the wrist, fingertips toward the floor and back under, and grasp the short end of the rope between the first and second fingers. Keep hold of that end and shake the loop down off the back of the hand, so it falls to form a knot on the hanging rope. With practice, this can be done so swiftly that the sudden appearance of the knot really looks like magic. Show the knot and untie it.

INSTANT ONE-HAND KNOT

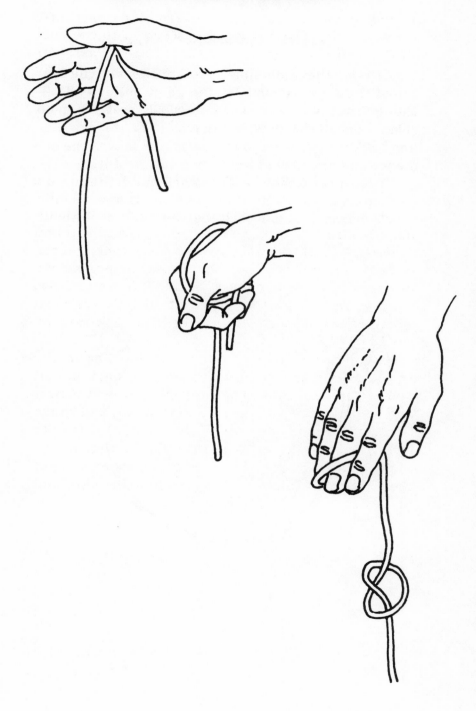

The Impossible Knot

It *would* be impossible to tie this knot at the center of the rope without letting go of either end, although that is what you seem to do. Secretly, you do release one of the ends, but in a way that brings that end back into your hand instantly and leaves the audience convinced that you never let go of it.

Take an end of the rope in each hand, thumbs up and palms toward you. Hold your hands apart so the rope's center hangs loosely between them. Without

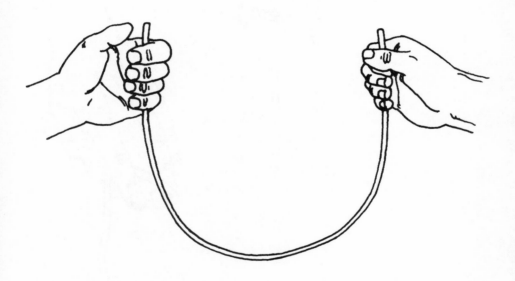

THE IMPOSSIBLE KNOT

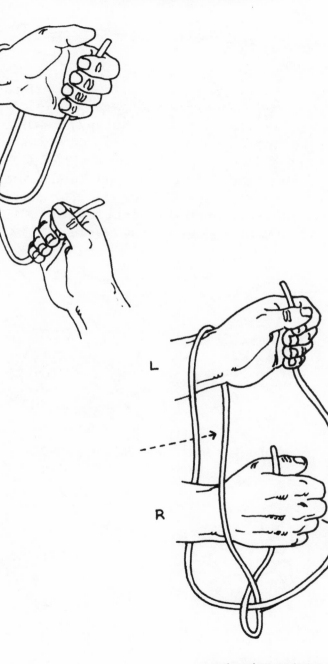

L

R

continued on next page . . .

THE IMPOSSIBLE KNOT—continued

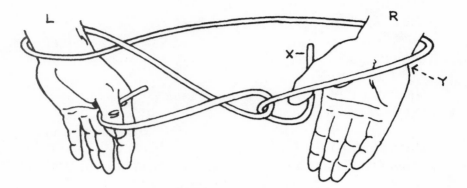

RIGHT THUMB RELEASES END "X" _
HAND CLOSES AROUND ROPE AT "Y"

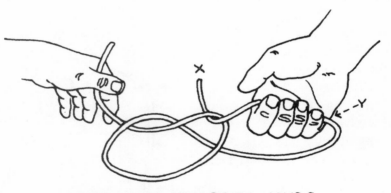

LOOPS DROP OFF BOTH HANDS

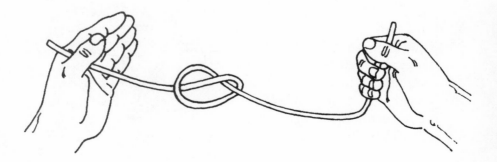

letting go of either end, bring your right hand up to the top of the left wrist and over the back of it to form a loop by draping the center of the rope over the top edge of the left wrist. Continue to draw your right hand down from the back of the left wrist until the right hand is about a foot beneath the bottom of the loop.

Lift your right hand toward you slightly and then push that hand *out from you* through the left side of the loop, to the *left* of the vertical strand that hangs down at the back of the loop. Twist the back of the right wrist out around that vertical strand, and then draw the right hand *in toward you* again, through the loop. Lift the right hand out to hold it in front of you, opposite the left hand.

At this point, a loop has been formed around each wrist, each hand still holds its end of the rope, and the knuckles of both hands are toward the front, thumbs up. The looped and twisted rope should be held tautly between them. You can pause, if you wish, to display the apparent knot that has been formed by the twisted loops. But from here on, the rest of the moves should be one continuous action, smoothly blended together without hesitation.

Turn both hands down toward the floor to let the loops fall off both wrists and, as you do that, secretly close the right fingers around the part of the rope that slides off the wrist into them, and release the end the right hand has been holding. As the loops fall, immediately draw both hands apart to tighten the knot that forms at the center of the rope, sliding your right hand out to its end, which seemingly has never left that hand. Hold up the rope, still gripped at both ends, and tell the audience, "Well, they say it's impossible ... Try it when you get home."

TWO MORE WITH ONE HAND

The Instant One-Hand Knot, previously explained in the *Basic Tricky-Knots Routine*, is among
the showiest and most impressive of all knot flour-
ishes. Here are two additional easy ways of performing it, both of which avoid the sometimes awkward
positioning and wrist-twisting of the standard method.

Simplicity One-Hand Knot

How it looks

You hang the center of a rope over one hand,
bring up the two ends, and hold them with the open
palm of the hand toward the audience. Without any
tricky moves, you simply drop one end and give the
rope a sharp downward shake. A knot suddenly appears, tied at its center.

What you do

Hold your right hand with its palm toward you,
thumb up, and fingertips to the left. Drape the center of the rope over the top of that hand, close to the
thumb. Half the rope hangs down over the back of
the hand and the other half hangs down over the
palm.

Close your left hand into a loose fist around both
hanging parts of the rope, slide the hand down to the

SIMPLICITY ONE-HAND KNOT

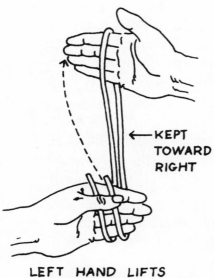

← KEPT
TOWARD
RIGHT

LEFT HAND LIFTS
BOTH ENDS

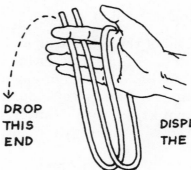

DROP
THIS
END

DISPLAYING
THE ROPE

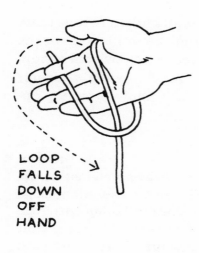

LOOP
FALLS
DOWN
OFF
HAND

bottom, lift both rope ends up together toward you, and bring the ends up to hold them between your right first and second fingers. (Be careful not to twist the ends as you lift them. The end that hangs down from the back of the right hand should be kept to the right.)

Turn the palm of your right hand to the audience to display the rope. When you are ready to produce the knot, drop the forward end of the rope from between your first and second fingers, keep hold of the other end, and in one continuing motion tilt your fingertips down toward the floor as you give your hand a sudden downward shake. The remaining loop will fall off your hand and form an instant knot at the rope's center.

Loop-Around One-Hand Knot

How it looks

Holding one end, you casually loop a rope around your hand, and turn the palm toward the audience so it can be seen that the rope is not twisted in any tricky way. Swinging the hand toward yourself again, you flick it down, and a knot instantly appears.

What you do

Start with the right palm toward you, thumb up, and fingertips to the left. Place one end of the rope into the crotch of the right thumb to hold it. Run your left hand down the rope to its center, bring that part up around the *back* of your right hand, and drape the center over the top edge of the right fin-

LOOP–AROUND ONE–HAND KNOT

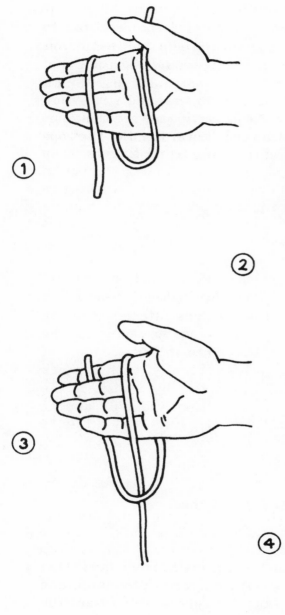

①

②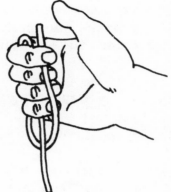

③

④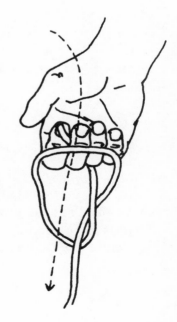

gers so the rope's other end hangs down across the palm. Remove your left hand.

Turn your right palm toward the audience to show the rope and then swing the palm toward you again. Quickly close your fingers against the palm, take the end of the rope out from under your thumb with your first and second fingers, and straighten out your hand. Tilt your fingertips toward the floor, give the hand a downward shake, and the knot appears at the center of the hanging rope.

A SPECTACLE OF KNOTS

How it looks

Here's a brief routine based on the tying of a single knot. You start by tying an ordinary Ring Hitch in the standard way, then demonstrate how it can be tied instantly with only one hand. Spreading out the knot's loops, you form them into an imitation pair of old-fashioned "spectacles." Finally, with a quick twisting of the loops, you magically transform the Hitch into two other knots that suddenly appear along the rope—an Overhand Knot and a Figure Eight.

What you need

A 4-foot length of soft clothesline.

What you do

To "set the stage" for the instant one-hand tying that is to come, you first tie a Ring Hitch with both hands, as follows. Take the rope at its center with your right hand and turn the left palm toward you. Place the center loop under the left thumb to hold it there, with about 2 inches of the loop extending above your left hand. Grasp both bottom ends of the rope with your right hand and bring them up together in front of the palm, over the left thumb, and through the center loop. Pull them down to form the ordinary Ring Hitch around the left thumb and turn the hand palm-outward to display it.

"This knot has a dozen different names and a hundred different uses," you say. "It is called a Cow Hitch, a Carriage Hitch, a Sling Hitch, a Hoist Hitch, a Ring Hitch, and most of us know it as a Tag Knot, used for tying price tags to things."

The One-Hand Ring Hitch

As you speak, untie the Hitch from your left thumb by pulling out the two ends, and take the center of the rope with your left hand. Hold out your right hand with its palm toward the floor, fingertips toward the right, and the tip of the thumb thrust straight out toward the audience. Drape the center of the rope over the right thumb, so both ends hang down evenly at the bottom.

"Sailors sometimes called it a Lanyard Hitch," you say, "and some old salts could tie it quicker than you can blink . . . and with only one hand."

Bend your right fingers down and back toward you to grasp between the first and second fingers the part of the rope that hangs nearest to your body. Twist your hand toward the rear and then up and straight out to the right again, palm down as at the start. This catches a little loop around the tip of the

ONE-HAND RING HITCH

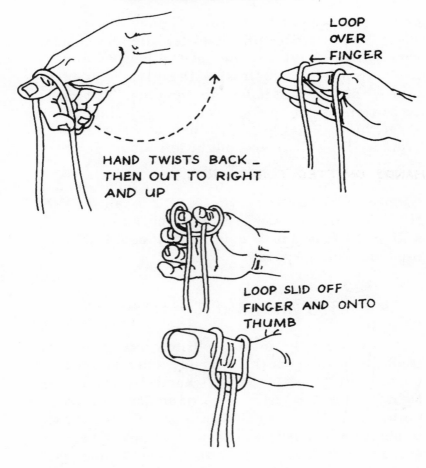

LOOP OVER FINGER ←

HAND TWISTS BACK — THEN OUT TO RIGHT AND UP

LOOP SLID OFF FINGER AND ONTO THUMB

A PAIR OF SPECTACLES

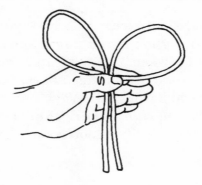

TWO KNOTS FROM ONE

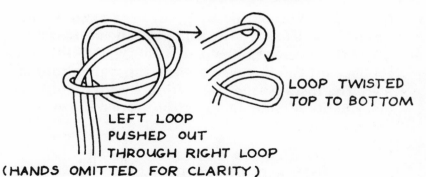

LOOP TWISTED
TOP TO BOTTOM

LEFT LOOP
PUSHED OUT
THROUGH RIGHT LOOP
(HANDS OMITTED FOR CLARITY)

LEFT END
PUT THROUGH
LOOPS — PULLED
OUT TO FRONT

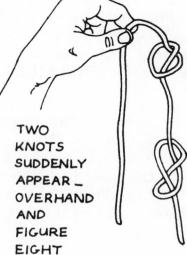

TWO
KNOTS
SUDDENLY
APPEAR —
OVERHAND
AND
FIGURE
EIGHT

first finger. Without pausing, turn the hand thumb-upward, palm toward the audience, and press the tip of the first finger against the tip of the thumb. Slide the loop off the finger and on to the thumb to complete the instant One-Hand Ring Hitch, timing the movements of your hand to the words as you say, "Just . . . like . . . this!"

A Pair of Spectacles

Hold your right hand high to show the Hitch tied around your thumb, then bring that hand down in front of you, palm toward you. Bring your left hand, palm toward you, over beneath the right thumb, and slide the bottom of the loop down about 2 inches. Grip it there, along with the two hanging strands, between your left thumb and first finger, and slide the Hitch off your right thumb. (Your left hand will hold the rope as it is until the end of the routine.)

With your right hand, turn the two side loops of the Hitch out flat to the left and right and shape them with your fingers to look like a pair of large eyeglasses. Turn your left palm out to show the "glasses" and say, "A pair of old-fashioned spectacles." Lift them to your eyes and look out at the audience through them. *"Spectacular—isn't it?"*

Two Knots from One

Bring your left hand down in front of you, turn-ing the palm toward you again. With your right hand, bend the left loop over to the right, push it out through the right loop from back to front, and then give it one quick downward twist from top to bottom, moving your left thumb a little to take a fresh grip on the two loops at their base.

"We had one knot," you say, as you reach down with your right hand to take the end of the rope that is hanging to the *left* and hold it up. "But if this goes into that ... " Push that end of the rope through both loops at once, from back to front, and draw the end out to the front as you release the loops from under your left thumb to hold the rope stretched between your hands. Two knots suddenly appear, spaced along the rope — "... now we have two, a pair of knots everybody knows."

Drop the end of the rope from your right hand, hold the dangling rope high with your left hand, and point with your right finger to one knot and then the other. "An Overhand Knot and a Figure Eight."

KNOT A ROPE AND CATCH A RIBBON

How it looks

You show a rope, tie it into a large loop and, as you pull your hands apart and tighten the knot, a bright red ribbon suddenly appears, tied to the center of the rope.

What you need

A 4-foot length of soft white clothesline.
A 3-foot length of red satin ribbon, 1 inch wide.
A wire twist-tie, the kind made for tying plastic sandwich bags.

The secret

The ribbon, tightly rolled into a small coil around the rope, is secretly hidden in one hand from the time the rope is first shown. But the rope is so freely displayed and drawn back and forth through the hand that the sudden appearance of the ribbon tied to the rope takes the audience by surprise.

Lay the ribbon out horizontally flat on a table top. Place the center of the rope vertically on top of the center of the horizontal ribbon. Fold the left side of the ribbon over to bring both ends together at the right, so the ribbon is now at a right angle to the rope.

Take both ends of the ribbon together and start rolling the doubled ribbon tightly in upon itself toward the center of the rope, continuing until the entire ribbon has been rolled up beside the rope.

Wrap the twist-tie tightly around the rope and ribbon to hold them together. The twist-tie is used simply to keep the rolled ribbon securely in place, so you can prepare the rope in advance and carry it with the rest of your props. The final set-up, done just before your performance, takes only a second. Place the rope on the table with its center hidden behind some other prop, and then unfasten the twist-tie and discard it, leaving the coiled ribbon lying beside the rope's center and to its right.

What you do

Take up the rope at its center with your right hand, by closing your fingers into a loose fist around both the rope and ribbon. Turn the back of your hand toward the audience and lift up the rope to show it, keeping the ribbon hidden inside your fingers.

With your left hand, take the end of the rope that hangs down nearest you. Draw that end down, pulling the rope down through your right fist and the concealed ribbon until only about 3 inches of rope extend above the top of the right hand. Then, lift your left hand, with the end of rope it is holding, up opposite your right hand. At this point, each hand should be holding one end of the rope in a similar way, fingers closed around it and backs of the hands toward the audience. Pause a moment to display the plain rope hanging down between your hands.

Bring your left hand over to your right hand, and lay the left end of the rope across the right end to tie a knot that forms a big loop. Then, take both rope ends and hold them with the left hand. Without opening the right hand, slide it and the hidden ribbon down the rope to its center at the bottom of the loop.

Immediately, raise the right hand up again, lifting the center part of the rope that your hand is still closed around. Quickly take the right end of the rope away from your left hand, by gripping that end between your right thumb and first finger. Keep the other rope end in your left hand and suddenly pull both hands wide apart and out to the sides, finally opening your right fist to release the ribbon.

The outward pull of your hands jerks the suddenly unrolling ribbon into view and tightens the knot around it as it magically appears, tied at the center of the rope.

KNOT A ROPE AND CATCH A RIBBON

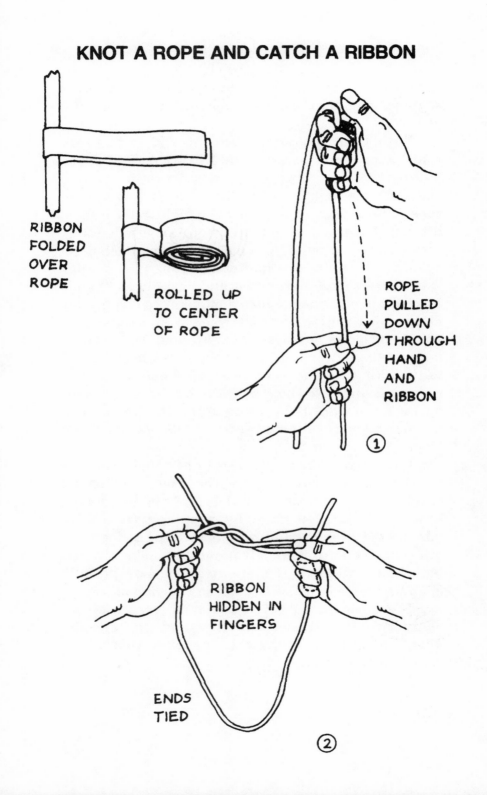

RIBBON
FOLDED
OVER
ROPE

ROLLED UP
TO CENTER
OF ROPE

ROPE
PULLED
DOWN
THROUGH
HAND
AND
RIBBON

①

RIBBON
HIDDEN IN
FINGERS

ENDS
TIED

②

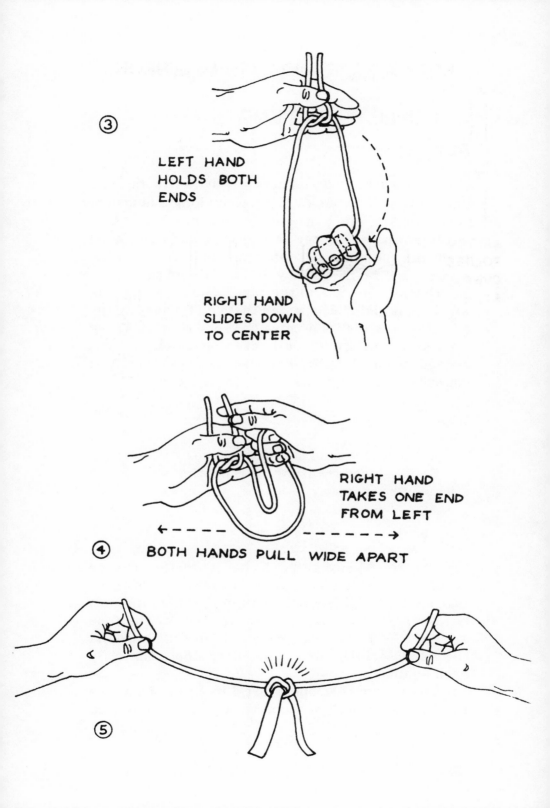

③ LEFT HAND HOLDS BOTH ENDS

RIGHT HAND SLIDES DOWN TO CENTER

RIGHT HAND TAKES ONE END FROM LEFT

④ BOTH HANDS PULL WIDE APART

⑤

TRIPLE FLYING KNOTS

How it looks

"One knot ... Two knots ... Three knots," you
say, as you tie three knots, spaced along a length of
rope. Holding one rope end in each hand, you suddenly snap the center of the rope forward, as if
throwing the knots out into the audience. All three
knots vanish. "There they go! ... Knots to you!"

Quickly you coil up the rope, take it by one end,
and hold it high. "Now watch them all fly back again.
... Knots to me!" You give the rope a sharp shake
and, as it uncoils, three knots appear once more,
spaced down along it. Pointing to each knot, you
count them aloud, "One ... Two ... Three!"

What you need

A 4-foot length of soft clothesline.

Double-faced transparent tape, the kind that is
sticky on both sides.

The secret

The rope has bands of the double-faced tape
spaced along it, which help you to tie a row of three
fake knots. The knots look genuine, but they instantly fall apart and vanish when the ends of the rope
are pulled. The way the rope is then coiled around
the hand secretly forms the three knots that "fly
back again."

To prepare the rope, start 6 inches in from one
end and wrap a 2-inch length of the double-faced

tape in a *tight* band around it. Move along the rope 6 inches and wrap another strip of tape tightly around it. Continue until you have wrapped six little strips of sticky tape around the rope, spaced 6 inches apart. (After the rope has been used a dozen or so times, the tape should be snipped off and replaced with new pieces.)

What you do

Pick up the rope and hold it with both hands about a foot in from the left end. The hands should be palms down, with the rope held between the thumb and first two fingers of each hand. Casually slide your hands a little apart along the rope until you feel the first two sticky bands of tape with your left and right fingers.

Holding those two bands, move your right hand forward toward the audience and then over to the left to form a loop in the rope that brings the two sticky tapes together. Give them a little squeeze with your left thumb and finger so they stick together tightly.

Keep that loop held as it is with your left hand. Slide your right hand loosely along the whole length of the rope to its right end. Take that end and put it in through the loop *from the front*, pointing the end toward yourself. Draw the end through, just as if tying a knot, then drop that end and bring your right hand back to hold the rope near its center. Remove your left hand and let the first knot dangle down.

Repeat the same moves to tie a second false knot with the second set of sticky tapes, and then a third knot with the third pair of tapes.

Hold one rope end in each hand, with the rope

hanging somewhat slackly between them, and display the row of knots. Swing the center of the rope forward, as if "throwing" the knots, and suddenly stretch both hands out to the sides to snap the rope taut. That pulls the stuck-together loops apart and all three knots instantly vanish.

Drop the left end of the rope from the left hand and turn the palm of this hand toward you. Bring the right rope end over and put that end into the crotch of the left thumb, closing the thumb to hold it there. Remove your right hand so the rope is left hanging down from your left hand.

What you seem to do now is to gather up the rope in a series of loops quickly and casually, hanging each of the loops over your left hand to coil the rope around it. But this looping is done in a way that secretly forms three knots that will appear when the rope is shaken out.

Bring your right hand, palm up, under the rope that hangs down from your left hand, so the rope lies across both palms and so the little fingers of both hands are about 6 inches apart. The right side of the rope should pass under the right thumb.

Close the right fingers to make a fist, and then turn your right hand counterclockwise, palm downward. A loop of rope now runs through your right fingers. Hang that loop over the outstretched fingers of your left hand and leave it there.

Turn the right palm up again and move it along the rope to where you can make a second loop the same way. Hang that loop over your left hand. Then, make a similar third loop and hang it over your left hand.

Now, put the first two fingers of your right hand

TRIPLE FLYING KNOTS—1

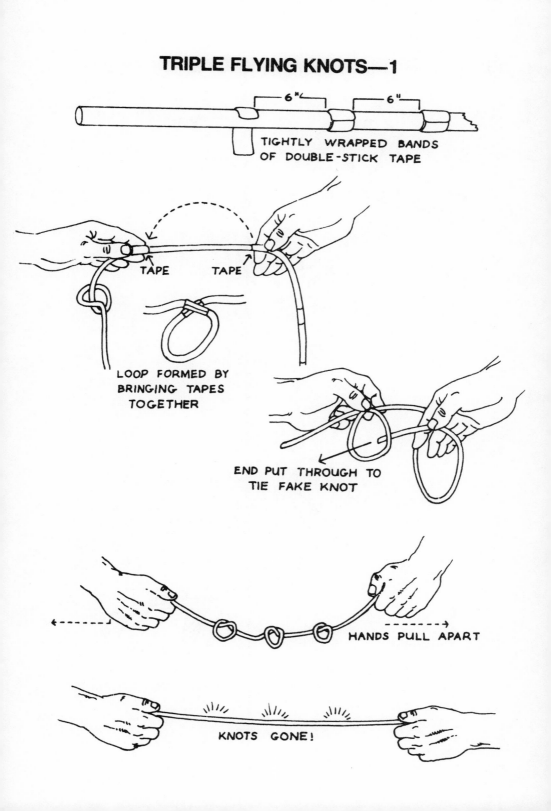

6" 6"

TIGHTLY WRAPPED BANDS
OF DOUBLE-STICK TAPE

TAPE   TAPE

LOOP FORMED BY
BRINGING TAPES
TOGETHER

END PUT THROUGH TO
TIE FAKE KNOT

HANDS PULL APART

KNOTS GONE!

TRIPLE FLYING KNOTS—2

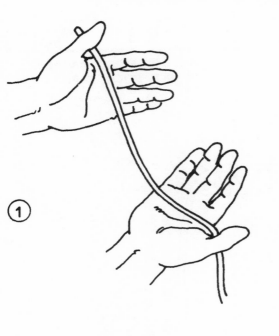

①

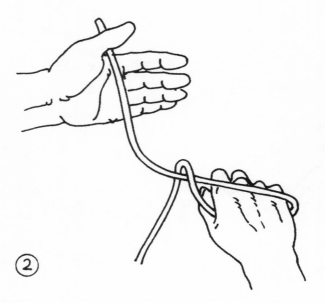

②

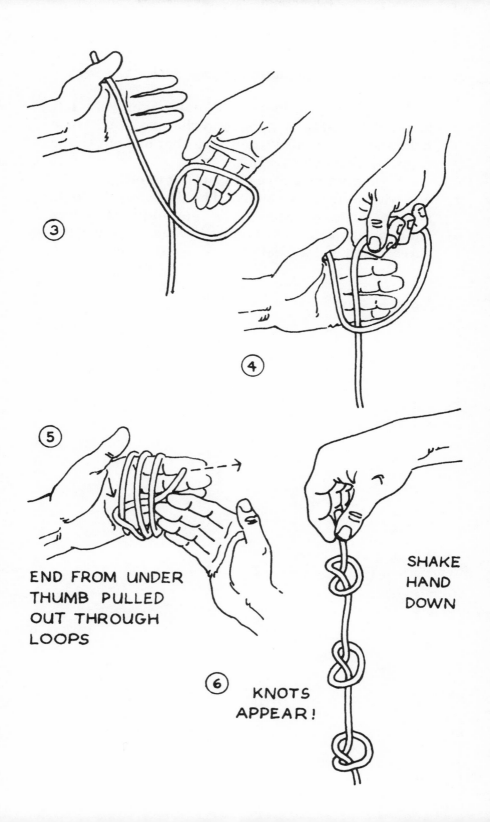

③

④

⑤

END FROM UNDER
THUMB PULLED
OUT THROUGH
LOOPS

⑥ KNOTS
APPEAR!

SHAKE
HAND
DOWN

in *through* all the loops that hang over your left hand. With those fingers, grip the end of the rope held under your left thumb. Pull that end out to the right, up through the coils.

Slide the coiled rope off your left hand, grasp the end with your right hand, and hold the rope up high, still coiled as it hangs from your hand. Give it a sharp downward shake and, as it comes uncoiled, the three knots will appear, spaced down along it.

3

PENETRATIONS

COFFEE, TEA, OR MAGIC

How it looks

You show a rope and drape the center of it over your hand so the two ends hang to the bottom. Then, you pick up a coffee cup and hold it by its handle with the same hand. "I call this one 'Coffee, Tea, or Magic,' " you say. "I'm sorry there is no coffee or tea to offer you. But there is—*magic*!"

You grip the cup with your other hand and quickly pull it down to leave it hanging at the center

COFFEE, TEA, OR MAGIC

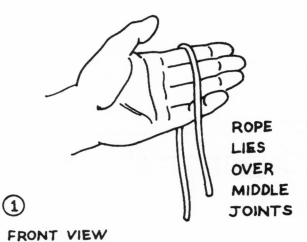

ROPE
LIES
OVER
MIDDLE
JOINTS

① FRONT VIEW

② SIDE VIEW

RIGHT HAND
PUTS CUP INTO
LEFT_ HANDLE
AGAINST MIDDLE
FINGERS

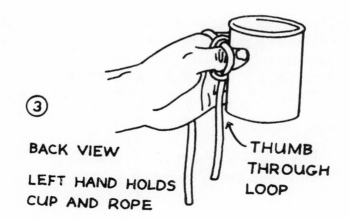

③

BACK VIEW

LEFT HAND HOLDS
CUP AND ROPE

THUMB
THROUGH
LOOP

CUP PULLED DOWN
OUT OF LEFT HAND

PULLS CENTER
LOOP DOWN

END PULLS UP
THROUGH
HANDLE

④

of the rope, magically linked to the rope by its handle. Taking one end of the rope in each hand, you tilt the rope up and down so the linked cup slides back and forth on it. "At least, it's a new way to dry the dishes," you say. "Just hang them out on the line."

What you need

A 3-foot length of soft clothesline.
A coffee mug with a large handle.

The secret

As you place the cup in your hand at the start of the trick, you secretly push a small loop through the handle and hook it over the tip of the thumb holding the cup. When you pull the cup down, it automatically draws one of the rope's ends through the handle, but it happens so quickly spectators will be convinced the two ends were never out of sight.

There is nothing to prepare. Just have the cup and rope on your table.

What you do

Show the rope and hold it at the center with your right hand, so the two ends hang down. Hold your left hand out to the side of your body, fingertips to the left and palm toward the audience. Hang the center of the rope over the top of the left fingers, with the part that comes down the front of the hand lying against the fingers' middle joints.

Pick up the cup by holding the front of it, leaving the handle free, and bring it to the held-out left hand. As your hands come together, the cup and right hand partly hide the left hand from front view, which covers the one secret move you have to make. There's no need to hurry, but it should look as though you are merely taking the cup from your right hand with the left. Here, in detail, is what you do:

With your right hand, touch the back of the cup's handle against the two middle left fingers close to where they join the palm. Draw back the left second finger and with the tip of it push a little loop of rope through the handle toward you. Stick your left thumb up through that loop and hook it well over the tip of the thumb. Then, close the left thumb and fingers against the sides of the handle to hold the cup and remove your right hand.

Holding your fingers that way, you can show the cup and rope quite freely, since the secret loop is hidden behind the cup. Now, turn your left hand in toward you, with its back to the audience, and hold it high in front of you. When you are ready to link the cup to the rope, grasp the cup firmly with your right hand around the outside of it, fingers in front and thumb at the back.

Quickly pull the cup straight down toward the floor, closing your left hand around the two ends of the rope to hold them as they are drawn to the top of the hand and the center loop is pulled to the bottom. Swiftly pulling the cup down automatically draws the rope through the cup's handle.

Remove your right hand and leave the cup hanging at the bottom of the loop. Then bring the right hand up, take one end of the rope from your left hand, and spread your hands apart. Tilt your hands up and down so the cup slides back and forth on the rope stretched between them.

AT THE SPECTATOR'S COMMAND

How it looks

You thread a ribbon through a large brass ring, tie the ends of the ribbon so the ring hangs at the bottom of the knotted loop, and thread six smaller brass rings on the ribbon. Holding an empty paper bag open end downward with your other hand, you put the ribbon and rings up into the bag, pull the top end of the ribbon up through a slit in the bag, and hang that end over your finger so it remains in full view.

"Unless there is some magic that can pass solid metal through solid metal, there is no way the rings can be removed from the ribbon," you say, as you shake the upside-down bag to rattle the rings held on the ribbon inside it. You turn to one of the spectators. "Will you, sir, please command the magic to happen? Whenever you wish, just shout out the word 'Now!' "

The instant he shouts, the six small rings fall free, dropping from the paper bag to clatter on the table. You pull the ribbon up through the slit in the bag to show that the big ring still hangs at the bottom of the knotted loop. The other rings seem to have passed right through it at the spectator's command.

What you need

A 19-inch length of bright red satin ribbon, 1 inch wide.

A thick brass-plated metal ring about 3 inches in diameter.

Six smaller brass-plated rings, each about 1¼ inches in diameter. (Such rings are available in various sizes at sewing and needlework counters and at craft and hobby shops.)

A flat-bottomed brown paper "lunch" bag, approximately 10 inches high and 5 inches wide.

A pair of scissors.

The secret

The two ends of the loop are secretly switched when the ribbon is put up into the bag at the start of the trick. It is really the bottom end of the ribbon that is pulled up through the slit, instead of the ribbon's top end as the audience believes. Part of the ribbon is held pinched inside a corner of the bag by your fingers, holding the bag from the outside, which is what keeps the rings from falling off the ribbon until the spectator gives his command.

Open the paper bag, turn it bottom up, and use the scissors to cut a horizontal slit across the bottom to within ½ inch of each side. That is the only preparation. The props are not faked in any way. Have the opened bag on your table with its *bottom toward the audience* and the rings and ribbon beside it. (The bag is placed that way so you can pick it up to hold it at the corner where your fingers will need to be to hold the ribbon.)

What you do

Show the large ring and ribbon, thread the ring on the ribbon, and bring the two ribbon ends to the

AT THE SPECTATOR'S COMMAND

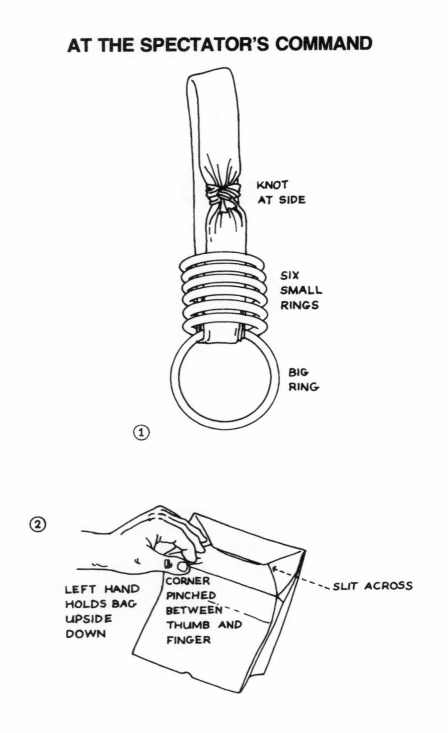

KNOT
AT SIDE

SIX
SMALL
RINGS

BIG
RING

①

②

LEFT HAND
HOLDS BAG
UPSIDE
DOWN

CORNER
PINCHED
BETWEEN
THUMB AND
FINGER

SLIT ACROSS

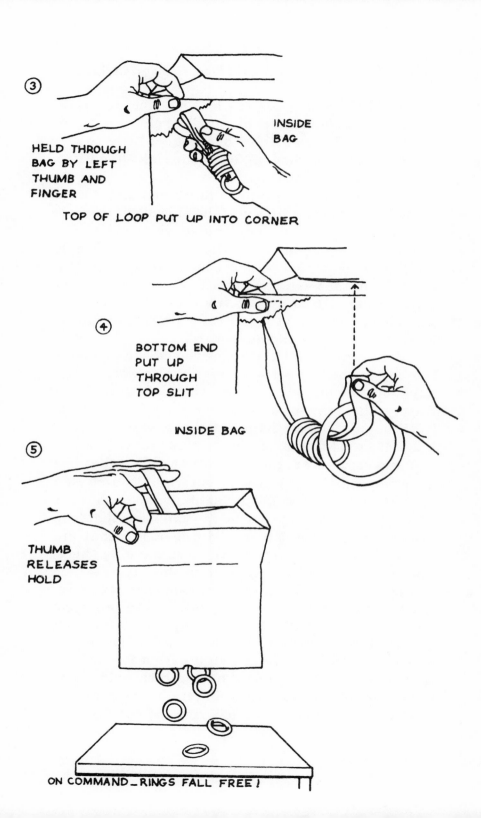

③ HELD THROUGH
BAG BY LEFT
THUMB AND
FINGER

INSIDE
BAG

TOP OF LOOP PUT UP INTO CORNER

④ BOTTOM END
PUT UP
THROUGH
TOP SLIT

INSIDE BAG

⑤ THUMB
RELEASES
HOLD

ON COMMAND — RINGS FALL FREE!

top so the ring hangs at the bottom. Hold the ends together and tie them with a small single knot. Show the knot by drawing the ribbon out a little to the right, so that the knot will be at the right-hand side of the loop, *not* at the top.

Take the small rings, one at a time, and thread them down over the ribbon to the big ring at the bottom. Then hold the ribbon loop about an inch from the top between your right thumb and first finger. Pick up the paper bag with the left hand by bringing the palm of that hand against the bottom of the bag at its upper left corner, so that you can hold it at that corner between the left thumb and first finger. Hold the bag open end downward.

With your right hand, bring the ribbon up inside the bag to the left corner. Pinch that corner of the bag from the outside between your left thumb and finger to hold the top end of the ribbon. Grip it tightly through the bag. Immediately move your right hand down a little inside the bag and pinch the *bottom* end of the loop, the part of the ribbon that lies over the big ring, between your right thumb and first finger. Pull that end straight up and push it out through the slit in the bag so you can hang that loop over your extended left second finger. Lift that finger so the audience can see the loop hanging there, and remove your right hand from the bag.

To the audience, this should look as if you merely brought the top end of the ribbon up through the bag and out the slit. But the ends have now been switched to turn the ribbon loop upside down. The small rings would fall right off it except for the fact that what was the top end is now secretly held inside the corner of the bag, gripped there by the pressure of your left thumb and finger from the outside.

Hold the bag that way with your left hand and rattle the rings inside it. Bring the open end of the bag down close to the top of the table, and tell the spectator, "Whenever you wish, just shout out the word 'Now!' "

When he calls his command, lift your left thumb slightly to release that end of the ribbon. The rings fall down and out of the bag to clatter to the table. With your right hand, pull the entire ribbon up through the slit in the bag and hold it high to show that the big ring still hangs at the bottom of it.

OFF-AGAIN, ON-AGAIN RING AND STRING

How it looks

You give someone a small plastic ring to hold for a moment while you show a string and bring its two ends together in your left hand so it forms a loop with its center at the bottom. Taking the ring, you thread it on the string and knot the ends of the string together. The ring hangs at the bottom of the loop.

Reaching down with your right hand, you magically pull the ring right through the string, and it visibly comes off into your hand. Then, you put the ring into the hand holding the string, pull it down along the string again, and the two become linked. The ring is back on the tied loop of string, and the ring and string can be thoroughly examined.

What you need

A 3½-foot length of string.

Two identical plastic curtain rings, ¾ inch in diameter.

A facial tissue.

A coping saw or other small handsaw for cutting thin plastic.

The secret

Although the audience is aware of only one ring, two rings are used, one of them faked by being cut. The fake is made by simply clamping one of the rings upright and sawing straight down through one side. Because of the springy plastic, the cut ends hold together, leaving a small slit that can be pushed open to pass the string through it. The rings are handled so that nobody gets a close look at the cut one.

Thread the faked ring on the string and bring it to the center, with both ends of the string hanging down from the ring. Loosely gather up the string and put it into the left pocket of your jacket so that the threaded ring lies on top of the bunched string. Crumple the facial tissue and stuff it down inside your breast pocket to slightly bulge open the top of that pocket. Have the unfaked ring in your right pocket.

What you do

Take out the unfaked ring, show it, and say, "This ring has a hole in it." Give it to someone and ask, "Can you find the hole?" While he is examining it, reach into your left pocket with the left hand. Get the edge of the faked ring into the crotch between your first and second fingers, so you can hold it between the sides of those fingers at their base, and then bring out the bunched string with the back of that hand toward the audience.

Shake out the string so both ends hang down. Take the end that is toward you, bring it up to the top, and drop it down over the back of your left hand. You can now draw the string back and forth through your hand and through the ring that is secretly threaded on it, and it looks to the audience as if you were merely holding a length of string.

Draw the string down until about 3 inches extend above the top of the left hand. Bring the bottom end up and hold both ends beside each other at the top, forming a loop with its center hanging at the bottom.

Ask the person who is examining the ring, "Did you find the hole?" Then smile, and explain, "The hole in the ring is the part in the center—like the hole in a doughnut." (This little joke provides a way to have the ring examined and also lets you take your time getting the string and faked ring out of your pocket and positioned properly.)

Take the unfaked ring from the spectator. Hold it by one side between your right thumb and first finger and thread it over the top left end of the string. Bring it down inside your left hand until that ring rests on top of the split ring hidden there. Press your left thumb against both rings to hold them together and remove your right hand for an instant. Then, bring your right hand up inside your left hand again. Draw the bottom ring (the split one) down the string to the bottom of the loop and leave it hanging

OFF–AGAIN ON–AGAIN RING AND STRING

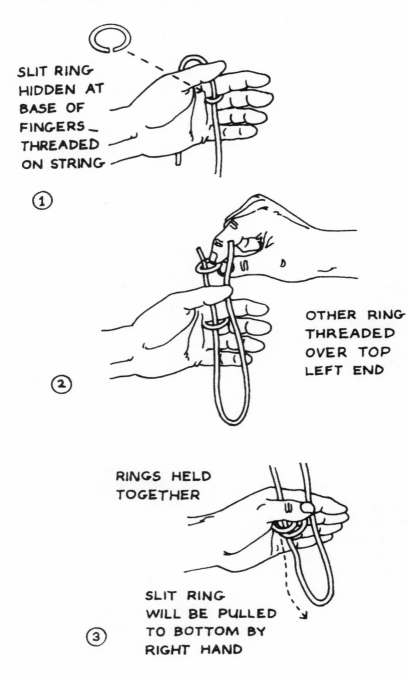

SLIT RING
HIDDEN AT
BASE OF
FINGERS
THREADED
ON STRING

①

OTHER RING
THREADED
OVER TOP
LEFT END

②

RINGS HELD
TOGETHER

SLIT RING
WILL BE PULLED
TO BOTTOM BY
③ RIGHT HAND

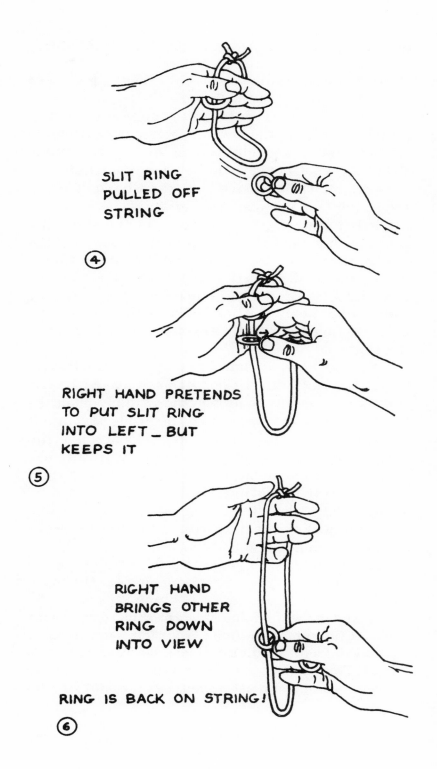

SLIT RING
PULLED OFF
STRING

④

RIGHT HAND PRETENDS
TO PUT SLIT RING
INTO LEFT — BUT
KEEPS IT

⑤

RIGHT HAND
BRINGS OTHER
RING DOWN
INTO VIEW

RING IS BACK ON STRING!

⑥

there. Your left thumb keeps the other ring pressed against the inside of the fingers.

Use both hands to tie the top ends of the string together, keeping the lower fingers partly closed so the left hand can hide its ring during the tying. Draw the knot out a little between your hands to show it, and then remove your right hand, keeping the string held up with your left hand.

Bring your right hand down to the split ring that now hangs at the bottom of the loop. Take the ring in that hand, feeling around it with the thumb to find the split. Secretly push it open and pull the ring right off the string. Show the ring with your right hand, holding it up between the thumb and first two fingers, with the tip of the thumb covering the split.

Now, bring your right hand up to your left, as if to put the ring into the left hand to leave it there. But as your hands come together, simply push the front edge of that ring against the inside of your left hand, so the ring is pushed back into your right fingers where your thumb can hold it. Keep the fake ring in the right hand. With the tips of your right fingers, pull the other ring (the unfaked one) straight down along the string out of your left hand. They appear linked again, with the ring back on the string, hanging at the bottom.

Keep the backs of your right fingers toward the audience and bring the right hand up near the top of the loop. With that hand, take one strand of the string and draw the hand straight back toward your body. At the same time, move your left hand straight out to the front, holding the loop between your two hands. This brings your right hand directly above your bulged-open breast pocket. Let the split ring secretly drop from your right hand into that pocket and immediately swing both hands out horizontally in front of you, tilting the loop up and down to slide the other ring back and forth on it.

You are now "clean," with nothing to hide, as you hand the knotted string and the ring to the spectator, and say, "I told you there was a hole in the ring—but that has nothing to do with the magic."

DISCO MAGIC

How it looks

"Here's something you can do with old records when you're tired of playing them," you say, as you show two phonograph records and a red ribbon. You thread the ribbon through the hole in one of the records, tie it around, and then hang the other record on the ribbon. "Just string them up like this, hang them from the ceiling, and you've got yourself a work of art—a disco mobile! It's practically priceless. *Nobody* would pay *any* price to have it."

You take one end of the ribbon in each hand, so the records hang fastened at its center. "I could tell you that this mobile is an artistic expression of the Thirteenth Dimension," you say. "But you wouldn't know what I was talking about—and neither would I. All I know is that if you watch it long enough, you get the sensation that these records melt right through the ribbon and flip themselves off into space. Of course, it doesn't really happen. But it sure *looks* like it happens."

As you draw your hands apart, the two records

pop up into the air and fall free, seeming to visibly penetrate the ribbon. "There they go!"

What you need

A 42-inch length of red satin ribbon, 1 inch wide.

Two standard 45 RPM phonograph records. These have center holes about 1½ inches in diameter. (Choose records you no longer want to play, because using them in the trick will scratch them.)

The secret

The records and ribbon are unprepared and nothing else is used. The whole secret is in the handling of the ribbon, which involves an easy and convincing switch of the two ends. Have the records and ribbon on your table.

What you do

Hold one of the records upright with your left hand by placing that hand around the left side of the record near the top, fingers in front, and thumb at the rear. Hang the center of the ribbon over the top edge of the record, then pull the ribbon at the back down a few inches so the front end is a little shorter than the back end.

Place the tip of your left thumb on the left edge of the ribbon that hangs down at the back. Your thumb should be just above and slightly to the left of the record's center hole. Keep the left edge of the ribbon held under your thumb during the moves that follow.

What you *seem* to do now, as the audience sees

it, is to bring the front end of the ribbon in through
the hole in the record, then up over the top, and back
down through the hole again. But what you *really* do
is switch the two ends of the ribbon. The switch is
almost automatic.

Start with your right hand at the front of the
record. Push part of the ribbon in through the center
hole from the front, so that a small loop hangs
through toward the back. Move your right hand to
the back with its palm toward you. Put your first finger through the ribbon loop, and then bring the rest
of the fingers beneath the ribbon that hangs down
over the back of the record.

Now, simply slide your right hand straight
down the ribbon to the very bottom end. This pulls
the rest of the front end of the ribbon in through the
hole. But since that end was shorter, moving your
hand down also pulls the short *front* end out of your
fingers and leaves them holding the bottom end of
the *back* part of the ribbon. (This has been explained
in detail so you will understand what happens, but
you don't have to think about it while performing
the trick. Just bring your hand straight down along
the ribbons and the switch is automatic.)

Without pausing, lift the bottom ribbon end
right up over the top edge of the record, down the
front to the center hole, then push that end through
the hole, front to back.

The edge of ribbon your left thumb has been
holding since the start of the trick will be twisted
into a loop by this switching of the ribbon's ends.
That loop, hidden at the back behind the top of the
record, is the real center of the ribbon. Hold that
loop firmly with your left thumb. Bring your right
hand down to the two bottom ends of the ribbon and

DISCO MAGIC

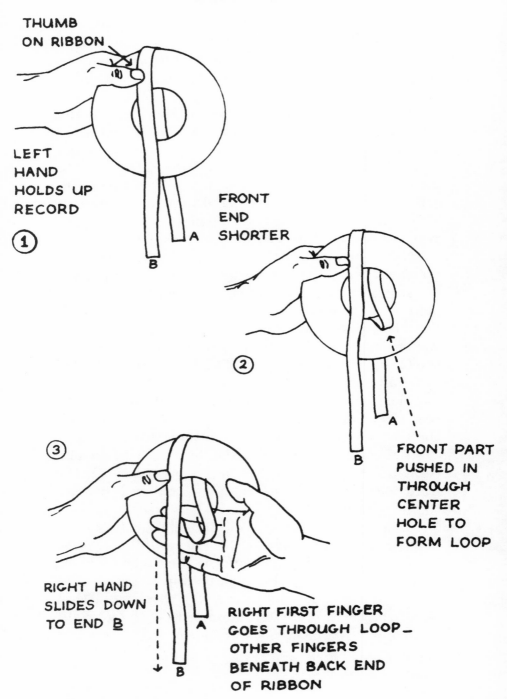

THUMB ON RIBBON

LEFT HAND HOLDS UP RECORD

①

FRONT END SHORTER

B

A

②

A

B

FRONT PART PUSHED IN THROUGH CENTER HOLE TO FORM LOOP

③

RIGHT HAND SLIDES DOWN TO END B

A

B

RIGHT FIRST FINGER GOES THROUGH LOOP — OTHER FINGERS BENEATH BACK END OF RIBBON

TOP OF OTHER RECORD
WILL GO HERE

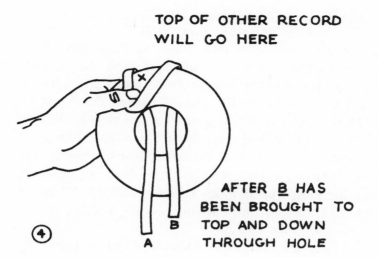

④

AFTER **B** HAS
BEEN BROUGHT TO
TOP AND DOWN
THROUGH HOLE

⑤

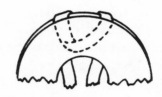

LOOP SANDWICHED BETWEEN
TOP EDGES OF RECORDS

BOTH RECORDS
HANG ON RIBBON

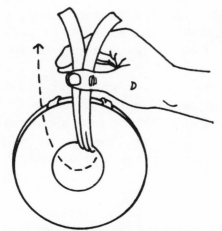

TWO ENDS PULLED THROUGH
HOLE IN SECOND RECORD—
THEN UP TO TOP

give them a slight downward tug, to "demonstrate" that the ribbon is tightly looped around the record.

Take up the second record with your right hand. Place the top side of the second record flat against the top side of the first, pressing them together to trap the loop of ribbon between them. Remove your left thumb from between the records and take a new grip with that thumb to hold both records together. With your right hand, draw the ribbon ends through the center hole of the second record, pulling them through from front to back.

Lift the two ends of ribbon together straight up to the top and remove your left hand. The two records now hang on the ribbons that are held at the top by your right hand. (The weight of the second record, resting against the hidden loop, holds them on the ribbon together.)

Display the records hanging that way as you talk about the "mobile." Then, take one end of the ribbon in your left hand, the other end in your right hand, and *gently* draw your hands apart. The hanging records will remain on the ribbon as long as they are kept *vertical*. But as soon as you spread your hands far enough apart so the records are *horizontal*, the hidden loop will pull free and the records will fall from the ribbon.

You can release the records whenever you wish, timing it to your patter. Spread your hands with a sudden little outward and upward snap of the ribbon and the records will pop up into the air and fall free to the floor while the ribbon remains stretched out between your hands.

LIGHTNING RING ON ROPE

How it looks

You show a large brass ring and hang it over the open palm of your hand. Then you take two ends of a rope in the same hand and hold the ends in full view, with the rest of the rope hanging down in a long loop.

"I'm about to do two things at once," you say, "both of which may seem quite impossible. Without letting go of the ends of the rope, I am going to tie a knot in the center of it. At the same time, I intend to pass this metal ring right through the rope and link it into the middle of that knot. And it all happens much faster than I can hope to explain it to you."

You take hold of the ring with your other hand, swiftly pull it down over the rope, and the ring instantly becomes linked and tied with a knot that appears at the center, as you say, "Just ... like ... that!"

What you need

A brass-plated ring about 5 inches in diameter (big enough to fit easily over your hand).

A 4-foot length of soft clothesline.

The secret

The rope and ring are unprepared. The trick is accomplished with one simple move that instantly forms a standard Ring Hitch.

LIGHTNING RING ON ROPE

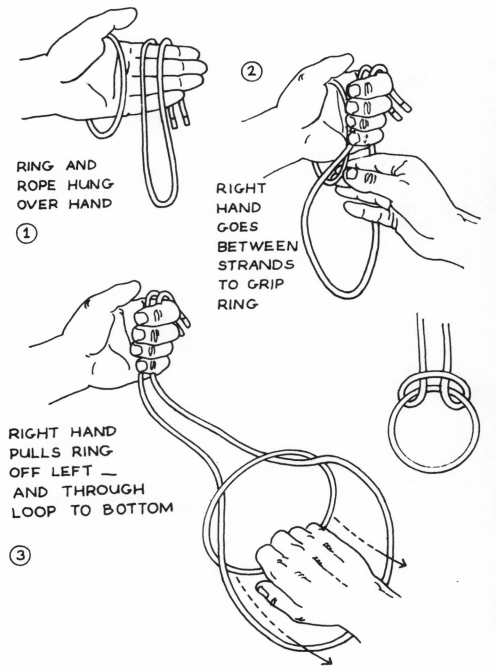

RING AND
ROPE HUNG
OVER HAND

① 1

② 2

RIGHT
HAND
GOES
BETWEEN
STRANDS
TO GRIP
RING

RIGHT HAND
PULLS RING
OFF LEFT —
AND THROUGH
LOOP TO BOTTOM

③ 3

What you do

Show the ring and turn your left palm up flat in front of you, thumb to the front, fingertips to the right. Hàng the ring over the hand, close to the thumb. Take one end of the rope in each hand, hold it stretched out between them to show it, and bring both ends evenly together. Lay the two ends on your left fingers, to the far right of the ring, with the ends hanging over the front edge of the hand by a few inches so they will remain in full view, and the long center loop hanging down toward the floor.

Display the ring and rope lying separately on your outstretched hand. Then, close your fingers over the parallel strands to hold them tightly, and lift your hand with its back to the audience and palm toward you. What you do now should all be performed in one swift, continuing motion. Bring your right hand over beneath your left hand. Slide your right fingers *in between the two strands* and grip the *bottom* of the ring with them. Pull the ring to the right, off your left hand, and then lift the bottom of the ring *up toward you through the strands*, and swiftly pull the ring down to the bottom of the loop. (This automatically forms the Hitch that knots the rope around the ring.)

Give the ring a quick downward tug to tighten the knot that now holds it tied at the bottom of the loop and take your right hand away. *Immediately* bring your right hand up to take one of the top ends of the rope from your left hand. Spread your hands apart to show the ring knotted at the center of the rope stretched between them.

After the trick is over, be careful about how you

untie the ring from the center of the rope in front of the audience. Don't do it by simply pulling out both strands of the Hitch together, because that gives the trick away by revealing that what looks like a "knot" is only a simple Hitch. Untie it by drawing out one strand at a time, as if you were untying an ordinary Overhand Knot.

COMEDY SOAP AND ROPE

How it looks

"We come now to the educational part of this program," you say. "Here's a household hint that can save you a little money—and make it safer to take a shower."

You hold up a large bar of soap that has a rope threaded through a hole cut in its center. The rope is tied in a loop, and you untie it and remove the soap.

"You all know what shower soap is—the kind you hang around your neck so that when the water is splashing in your face you don't have to grope for the soap," you say. "Most shower soap is expensive; but you can easily make your own at home. Just take any cake of soap, cut a hole through the center with a kitchen paring knife, and string it up on a rope. Tie the rope through twice, like this."

As you explain, you demonstrate by threading the rope through the soap, and again tying it into a loop, which you put over your head so the soap hangs down in front of you. "There you are. You've got your own inexpensive shower soap in your favorite brand." You hold up the roped bar. "But there *is* one problem with shower soap. When you've got it hanging around your neck like this, how do you reach down with the soap to wash your toes?"

You awkwardly show how hard it would be to reach down to your feet with the soap. "Of course, you could untie it from the rope," you say. "But there's a simpler way. You just use magic . . . and pull the soap right through the rope!" Suddenly you pull the bar of soap free from the loop that hangs around your neck. "There it goes . . . And now you can wash your toes!"

What you need

A 5-foot length of soft clothesline.
A large (bath size) bar of soap.
A sharp-pointed kitchen paring knife.
A penny.
White cloth adhesive tape.
A ruler.

The secret

The ends of the rope are switched during their threading through the soap, secretly doubling the rope upon itself and forming a small loop. The loop is drawn inside the hole where it jams into a position that keeps the soap on the rope until you are ready to release it.

With the ruler, find the center of the soap, front and back. Press the penny into the soap, first one side and then the other, to mark a circle around those centers, and cut the hole through with the knife.

Bind each end of the rope with a short horizontal strip of white tape, to prevent fraying and to make it easier to thread the rope.

COMEDY SOAP AND ROPE

RIGHT
THUMB
AND
FINGER
TAKE
PART
THAT
HANGS
TO FRONT

HAND
MOVES
UP TO
BACK
OF
SOAP

①

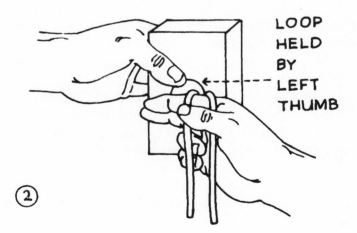

LOOP
HELD
BY
LEFT
THUMB

②

RIGHT HAND
MOVES BACK TO
TAKE OTHER END

③

AFTER
BACK END
HAS BEEN - - - →
PUT
THROUGH
LEFT
SIDE
OF HOLE

④

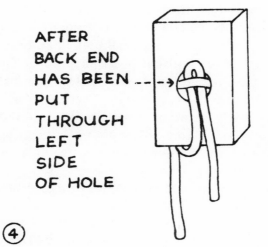

Put one end of the rope through the hole from back to front. Draw half the length of the rope through, bring it around the bottom of the soap, and then put that *same end* through the hole from back to front again. Bring both ends to the top and tie them into a loose Square Knot, so the soap hangs at the bottom of the long loop.

The soap is now really tied on the rope and that is the way you first show it to the audience, so they can watch you untie it, which helps convince them that the later retying of it is genuine.

What you do

Start by showing the soap tied on the rope. Untie the top knot, unloop the rope, and remove the soap from it. After explaining about the "shower soap," what you seem to do is tie it back on the rope in the way it was tied before. The following moves should be practiced until you can do them smoothly and deliberately, without hesitation.

Hold the soap upright with your left hand, fingers at the front around the left edge, and thumb at the back just above the center hole. Take one end of the rope with your right hand and push it through the hole from back to front. Draw the rope out until the two ends hang even at the bottom. Move your right hand, with its palm toward you, down about 2 inches below the bottom of the soap. Bring that hand around *both parts* of the hanging rope, so they hang down through your fingers.

Grip the part of the rope that hangs down from the *front* of the soap between your right thumb and first finger and move your right hand straight up against the back of the soap to just above the center hole. This forms a little loop across the top of your right first finger. Put that loop under the tip of your left thumb and hold it with that thumb against the back of the soap.

Leave that part of the rope hanging and slide your right hand back toward you along the *other part* of the rope to the end of it. Take that other end and push it from back to front through the left side of the hole in the soap. Draw that end out through the hole to the front until it draws the little loop into the hole. Continue to pull that end *gently* forward until the little loop is jammed inside the hole.

Bring both ends of the rope to the top, tie them into a Square Knot, and put the loop over your head so the soap hangs on the rope in front of you. Joke about the problem of trying to wash your toes while the soap is tied around your neck.

"Of course, you could untie it from the rope," you say. "But there's a simpler way." Take the bar in your right hand. "You just use magic . . . and pull the soap right through the rope!" As you speak, pull the bar out toward the right, away from the rope, and it will come free, leaving the tied loop still hanging around your neck. "There it goes . . . And now you can wash your toes!"

WITH A LOOP OF STRING

This is magic using only your hands and a simple loop of string. It's a series of penetrations all based on the ancient puzzle-like trick of seeming to pull a string through the thumb, but with variations that build it into an amusing little close-up routine.

How it looks

You hang one end of the loop over your thumb, wind the string around it, and ask someone to hold up one of his thumbs. Dropping the other end of the loop over his thumb, you have him pull on the string as he counts aloud. At the count of "three," he magically pulls the string right through your thumb, so your thumb is free and the loop is left hanging from his.

Taking the loop from him, you wind it around the back of your hand and give him the other end to hold. Once more, he works the magic, and tugs the string through your hand. You then hang it over your wrist, wrap it around, and he pulls it through your arm.

What you need

A 30-inch length of Venetian blind cord, or other smooth-finished and pliable string.

The secret

Basically, each of the penetration tricks depends on the same move, but done somewhat differently each time—a secret figure-eight twist that reverses the strands and lets you control the release of the string. The only preparation is to tie the ends of the string together with a small and tight Square Knot, and to trim the ends off close to the knot.

What you do

Through the Thumb

With the palm of your left hand toward you and the thumb upright, hang the unknotted end of the loop over the thumb. Bring your right hand under the bottom end of the loop, palm upward and fingertips toward the left. Put those fingers up through the loop from left to right, closing your hand around it. Lift your right hand up until the loop is stretched horizontally between your hands.

Twist your left fingers in toward you, hook the tip of your second finger over the strand nearest to your body, and pull that strand back over the top of the other one and around to the back of your thumb. Immediately turn your partly closed left hand palm downward. With your right hand, hang what is now the forward strand over your left thumb, and then draw the string taut between your hands again.

Reversing the strands has formed a small loop around the tip of your left second finger, hidden now by the closed fingers of that hand. Press that secret loop against the base of your left thumb and keep it held there until the end of the trick. At this point, the doubled string has really been just bent around your thumb, although the thumb appears to be firmly bound.

Ask someone to hold up one of his thumbs. Put the right-hand end of the loop over his thumb. Tell him he is about to perform the magic and explain that he is to pull on the string with his thumb while he counts aloud to three. At his count of three, secretly release the little loop from under your left fin-

THROUGH THE THUMB

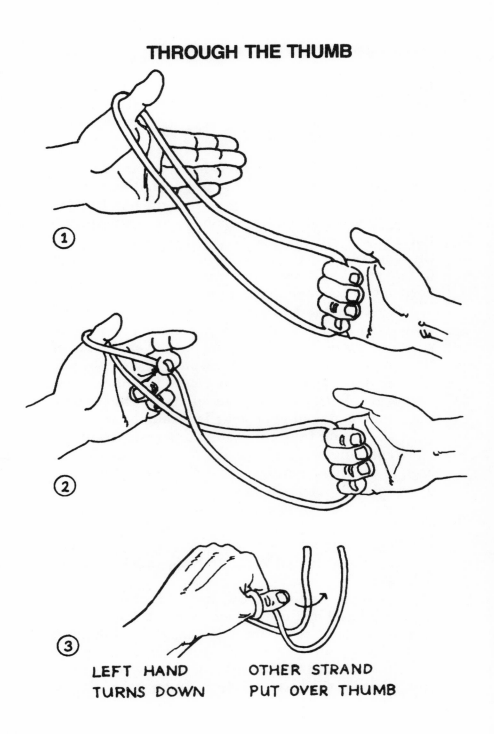

①

②

③ LEFT HAND TURNS DOWN   OTHER STRAND PUT OVER THUMB

ger so the string pulls free from your thumb and hangs from his. "You've pulled it right through my thumb," you say. "Now that you know how to do it, let's try something a little more difficult."

Through the Hand

Take the string from the spectator. Turn your left hand palm downward, thumb pointed toward you and fingertips toward the right. Hang the un-knotted end of the loop over the back of that hand, so that the rest of the string hangs down beneath it. (The loop should *not* encircle the thumb, which is kept free.) Bring your right hand, palm down, to the bottom end of the loop. Put your right fingers down through it, from right to left, and close them around it.

Bend your left fingers down and catch the side of your left second finger against the outside of the strand that is nearest to your body. With that finger, pull that strand out away from you, over the top of the other strand, and then hook that same fingertip down between the two strands.

Without pausing, lift your right hand, with its end of the string, straight up above the back of your left hand. This automatically brings part of the string up inside your left hand. Close your left fingers into a loose fist. Inside the fist there are now two little loops caught around the tip of your second finger. Each of the strands has been doubled upon itself, and all that holds the string around your hand is your finger in those loops.

Have the spectator take hold of the top end of the loop, the part your right hand has been holding a

THROUGH THE HAND

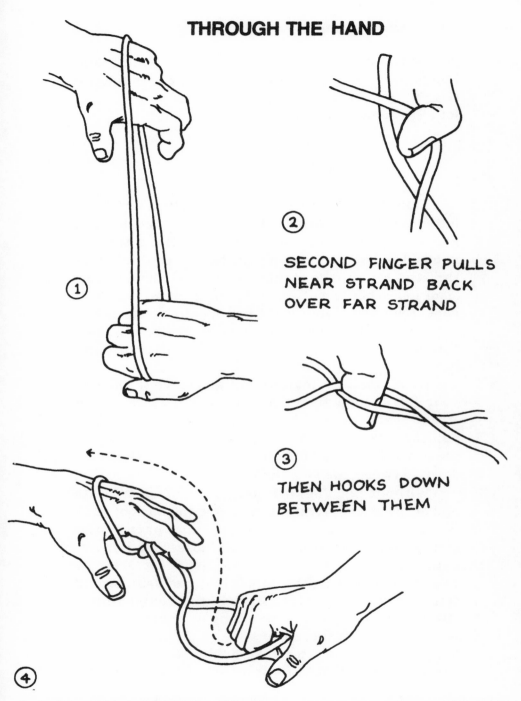

①

② SECOND FINGER PULLS NEAR STRAND BACK OVER FAR STRAND

③ THEN HOOKS DOWN BETWEEN THEM

④ RIGHT HAND BRINGS ITS END UP OVER BACK OF LEF

THROUGH THE WRIST

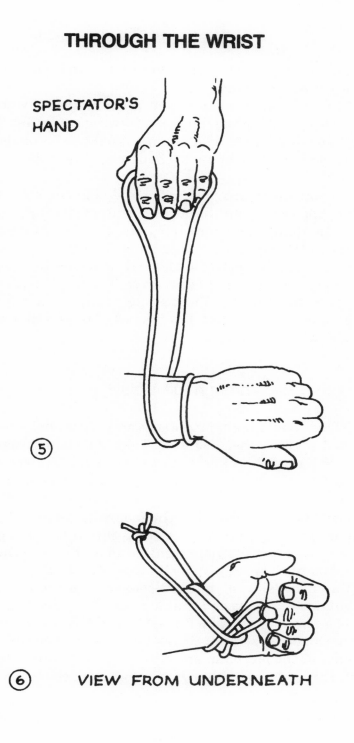

SPECTATOR'S HAND

⑤

⑥ VIEW FROM UNDERNEATH

few inches above the back of your left hand, and remove your right hand.

"I want you to imagine you are a magician who
is about to perform the illusion of sawing a woman in
half," you say. "How would you pass the solid blade
right through her body without causing her any
harm?"

As you speak, lift your left hand slightly, so the
string between your hand and the spectator's is
slack. Suddenly open your left hand out flat, fingers
straight and wide apart. This pulls the little hidden
loops off your fingertip so the string seems to pass
through your hand and comes free, leaving it hanging from his hand. "That's the idea," you say.
"You've done it! ... But I'm just as glad you didn't
use a saw!"

Through the Wrist

"This time, I'll bind my arm and you can help me
escape," you tell the spectator. Take the string from
him and hang the unknotted end over your left wrist
just above your hand. Turn your left hand palm
down.

Take the bottom end of the loop with your right
hand by putting your fingers down through it. Keep
the loop taut and lift your right hand up to the right
until it is horizontally opposite the left hand.

Catch the side of your left second finger against
the outside of the strand that is nearest to your body
and then hook that same fingertip down over the far
side of the other strand. Draw that finger up against
the base of the left palm and close your left hand into
a fist. Lift your right hand, with the end of the loop it

is holding, up over the back of your left hand and out to the wrist. (This doubles the strands upon themselves and forms a small hidden loop at the tip of your left second finger, which it holds tightly pressed to the base of the left palm. The string can be tugged, but won't pull free until you are ready to release it from your finger.)

Give the spectator the knotted end from your right hand, and say, "All you have to do now to work your magic and free me is just to pull the string *gently* .... Pull it right through my arm." Let him tug at the string once or twice, and tell him, "Maybe you should say some magic word. Why don't you say the name 'Houdini'?" Have him pull on the string again as he says "Houdini," and release the string so it suddenly "penetrates" your arm and comes free.

4

CUT
AND RESTORED

IMPROMPTU REPEAT CUT ROUTINE

This direct, fast-moving routine has been planned to keep both the rope and your hands in action during the two minutes or so it takes to perform—it gets right to the point of cutting and restoring a rope twice without any distractions from the simple main plot. The first cutting sets things up for the second cutting, and it can be done almost anywhere, with no advance preparation.

How it looks

With one end of the rope held in your left hand, you run your open right palm out along the rope to the center, bring the center to your left hand, draw it up into a loop, then lift the other end up beside it. You cut through the center, take two ends in each hand, and spread your hands apart to show the two cut pieces. Touching the four ends together so the hanging pieces form a circle, you immediately shake out the rope to show it whole again.

You then take one of the ends in your left fist and lift the center of the rope up to the level of your head. Holding the center between the right thumb and first finger, you pull the end out of your left fist so it swings out and down to hang beside the other end. Bringing the center over to your left hand, you again cut the rope in two and continue to snip pieces off it, cutting it several times. Looping the rope once, you draw it out between both open hands to show it restored once more.

What you need

While any reasonable length of soft clothesline or even thick cord or string can be used, the cutting will leave the rope several inches shorter at the end of the routine than it was at the start, so it is best to begin with a piece about 6 feet long.

Sharp round-ended scissors that will fit into your jacket pocket.

The secret

Both parts of the routine depend on variations of long-standard sleight of hand methods of cutting and restoring a rope. The moves have been simplified so they shouldn't be difficult to learn, but it will take practice to learn to do them smoothly. The first part of the trick leaves you with an extra-short piece, which becomes the loop that you cut through and snip away for the second restoration, so that at the end you again have a plain length of rope.

What you do

Each part will be explained as a separate trick, first the *End to End* effect and then the *Cut and Trim*. Either part can be used as a trick by itself, if you prefer not to show a repeat cutting. Start with the scissors in your right-hand jacket pocket and have the rope in the pocket with them, or else keep it handy on your table.

End to End

Take one end of the rope in your left hand, with the back of the hand toward the audience. Hold the end clipped between the side of the thumb and base of the first finger so that about 2 inches of the end extends above your hand.

Turn your right hand palm up, out flat, fingertips to the front and thumb opened out to the right. Bring that palm up under the rope and close to your

END TO END

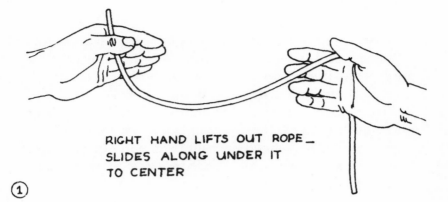

RIGHT HAND LIFTS OUT ROPE —
SLIDES ALONG UNDER IT
TO CENTER

①

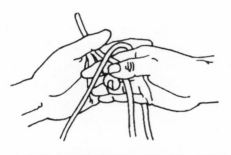

RIGHT SECOND FINGER HOOKS
PART OF LEFT END

②

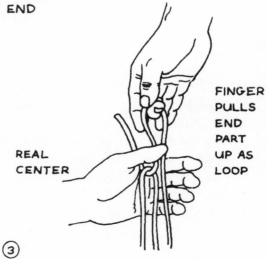

REAL
CENTER

FINGER
PULLS
END
PART
UP AS
LOOP

③

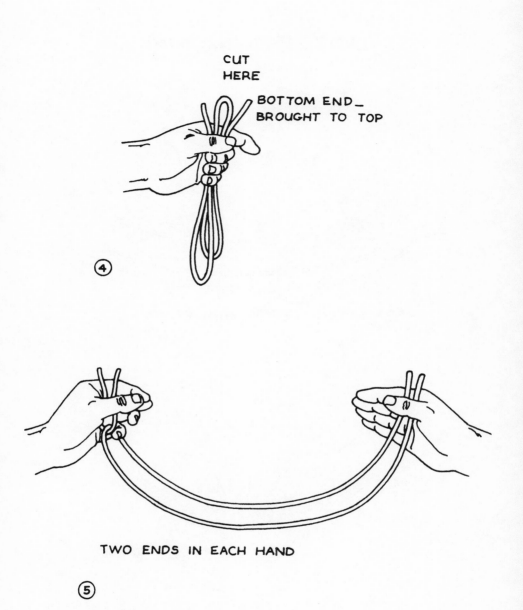

CUT
HERE

BOTTOM END_
BROUGHT TO TOP

④

TWO ENDS IN EACH HAND

⑤

continued on next page . . .

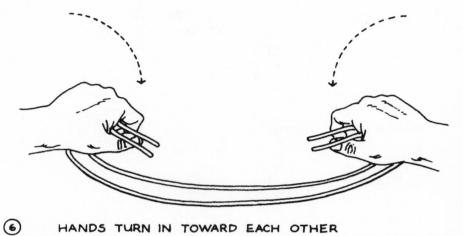

⑥ HANDS TURN IN TOWARD EACH OTHER

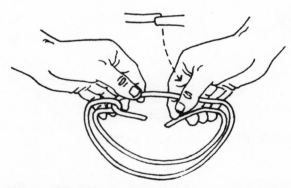

HANDS COME TOGETHER_ RIGHT THUMB PRESSES
OVERLAPPING LEFT AND RIGHT ENDS AGAINST
INSIDE OF FINGERS

⑦

left hand, so the rope hangs down over the right edge of the fingers. Lift the rope out to the right by sliding the open palm along the underside of it to the center. Then, turn that palm toward you, fingertips to the left, leaving the free end of the rope hanging down over the back of the right fingers.

Bring your right hand over inside the left palm and, as your hands come together, hook the right second finger under the part of the rope that hangs down beneath the left thumb. Tilt the right fingers down behind your left hand so the center of the rope slides off them, and then immediately lift your right hand up, drawing the part that is hooked over the second finger into a small loop that extends about 2 inches above your left hand. Close the left fingers to hold the loop and remove your right hand. (In a simple and natural way, you have secretly switched the center of the rope for the small loop formed by one end. The real center now hangs at the bottom of that loop, hidden behind your left palm. Your left hand appears to be holding one upright end of the rope, with the center loop extending up beside it.)

Without pausing, bring your right hand down and take the bottom end of the rope. Lift that end up to place it to the right of the loop and hold it with the other end and loop in your left hand. Then, take the scissors from your pocket with your right hand. Cut through the center of the upright loop and spread the cut ends apart. Drop the scissors, points down, into your outer breast pocket.

You seem to be holding four rope ends with your left hand. With your right hand, take the two ends that are at the right, gripping them between thumb and fingers. Continue to hold the other two ends with your left hand and spread your hands apart so the rope hangs slackly between them. With two ends in each hand, show the two "cut-in-half" pieces.

The restoration should happen quickly, as though you merely touch the four ends together in a circle for an instant, then shake out the rope to show it whole again. Here is how it is done:

Holding two rope ends in each hand, turn both hands in toward each other, palms down, and left thumb opposite right thumb. Bring your hands together so the sides of the left and right first fingers touch. This also touches the four ends together.

Grip what is now the *forward* left rope end and the *forward* right end together between your right thumb and first finger. Slide the thumb to the right to squeeze those overlapping ends against the inside of your right fingers and hold them tightly as one. Drop the other ends and the rest of the rope completely from both hands and lift the right hand up and out to the right to hold it high. Shake out the rope to show it restored. (Your closed right hand conceals the overlapping pieces so that the extra cut piece, hanging out of the hand, looks like the top end of the rope.)

Cut and Trim

The restored rope now hangs down from your right hand, with the overlapping pieces pressed against the inside of the fingers by the tip of the thumb. The visible end of the cut piece should hang out of the top of your right hand *toward the audience*. (If it doesn't, shake your hand a little to flop the end over in that direction.)

Lift your left hand up in front of you, palm to-

IMPROMPTU REPEAT CUT ROUTINE
CUT AND TRIM

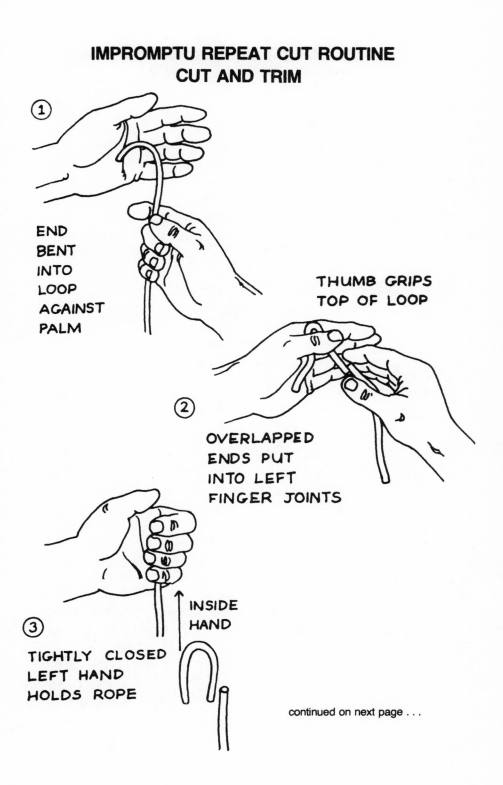

① END
BENT
INTO
LOOP
AGAINST
PALM

THUMB GRIPS
TOP OF LOOP

② OVERLAPPED
ENDS PUT
INTO LEFT
FINGER JOINTS

③ TIGHTLY CLOSED
LEFT HAND
HOLDS ROPE

INSIDE
HAND

continued on next page . . .

CUT AND TRIM—continued

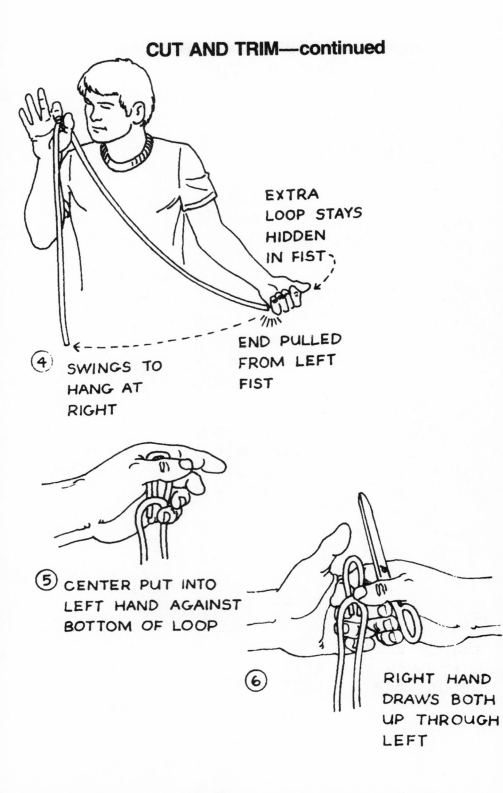

EXTRA
LOOP STAYS
HIDDEN
IN FIST

END PULLED
FROM LEFT
FIST

④ SWINGS TO
HANG AT
RIGHT

⑤ CENTER PUT INTO
LEFT HAND AGAINST
BOTTOM OF LOOP

⑥ RIGHT HAND
DRAWS BOTH
UP THROUGH
LEFT

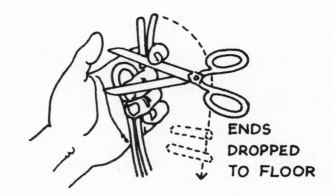

ENDS
DROPPED
TO FLOOR

BLADES HELD FLAT TO PRETEND
CUTTING LAST PIECES

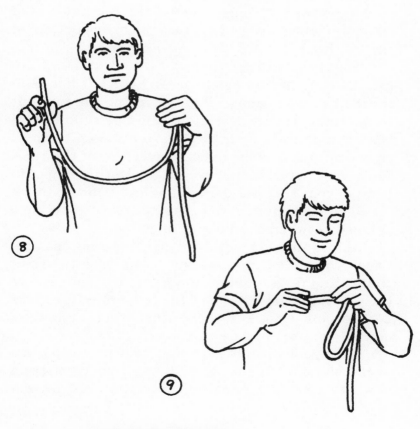

FRONT VIEWS

ward you, and fingertips to the right. Bring your
right hand down to the left. Touch the end of the cut
piece against the base of the left palm so the end
folds over to form a small loop across the inside of
the palm, and close your left thumb over the top end
of that loop. Without pausing, place the overlapping
parts against the middle joints of your two lower left
fingers. Quickly close your left hand into a fist to
hold the rope as you remove your right hand. (The
bending of the cut piece into a small loop happens
almost automatically as you push the hanging end
against the left palm. The transfer of the overlapping parts from your right thumb and fingers to the
joints of your left fingers leaves the real top end of
the rope tightly gripped against the inside bottom of
the left fist.)

Now, grip between the right thumb and first finger the rope that hangs beneath your left fist. Run
these fingers out along the rope, lifting the rope out
to the right. Turn your head to the right and look at
that thumb and finger, to fix attention on them as
they continue to slide out to the center of the rope.
Keep your left fist, holding its end of the rope, in
front of your chest, and lift your right hand up to the
level of your head, with the center of the rope
gripped between thumb and finger.

As you draw the upward-slanting rope taut between your hands, pull on the center with the right
thumb and finger, giving it a little tug, and release
the end from the bottom of the left fist so it swings
out free and drops beside the other end that dangles
down from your right hand.

Turn your head to glance at your breast pocket,
as if looking for the scissors. Bring your right hand
down to your left hand, opening your left fingers

enough so you can put the center of the rope into that hand against the bottom of the hidden loop. Close your left fist again to hold them both, and immediately reach with your right hand and take the scissors from your breast pocket.

Hold the scissors, handle end down, loosely in your right palm, leaving your thumb and first finger free. With the right thumb and first finger, reach down inside your left hand, opening the left fingers to let you grip both the lower part of the extra loop and the top part of the real center. Draw them up until most of the extra loop extends above the top of the fisted left hand and the real center is just below the inside of the left first finger. Press the left thumb against the finger to hold them there.

Hold your left hand chest-high so the loop can be seen clearly. With your right hand, bring the blades of the scissors over behind the loop. Cut the loop in two through the center. Then, cut a piece off each of the cut ends. Move the scissors down, so the blades are partly below the left first finger, keeping the blades flat against the cut loop. *Pretend* to cut twice more, as though still trimming bits off the rope, but really just work the scissors. Lift the left thumb and let the remaining pieces of the extra loop drop to the floor as the other cut pieces did.

Drop the scissors back into your breast pocket. You are still holding the real center of the rope doubled inside the left fist. With your right hand, pick up one of the rope's bottom ends. Bring it up to hold it between your left thumb and first finger. Remove your right hand for a moment and turn your fisted left hand palm down, thumb toward the right. Take the same end between the first finger and thumb and *slowly* draw the rope out to the right, pulling it through your left hand as that hand slides along the rope to the left. Grip the rope between the left first finger and thumb, opening the other fingers wide, and hold it out between both hands to show it is whole again.

RING A STRING

How it looks

"Here's a little puzzle you might want to put together to show some of your friends," you say, as you take out a small ring and a long string. "I should warn you that it's a puzzle with a catch to it." You thread the string through the ring, then bring the bottom end up to the middle and tie a knot. Holding the string by its top end, so the ring hangs at the bottom of the knotted loop, you explain, "Now this is the puzzle. ... How can you get the ring off the string without untying the knot or breaking the string?"

You let watchers think about it for a moment, and then say, "The answer is—that you cheat a little." Reaching into your pocket, you take out a small pair of scissors and cut through the string, letting the ring slide free to the table. You hold up the cut string with its two pieces knotted at the center. "I said 'without *breaking* the string.' I didn't say anything about not *cutting* it."

As if you had finished explaining the puzzle, you quickly wind the string around your fingers. "It's a silly little stunt. But it is fun to do at a party. If you show it to your friends, just keep them guessing for a minute before you bring out the scissors." You drop the scissors back into your pocket. "Of course, it does leave you with a string that has been cut in half. But that's another problem—and the way to solve that ... is with magic!"

You snap your fingers over the cut string and unwind it, to show that the knot has vanished and the string is whole again. "The ring has been removed and the string is all in one piece," you say. "So I didn't *really* cheat—well, not *much!*"

What you need

A 3-foot length of soft, smooth-finished cotton string.

A small ring.

Small scissors with round-ended blades that will fit easily into a jacket pocket.

The secret

The loop is tied in a way that makes it look as if you are cutting through the center of the string, but you really cut one end. Then, you secretly slide the knotted cut piece off the string as you wind the string around your other hand, and you get rid of the knot when you drop the scissors back into your pocket.

There is nothing to prepare in advance. Just have the scissors in your right-hand jacket pocket and the ring and string in another pocket. (This is a close-up trick that should be performed near a table or counter that you can rest the ring upon.)

What you do

Explain that you want to show those who are

RING A STRING

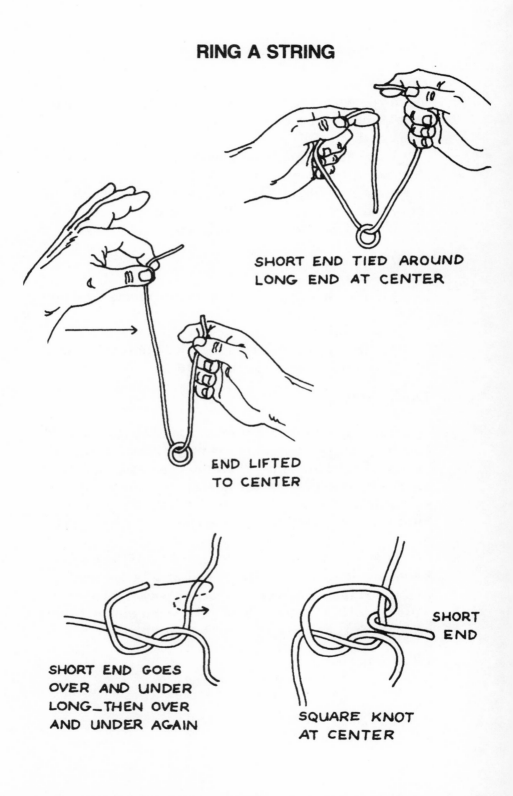

SHORT END TIED AROUND
LONG END AT CENTER

END LIFTED
TO CENTER

SHORT END GOES
OVER AND UNDER
LONG_THEN OVER
AND UNDER AGAIN

SHORT
END

SQUARE KNOT
AT CENTER

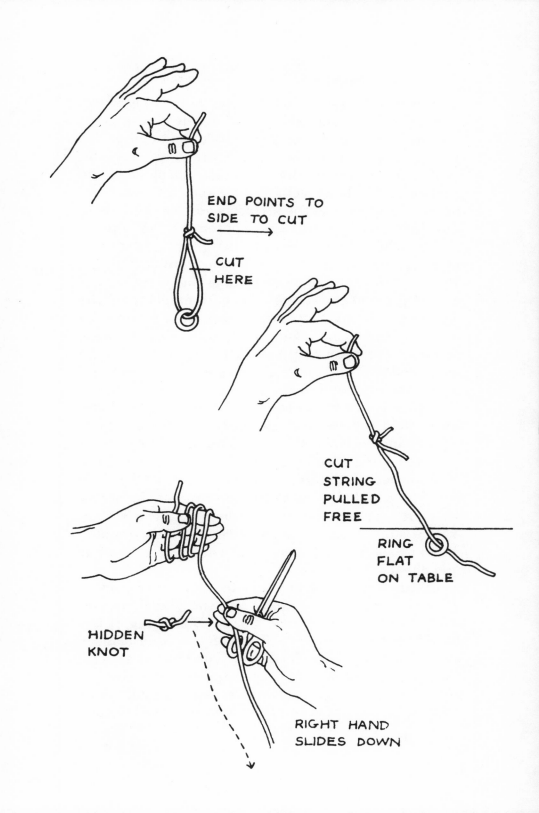

END POINTS TO
SIDE TO CUT

CUT
HERE

CUT
STRING
PULLED
FREE

RING
FLAT
ON TABLE

HIDDEN
KNOT

RIGHT HAND
SLIDES DOWN

watching a little puzzle that they may enjoy showing to others, and take out the ring and string.
Thread the ring on the string, take one end of the
string in each hand, and slide the ring back and
forth a few times, finally letting it slide down to the
bottom end held by your right hand. Lift your left
hand straight up so the string is vertical and bring
the right end up next to the center of the string.

Hold both strands with your right hand for a moment and drop the top end from your left hand.
Bring your left hand down to take the left strand of
string again at the center. Use both hands to tie the
short right-hand end into a *Square Knot* around the
center. (It must be a genuine Square Knot because
the trick won't work with any other knot. Just tie the
short end *over and under* the long end, then *over and
under* the long end again.)

After the knot has been tied, slide your left hand
up to hold the top end as before and remove your
right hand to leave the string hanging down from
your left hand. The ring hangs at the bottom of the
loop formed by the knot tied at the center. Explain
that the puzzle is how to get the ring off the string
without untying the knot or *breaking* the string.
Wait a moment, as if you were really offering a puzzle to be solved, and then say, "The answer is—that
you cheat a little."

With your right hand, reach into your pocket,
take out the scissors, and click the blades as you
show them. Lower your left hand so the ring at the
bottom of the string rests flatly on the table. (This is
so it won't fall to the floor after you cut the string.)
Cut through the *one side* of the loop that has the *end
of the knot* sticking out from it, making the cut about
an inch below that knot. (It makes no difference how

the string may have twisted after the knot was tied, as long as you remember to cut through the strand *below* where the end of the knot sticks out. That end "points" to the side that should be cut. If you cut the other side of the loop, the string will really be in two pieces!)

Keep the scissors loosely held in your right hand. With your left hand, draw the string up so the ring comes free and remains lying on the table. The hanging string appears to have been cut in half, with the two parts knotted at the center. Explain that the catch to the puzzle was not to *break* the string, "but I didn't say anything about not *cutting* it."

Act as if the stunt were over, so that restoring the string will come as a surprise. With your left hand still holding the top end of the string, bring your right hand around the knot at the center. Close your fingers around it, pressing the knot against the inside of the fingers with the thumb. Lift the string and quickly wind it up around the extended fingers of your left hand, sliding your right hand down along the string as you wind it, and secretly sliding the knot down with it. As you finish the winding, the knot will slide right off the end of the string into your closed right hand.

The fact that you still have the scissors in your right hand provides a reason for keeping the hand closed and helps hide the knot. It looks to those watching as if the knot had been wound into your left hand with the rest of the string. Just as you secretly slide the knot off the end, lift your right hand and gesture with the scissors, as you say, "If you show it to your friends, keep them guessing for a minute before you bring out the scissors."

Drop the scissors into your pocket and leave the knot there with them as you turn your head and look at the string wound around your left hand, lifting that hand a little to fix attention on it. "Of course, it does leave you with a string that has been cut in half," you say. "But that's another problem—and the way to solve that . . . is with magic!"

Snap your fingers over the string and unwind it. Take it between your hands to show that it has been restored. Point to the ring lying on the table, and say, "The ring has been removed and the string is all in one piece. So I didn't *really* cheat—well, not *much*!"

TOSS AND CUT

How it looks

You take a small ball of rope from your pocket, toss it from hand to hand, showing both hands empty, then shake out the rope to uncoil it. Holding the rope dangling straight down from one hand, you bring the other hand to the center and draw the rope up through that hand. Picking up a pair of scissors, you cut through the center of the rope and cut away several pieces, but as you stretch the rope out it instantly becomes whole again.

What you need

A 3½-foot length of soft clothesline with the core removed.

A 6-inch piece of the same clothesline.

Scissors.

The secret

As with many other such tricks, you cut through a loop made of the extra piece instead of through the real center of the rope. But the whole thing is self-contained and there is nothing to hide in your hands at the start or to get rid of at the end. The ball of rope is fixed to deliver the extra loop into your hand when and where you need it, by the simple action of taking away the rope with the other hand to uncoil it.

Bend the small piece of rope into a loop with the two ends touching at the bottom. Lay one end of the long rope vertically on top of the small loop so that end extends 2 inches above the loop.

Take the part of the long rope that is just below the loop and start winding it around the loop and the end. Wind it around in four flat turns, then continue winding the rest of the rope upon those first turns until you have a small ball. All the windings should be kept toward the bottom of the loop so that the loop and the top end of the rope stick up out of the center of the ball. Use the point of the scissors to tuck the last end of the rope in under one of the strands to hold the ball together.

Put the ball of rope into the right-hand pocket of your jacket and have the scissors on your table.

What you do

Take the ball of rope out of your pocket with your right hand and show that your left hand is empty. Toss the ball from your right hand into the left and show the right hand empty.

TOSS AND CUT

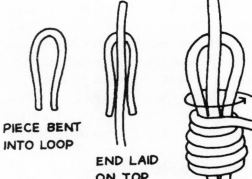

PIECE BENT
INTO LOOP

END LAID
ON TOP
OF LOOP

ROPE
WRAPPED
AROUND

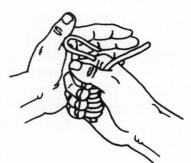

RIGHT HAND DRAWS ROPE DOWN
OFF LOOP CLIPPED UNDER LEFT THUMB

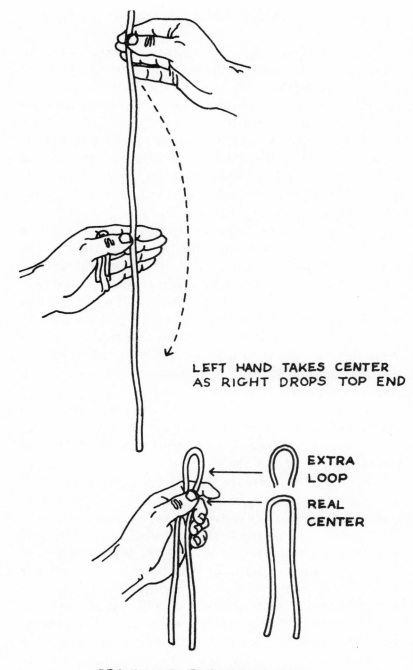

LEFT HAND TAKES CENTER
AS RIGHT DROPS TOP END

EXTRA
LOOP

REAL
CENTER

DRAWN UP THROUGH HAND
AND HELD FOR CUTTING

Hold the back of your left hand toward the audience and bring your right hand to the palm of the left to take the ball of rope. As your hands come together, push the top end of the loop that is sticking out of the ball into the crotch of your left thumb. Press the side of your thumb over the loop to hold it tightly. Then, close your right fingers around the ball and draw it down away from your left hand. This draws the ball down off the extra loop, which remains clipped under your left thumb.

Lift your right hand high and give it a sharp downward shake to uncoil the ball so the rope hangs straight down from that hand. Bring your left palm against the center of the hanging rope. Hold the center between the tip of your left thumb and first finger. Release the top end of the rope from your right hand and let it fall back and to the bottom. Close your left fingers into a loose fist, which brings the real center of the rope over against the extra loop hidden inside the hand.

With your right thumb and fingers, reach into the top of your left hand and draw the extra loop up so the top of it extends well above the hand. Hold it there with your left thumb.

Pick up the scissors with your right hand. Cut through the fake center loop and spread the two ends apart so everybody can see it has been cut. Then, continue to snip little pieces off each of the cut ends until the entire extra loop has been cut away.

Keep your left hand as it is, with the real center of the rope inside it. With your right hand, take one of the bottom ends of the rope and hold it straight up above your left fist. Rub the center of the rope with your left fingers, give it a little tug, and open your left hand wide to show that the rope has been restored to one piece.

DOUBLE DOUBLE

How it looks

You show a rope, draw it freely through your hands, and then hold it so it hangs straight down from one hand. Your other hand moves about one-third of the way down the rope, brings that part up into a loop, then moves down again and brings up a second loop.

With scissors, you cut through one loop and then the second loop, seeming to cut the rope into three parts. Folding the cut ends down into your hand, you snap the fingers of your other hand and instantly stretch the rope out between them to show that it is fully restored.

What you need

A 4½-foot length of soft white clothesline.
A second piece of clothesline, 10 inches long.
White cloth adhesive tape, ½ inch wide.
Scissors.

The secret

The short piece of rope is made into a double-looped gimmick with the adhesive tape; part of it also forms a small tube that slides up and down on the long rope. This permits a casual handling of the rope, as well as the instant restoration after the two fake loops have been cut.

Lay the long rope vertically on a table. Cut off a 10-inch length of tape and turn it *sticky side up*. With the sticky side out, wrap the tape upon itself, twice around the rope at a point about 4 inches up

DOUBLE DOUBLE

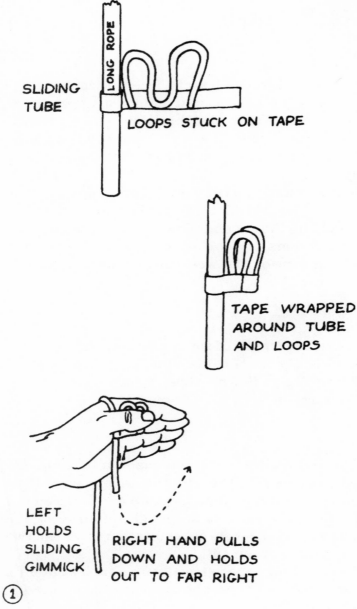

SLIDING
TUBE

LONG ROPE

LOOPS STUCK ON TAPE

TAPE WRAPPED
AROUND TUBE
AND LOOPS

LEFT
HOLDS
SLIDING
GIMMICK

RIGHT HAND PULLS
DOWN AND HOLDS
OUT TO FAR RIGHT

①

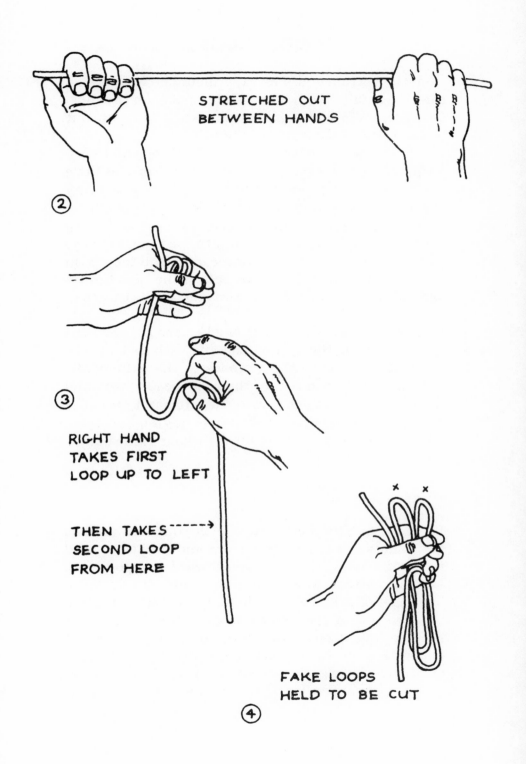

STRETCHED OUT
BETWEEN HANDS

②

③

RIGHT HAND
TAKES FIRST
LOOP UP TO LEFT

THEN TAKES - - - - - ➞
SECOND LOOP
FROM HERE

FAKE LOOPS
HELD TO BE CUT

④

from the bottom end. The tape should be wrapped so that the small tube it forms slides easily on the rope. Bring the remainder of the tape, sticky side up, out to the right of the rope on the table.

Take one end of the short piece of rope and stick it firmly to the tape just to the right of the little tube. Form a loop about 2½ inches high and bring the right side of that loop down to stick it to the tape. Then, form a second similiar loop beside it and bring the other end down to stick that to the tape. Fold the tape toward you so that the second small loop is on top of the first one. Wrap the rest of the tape tightly around the tube and the bottom ends of the attached loops.

Keep the gimmick positioned on the rope about 4 inches up from the bottom end and with its two fake loops upward. Take the gimmick in the palm of the left hand. Fold the rest of the rope loosely back and forth upon it and put it into the left-hand pocket of your jacket. Have the scissors handy on the table where you can pick them up with your right hand.

What you do

Take out the folded rope with your left hand so the gimmick is against the palm and hold that hand in front of you with its back toward the audience. Unfold the rope with your right hand and drop the long part of it down over the back of your left hand.

Bring your right hand down to the short end of rope at the bottom of your left hand. Take that short end with your right hand and draw it horizontally out to the far right until all but a few inches of the rope has been pulled through the bottom of your loosely fisted left hand, drawing it through the sliding gimmick that remains hidden in your left hand. Hold the rope stretched out between both hands to show it.

Drop the rope end from your right hand and let that end swing down toward the floor. Hold the rope high with your left hand. Bring your right hand to the hanging rope about one-third of the length down from the top and take it between the right thumb and first finger. Lift that part up as a loop and place it inside your left hand against the bottom of the hidden gimmick, holding that loop with your lower left fingers. Again, bring your right hand down along the rope, move it lower down, and lift it as a second loop to hold with the first one inside your left hand.

With your right thumb and fingers, reach down into the top of your left fist. Draw the two fake loops up into view until the band of tape at the bottom of the gimmick is against the inside of the left first finger. Separate the two loops a little so they can be seen clearly and hold the gimmick in place there with the left thumb.

Pick up the scissors with your right hand. Cut through the center of one of the fake loops and separate the two cut ends. Then, cut through the center of the second loop and separate those ends. Put down the scissors and display the twice-cut rope with your left hand. Bring your right hand, palm toward you, to the *front* of your left hand and bend the four cut ends back down together into the left fist, closing the left fingers around them.

Lift your right hand away from the rope, hold it high and snap your fingers twice, as if "casting a spell" to restore the rope. With your right hand, take the hanging bottom end of the rope and pull it down and out to the right to unfold it quickly and show it whole, stretched horizontally between your hands.

Drop the rope end from your right hand and let it swing toward the floor. Then, take the top end with your right hand and draw the rope out through your left hand far enough to hold it stretched between both hands again. Finally, gather the rope with your right hand, put it into your left hand, and put the loosely folded rope away in your jacket's left pocket.

5

LONG
AND SHORT

LIGHTNING STRETCH

How it looks

"Give a magician enough rope and he'll do a rope trick," you say. "But I'm embarrassed to tell you that when I packed my things for the show, I forgot to give myself enough rope." From your pocket, you take out a rope less than a foot long. "This little scrap is too short to be much use for anything."

You bring the two rope ends together to show how short it is, then measure it around the open palm of your other hand. "It hardly goes around my hand." Holding the short rope so it hangs down from that hand, you take one end and pull it out through the hand. Instantly it stretches to more than three times its original length, as you say, "What I really need is a piece about *this* long!"

What you need

A 3½-foot length of soft clothesline with the core removed.
A nail file.

The secret

Most of the rope is folded upon itself into a small bundle that hangs between the two ends, and it is handled so it looks from the front like a little scrap of rope, until you pull it out to full length.

Start 6 inches from one end and fold the rope up and down in tight 1½-inch accordion folds until you are about 10 inches from the other end. Then, take the 10-inch end and wind it *tightly* twice around the accordion folds, crossing the second turn down over the first to hold the folds together. Finally, make a small loop and push it up under the wound-around strands, using the round end of the nail file.

You should now have two short ends, with the folded bundle hanging securely between them. Put the rope into the right-hand pocket of your jacket.

What you do

Reach into your pocket, get the bundled part of the rope into the palm of your right hand, close the fingers around it, and bring that hand out in front of

you with its back toward the audience. Use your left
hand to adjust the rope by drawing the top end up
until the bundle is just beneath the crotch of your
right thumb. Close the thumb to hold it there, drop
the end over the back of your right hand, and remove your left hand.

With the bundle hanging hidden behind your
right palm and the two ends in view, it looks from
the front like a little piece of rope. Take the bottom
end of the rope with your left hand and bring it up to
hold it for a moment with the tip of your right
thumb, showing both ends together at the top and a
short loop hanging beneath your right hand, and
say, "This little scrap is too short to be much use for
anything."

Release that end and let it fall to the bottom
again, so you are holding the rope as at the start.
Give your right hand a little *inward* shake, toward
your body, to toss the top end back so it falls over the
top of the right thumb and hangs to the inside of the
right hand.

Bring your left hand, palm toward you, over inside your right hand. Grasp the top end of the rope,
just above the bundle, in the crotch of your *left*
thumb, and turn both hands out to the left *together*
as you turn your body slightly in that direction. As
you turn your hands, bring the left palm toward the
audience, release the bundle from your right hand so
it is hidden *behind* the left, and immediately move
your right hand down from in back of the left to take
the bottom end of the rope with your right hand.
Without pausing, lift that bottom rope end to bend
the rope up over your left palm, and say, "It hardly
goes around my hand." Drop that rope end and remove your right hand as you extend your left palm

LIGHTNING STRETCH

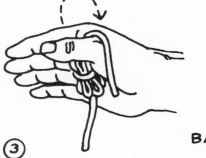

6"

6"

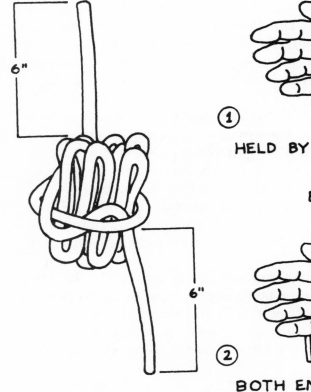

① HELD BY THUMB

BACK

② BOTH ENDS BROUGHT UP

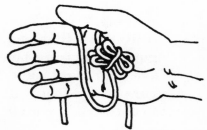

③ HAND SHAKES END OVER TOP OF THUMB

BACK

④ LEFT THUMB TAKES — BOTH HANDS SWING OUT TO LEFT TOGETHER

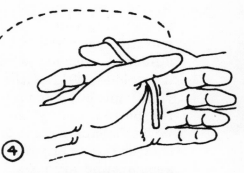

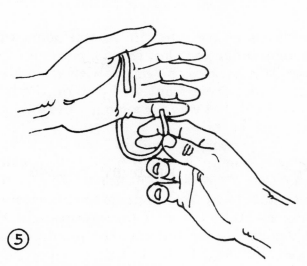

(5)

BUNDLE NOW HIDDEN
BEHIND LEFT HAND _
"IT HARDLY GOES AROUND MY HAND."

FRONT

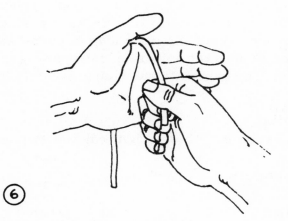

(6)

RIGHT HAND PULLS END

higher and farther out to the left. At this point, the top end is held under your left thumb, and the rope hangs down the back of the hand, with its folded bundle still hidden from front view behind the left palm. Keep it held that way for a moment to display the "little piece" of rope.

Then, bring your right hand up and take the top end of the rope, keeping your left hand as it is, palm toward the front. With your right hand, pull the end straight out and down from your left hand, closing the left fingers around it as it passes through. As you quickly pull out the top end, the bundle pulls loose against the back of your left thumb. The rope magically "stretches" to full length between your spreading hands, and you say, "What I really need is a piece about *this* long!"

RIBBON STRETCH

How it looks

You show a 2-foot length of bright-colored ribbon and tie its ends together to form a small loop. Taking one side of the little loop in each hand, you see-saw your hands up and down and gradually "stretch" the loop until the ribbon is 9 feet long.

What you need

A 3-yard length of bright-colored ½-inch satin ribbon.
A nail file.

The secret

Part of the ribbon is folded upon itself into a small bundle which is hidden by your hands. The way you hold the ribbon and secretly add to its length from the bundle gives the illusion of stretching it.

Start about 8 inches from the ribbon's top end and flatly fold it up and down upon itself in 1-inch accordion folds. When you have folded all but about 16 inches, wind it *tightly* around the folded bundle twice, in flat turns, and tuck about a 1-inch loop under those turns, using the round end of the nail file.

Have the prepared ribbon on your table behind some other prop that hides it from front view, so that you can quickly get it into proper position in your right hand before you hold it up to show the audience.

What you do

The ribbon should be held in your right hand so that the part of it just above the secret bundle lies at the crotch of your thumb, gripped there by the thumb. The top end of the ribbon hangs down over the back of the hand, which is toward the audience, and the bundle hangs hidden inside the palm, with the bottom end of the ribbon hanging straight down.

Hold it up that way to show what looks like a 2-foot length of ribbon. Let it be seen that your left hand is empty and bring that hand over to the inside of your right hand to take the ribbon. Do this by closing your left fingers into a loose fist around the bundle, so it is hidden within the three lower fingers,

RIBBON STRETCH

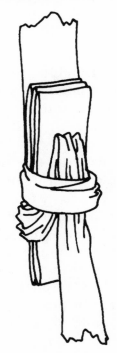

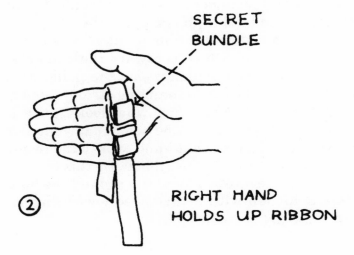

(1)

TIGHTY WOUND AROUND
AND TUCKED UP UNDER

SECRET
BUNDLE

(2)

RIGHT HAND
HOLDS UP RIBBON

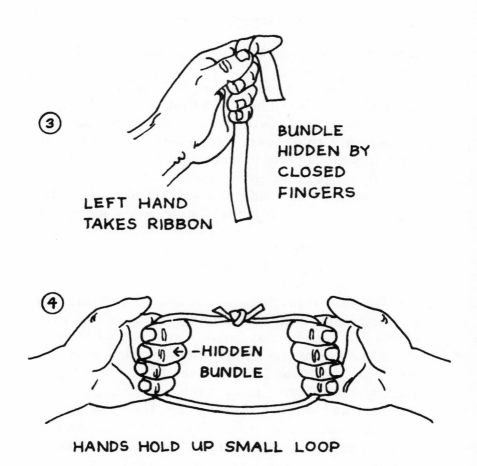

③ LEFT HAND
TAKES RIBBON

BUNDLE
HIDDEN BY
CLOSED
FINGERS

④ ←—HIDDEN
BUNDLE

HANDS HOLD UP SMALL LOOP

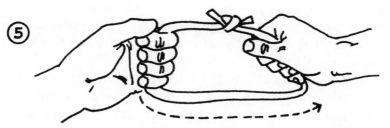

⑤

TURNING RIGHT HAND PULLS SOME
OF HIDDEN RIBBON FROM LEFT HAND

with the ribbon's top end hanging out over your first finger.

Immediately bring your right hand down to the bottom end of the ribbon. Lift that end up and lay it across the end that extends from the top of your left hand. Hold the crossed ends beneath your left thumb. With the help of your right hand, tie the two ends together in a tight Square Knot.

Take the right side of the little loop with the right hand by closing that hand into a loose fist around it. Hold up the loop to show it between your two fisted hands. You now pretend to stretch the loop as you tilt your fisted hands back and forth and very slowly draw them apart.

Tilt your right fist over toward the left until its thumb points to the left, pulling on the *bottom* part of the loop as your fist turns, which pulls a little of the ribbon from the bundle hidden inside your left fist. Then tilt your left fist over toward the right. Continue to tilt one fist and then the other, pulling a little on the bottom of the loop each time you tilt the right fist, rocking your fists back and forth. As you do that, keep sliding your right fist down its side of the loop so that the knot remains centered at the top, between your hands.

All of this is done in one continuous series of motions, rocking your hands back and forth until the full loop is stretched out. Finally, open both hands wide and display the giant loop hanging between your two thumbs.

If you wish to use the ribbon for a follow-up trick in a ribbon routine, you can untie the ends quickly. Just pull one end to upset the Square Knot and slide it free.

GREAT GRANDMA'S MAGIC THIMBLE

How it looks

"There's a story in our family that my great grandmother owned a magic thimble," you say, as you reach into your pocket, bring out a thimble and show it, and put it back into your pocket again. "She was also the family's champion string saver. She never threw away any little scrap of rope or string."

You hold up three short pieces of clothesline that are knotted together at both their top and bottom ends. After unfastening them at the top to show three separate pieces, you knot two of them together again, tying them end to end. Then, you repeat the same process with the bottom ends, tying two of those together, so that the three tied pieces are strung out end to end.

"Whenever great grandma had saved a few little pieces, she would tie them all together, end to end, and wind the pieces into a ball," you explain, as you wind the knotted rope around one hand. "Then she would take out her magic thimble . . ."— reaching into your pocket, you bring out the thimble on the tip of your first finger—". . . and tap the tied-together little pieces three times—just like this."

You tap the thimble three times on the rope wound around your other hand. "And instead of just a few scraps, there would be one long rope—all put together as good as new." Quickly you unwind the rope to show that the knots have vanished and the three pieces have magically joined together as one. " 'Waste not, want not,' she always used to say."

What you need

A 6-foot length of soft clothesline.

Two additional pieces of clothesline, each 6 inches long.

A thimble.

The secret

The long rope is doubled, with one of the little extra pieces looped through each doubled end, so at the start you seem to have three tied-together short ropes. The extra pieces, after being tied as "knots," are secretly stolen away in your hand when you wind the rope around your other hand. The "magic thimble" provides a logical reason for reaching into your pocket to get rid of the extra pieces, so that at the end you are left with only the plain length of rope.

Prepare the rope in advance by laying it out vertically on a table and doubling it into three separate sections, with one loop at both top and bottom. Thread a short extra piece of rope through each of the end loops, bending the short pieces so their ends come together next to each real end of the rope.

Hold the top set of three "ends" together and tie all three with one wrap-around single knot. Draw it tight to conceal the looped part within the knot. Tie the bottom set of three "ends" together in the same way. You now have what looks like three short lengths of rope, tied together top and bottom so the audience will see three ends at the top and three more at the bottom. Have the prepared rope on your table and the thimble in your right-hand slacks pocket.

What you do

As you talk about "great grandmother's magic thimble," reach into your pocket, get the thimble on the tip of your right first finger, bring it out to show it, and then put it back into your pocket. This plants the idea right at the start that you later will be reaching into your pocket to bring out the thimble again. Explain that "great grandma" also saved scraps of rope and string, and hold up the "three" tied-together pieces to show the audience.

Use both hands to untie the large knot at the top, keeping your hands together so as not to reveal that two of the "ends" really are one looped short piece. Take the ropes in your left hand, between your thumb and fingers, with the back of the hand toward the audience. Your thumb covers the bottom of the short loop and the three "ends" extend above the top of your hand.

With your right thumb and first finger, lift the real end of the long rope out to the right. Hold it for a moment to show that the pieces are separate. Then drop that end, let it fall to the bottom, and remove your right hand. That leaves your left hand holding only the two ends of the short piece and the looped part of the rope that hangs beneath.

Bring your right hand back to your left hand and with both hands tie the short rope piece in a single knot around the rope. Keep the small loop hidden by your fingers until the knot is tied and then show the knot. This looks as if you had tied two of the ropes together, end to end.

Now, take the remaining large knot at the bottom and bring that to the top to untie it as you did

GREAT GRANDMA'S MAGIC THIMBLE

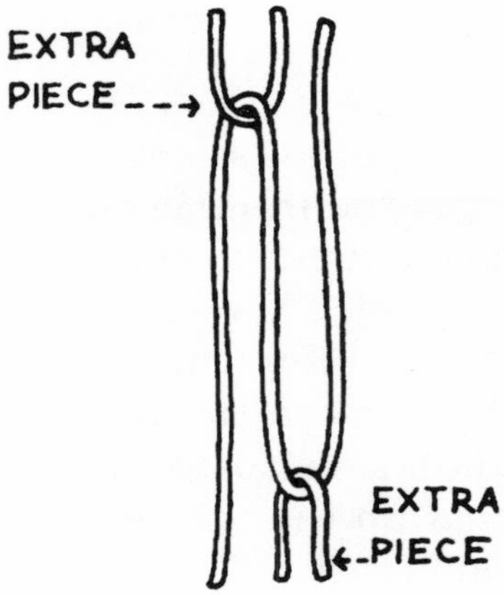

EXTRA PIECE ---→

←EXTRA PIECE

①

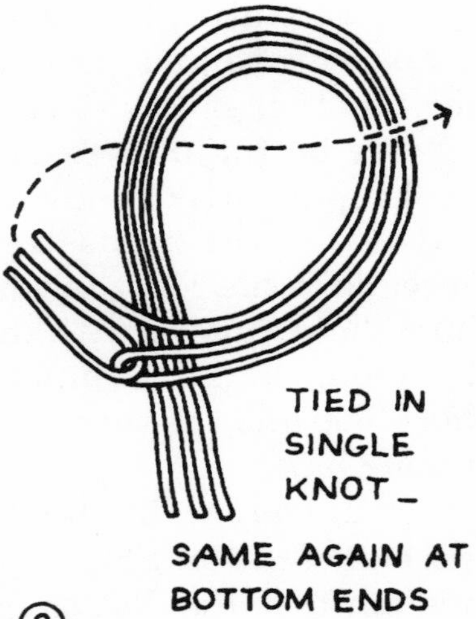

② TIED IN SINGLE KNOT —

SAME AGAIN AT BOTTOM ENDS

THIMBLE IN POCKET

③

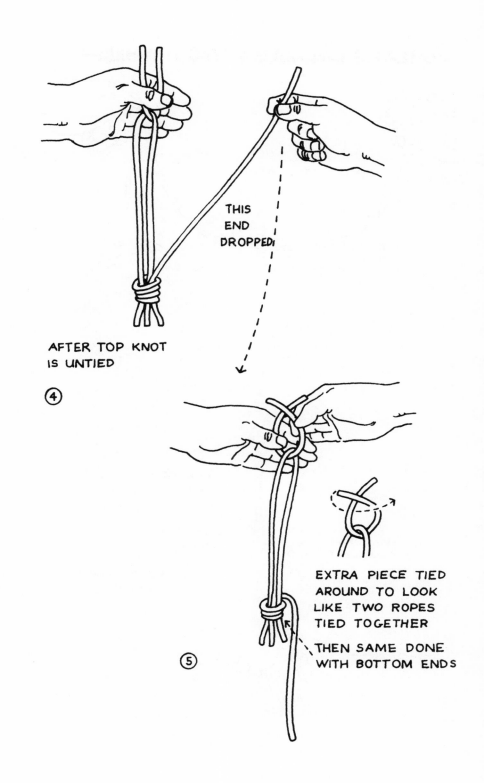

THIS
END
DROPPED

AFTER TOP KNOT
IS UNTIED

④

EXTRA PIECE TIED
AROUND TO LOOK
LIKE TWO ROPES
TIED TOGETHER

THEN SAME DONE
WITH BOTTOM ENDS

⑤

GREAT GRANDMA'S MAGIC THIMBLE—2

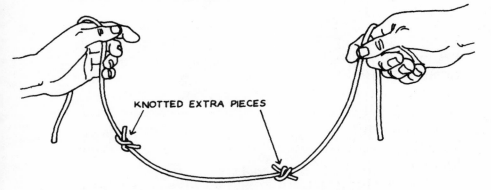

KNOTTED EXTRA PIECES

LOOKS LIKE THREE SHORT ROPES TIED END TO END

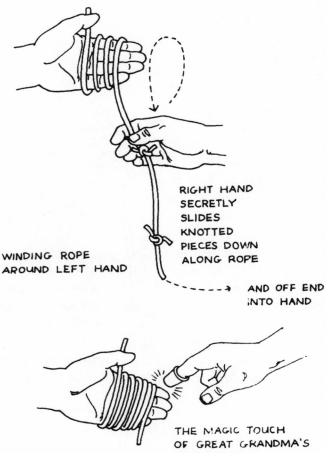

RIGHT HAND
SECRETLY
SLIDES
KNOTTED
PIECES DOWN
ALONG ROPE

WINDING ROPE
AROUND LEFT HAND

AND OFF END
INTO HAND

THE MAGIC TOUCH
OF GREAT GRANDMA'S
THIMBLE!

the first one. Repeat the same moves of holding the three "ends" between your left thumb and fingers, lifting the long end out to the right and dropping it to the bottom, then tying the short piece in a knot around the rope. Show what appears to be the three short ropes, knotted together and strung out end to end. (You really have one long rope, with the two little extra pieces tied along it to look like connecting knots.)

"Whenever great grandma had saved a few little pieces," you say, "she would tie them all together, end to end, and wind the pieces into a ball." Turn the palm of your left hand toward you. Hold one end of the rope with your left thumb and with your right hand begin coiling the rope around your left hand. As you wind the rope around your left hand, the hanging part naturally slides through the palm of your right hand, bringing first one of the knotted little pieces and then the second one into that hand.

Just keep both of the knotted pieces in the right hand, concealed by the fingers that are partly closed around the rope, and continue to slide the hidden knots down as your hand winds the rope. The audience thinks the knots are still on the rope coiled around your left hand.

As you finish coiling the rope, secretly slide both little pieces off the end of the rope into your right hand. Let that hand drop to your side for a moment with the two hidden pieces and lift your left hand high to show the coiled rope, as you say, "Then she would take out her magic thimble. . . ." Immediately put your right hand into your pocket to get the thimble the audience already knows is there. Leave the two rope pieces in your pocket, get the thimble on the tip of your right first finger, and bring it out to show it again.

The rest is simply acting out the story. Display the thimble as though it had some "magic power." Tap your thimbled finger three times on the rope coiled around your other hand. Then, unwind the rope and hold it out between your hands to show that the knots have vanished and the three short pieces have joined together as one.

ODD-EVEN ROPES ROUTINE

Magicians have invented scores of "patter" themes, moves and alternate plots for the popular trick of magically stretching a short, a medium-length, and a long piece of rope so that all three become the same length.

The presentation given here has been performed for more than twenty years before audiences of all ages, on stage, television, and in close-up magic. It sticks closely to the basic plot and deliberately keeps to the simplest, most direct method of accomplishing it. The trick itself will be explained first, followed by a working script of the patter and presentation.

How it looks

You show three pieces of rope, one a foot long, the second 2 feet long, the third 3 feet long. Holding the three pieces together with your left hand, you draw their top ends down over the back of that hand so those ends are even, then bring the three bottom ends up and hold all six ends with your left hand. You obviously still have three ropes of differing lengths: short, medium, and long.

Taking three ends in each hand, you spread your hands apart and visibly "stretch" the ropes until all three are the same length. You count them separately from hand to hand. But suddenly the ropes "shrink" again, so that you end the trick as you began it, with a short piece, a medium-length piece, and a long piece.

What you need

Three pieces of soft clothesline—1 foot, 2 feet, and 3 feet long.

The secret

The short rope is secretly looped around the long one behind your left hand and the ends are placed in that hand so that when the ropes are "stretched," the long one becomes doubled in half, with the short piece looking like two top ends.

Lay the three ropes side by side, short, medium and long, with the top ends even, and tie those ends together with a single wrap-around knot. They can be carried that way until you are ready to perform the trick.

What you do

Untie the ropes, hold each one up to show it, and turn the palm of your left hand toward you, fingertips to the right. Place the top end of the short rope under your left thumb, close to the crotch, then place

ODD-EVEN ROPES ROUTINE

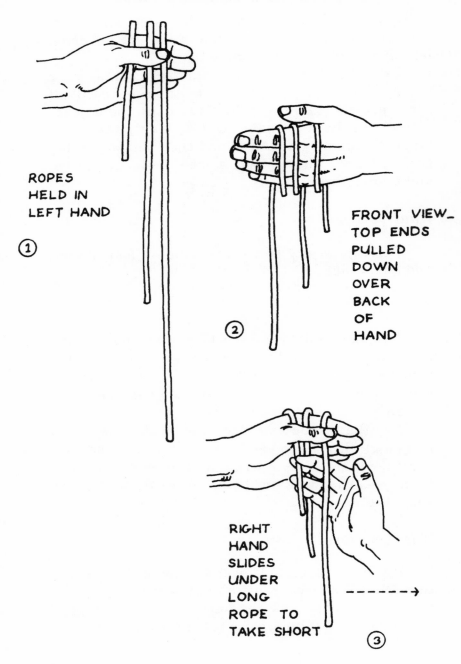

ROPES
HELD IN
LEFT HAND

①

FRONT VIEW_
TOP ENDS
PULLED
DOWN
OVER
BACK
OF
HAND

②

RIGHT
HAND
SLIDES
UNDER
LONG
ROPE TO
TAKE SHORT

③

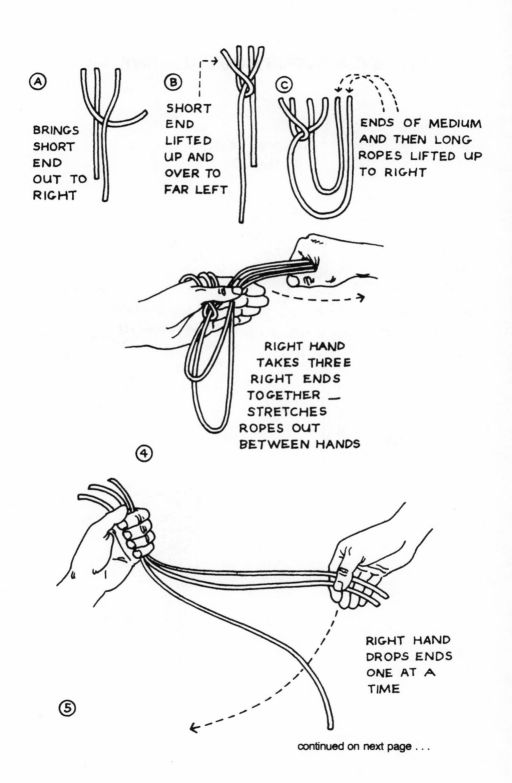

(A) BRINGS SHORT END OUT TO RIGHT

(B) SHORT END LIFTED UP AND OVER TO FAR LEFT

(C) ENDS OF MEDIUM AND THEN LONG ROPES LIFTED UP TO RIGHT

④ RIGHT HAND TAKES THREE RIGHT ENDS TOGETHER — STRETCHES ROPES OUT BETWEEN HANDS

⑤ RIGHT HAND DROPS ENDS ONE AT A TIME

continued on next page . . .

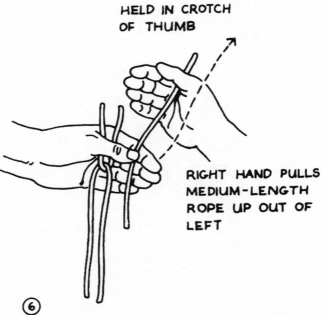

HELD IN CROTCH
OF THUMB

RIGHT HAND PULLS
MEDIUM-LENGTH
ROPE UP OUT OF
LEFT

⑥

COUNT:
"ONE!"

⑦

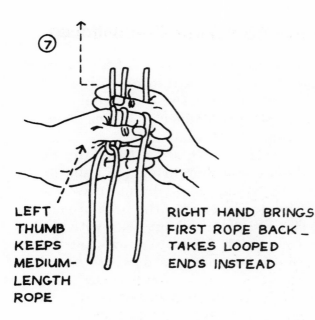

LEFT
THUMB
KEEPS
MEDIUM-
LENGTH
ROPE

RIGHT HAND BRINGS
FIRST ROPE BACK —
TAKES LOOPED
ENDS INSTEAD

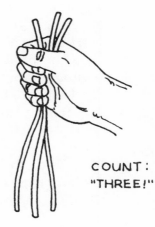

COUNT:
"TWO!"

RIGHT HAND
AGAIN PULLS
MEDIUM-LENGTH
ROPE UP OUT
OF LEFT TO ADD
TO REST

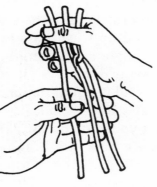

⑧

COUNT:
"THREE!"

the top end of the medium-length rope a little to the
right of that, and finally, place the top end of the
long rope to the right of both. The thumb holds all
three pieces side by side, with about 2 inches of the
ends extending above your hand.

Turn the left palm out to show the hanging
ropes to the audience and then bring the palm toward you again. With your right hand, draw the
three top ends down together over the back of your
left hand until those ends are about even with the
bottom edge of that hand. Pause to show that the
three top ends have been drawn down to equal
length.

Bring your right hand, fingertips to the left,
over inside the left palm. Slide your right fingers *under* the long rope, *over* the medium-length rope, and
grip the short rope just beneath where it is held by
the left thumb. Lift the short rope out to the right,
sliding the right fingers along to the end of it. Immediately bring that end up to the top and *over to the
far left* to hold it with your left thumb, to the left of
the other ends. Draw it down over the back of your
left hand until that end is equal in length to the others. (You have secretly looped the short rope around
the long one behind your left hand. This should look
as though you simply took the hanging end of the
short rope and brought it up to the top. Be careful to
keep the hidden loop below your left thumb so the
looping cannot be seen by the audience.)

Take the bottom end of the medium-length rope
and bring that up to the *right* of the other ends, to
hold that with the left thumb, and draw that end
down over the back of your left hand until its length
is equal to the others. Then, take the bottom end of
the long rope and bring it up to hold it to the *right* of
all the rest, drawing it down even with them.

Your left hand holds all six ends, which hang down at equal length over the back of that hand. With your right hand, separate the three ends that are to the right, so they are a little apart from the other three ends. Close your left hand into a loose fist around all the ropes and hold them up to show them as you remove your right hand.

You are now about to "stretch" magically the three ropes so they will visibly become the same length. Keep your left fist in front of you. Take the three top ends that are to the *right* with your right hand. Hold them together and draw your right hand horizontally out to the right, pulling the two hands apart as the loops seem to lengthen until all three ropes are equal. Keep the ropes as they are for a moment, so the audience clearly sees what has happened, and tug at the ropes stretched between your hands. Then, open your right hand enough so as to drop each of the rope ends separately and let them swing free to the bottom, one at a time.

Your left hand still holds what appears to be the other three ends, really the end of the medium-length rope and the two ends of the short rope that is looped through the center of the doubled long rope. Now, you seem to show each of the three ropes separately as you count them from hand to hand. But you "false count" them, in this way:

With the three top ends held by your left thumb, open the palm of your left hand toward you. Bring your right hand over against the *outside* of the left, so that the tips of the two lower right fingers touch against knuckles of the upper left. Grip the top end of the medium-length rope in the crotch of your right thumb and lift your right hand straight up to pull that rope completely out of your left hand, as you count aloud, "One."

Move your right hand back to your left hand as if to take a second rope, bringing both hands together again as they were, with the medium-length rope, which your right hand has just taken, hanging down inside your left hand. Press the tip of the left thumb against that rope to keep it in your left hand and grip the other two ends together with your right thumb and fingers. Draw those two ends straight up, closing your right fingers around the looped part to hide it, and pull those ropes out of your left hand, as you count aloud, "Two."

Now, take the remaining top end with your right hand and pull it up out of your left hand, as you count aloud, "Three." (This is really the medium-length rope that you are counting for a second time. You apparently have shown each rope separately as you transferred them from hand to hand.)

Keep the right fist closed around the ropes and hold them high to show that all three are of equal length. Wait for the applause, as if the trick were finished.

Then, put all three ropes together into your left hand, with the loop still concealed. Quickly take the three bottom ends with your right hand and bring those up to put them beside the other ends in your left hand. With your left palm toward you, open it enough so you can glance at the looping.

Take one of the short ends with your right hand and pull that short rope up out of your left hand, then take one end of the medium-length rope and pull that out, and finally pull out the long rope. Pass the ropes separately from hand to hand to show that they are once again as they were at the start: short, medium, and long.

Patter and presentation

Here is the full routine, in playscript form, for acting out the trick as explained:

Magician (speaks slowly, seriously): All of magic is make-believe, pretending, using your imagination. The whole of theater has its roots in that kind of magical illusion. When you go to a theater, you know that what happens on the stage isn't real. The scenery is painted, the words the actors speak are words that somebody wrote for them to say.

But if *you* pretend with them, if *you* make believe, then what happens on the stage seems real to you *while* it is happening. And that's the true joy of watching magic—making believe you can see something happen before your eyes that you know can't really happen at all.

(Picks up and unties the three ropes, shows each separately as he positions them in his left hand.) I'd like to show you what I mean with these three pieces of rope. There's a little piece, a middle-sized piece, and a long piece. *(Draws three top ends down over back of his left hand.)* If I were to draw these three ends down so they are equal, we might pretend, we might make believe, that we *have* three ropes that *are* the same length. *(Swings left palm out toward audience, runs right first finger down along each of the ropes.)* But we know we still have a little one, a middle-sized one, and a long one.

(Turns left palm toward himself again. Brings each of bottom rope ends up to hang evenly with top ends over back of his left hand.) If I were to bring *all* the ends up—the little one, the middle-sized one, and the long one—again, we might pretend that we have

three ropes the same length. (*Holds right palm flatly beneath the six hanging ends, as if measuring length, then gestures with right first finger toward the loops hanging beneath his left hand.*) But we know we still have a short loop, a medium one, and a long one.

(*Grips three right rope ends with his right hand. Stretches ropes between both hands, timing action to the words.*) Just for a moment, will you all *pretend* with me ... that there *could* be such a thing as *magic* ... that would *stretch* ... these ropes to *be* the same length. (*Tugs ends between his hands. Lets right-hand ends drop down, one at a time. Brings right hand to left hand and counts ropes separately from hand to hand.*) One ... two ... three. (*Holds right hand high, fisted around ropes.*) Thank you for pretending with me that there *is* such a thing as magic.

Accepts applause as if trick were ended. Transfers ropes together from right to left hand. Brings bottom ends up beside top ends in left hand. Then pauses and smiles to audience.) But of course, we *were* just pretending, just making believe. (*With right hand, quickly pulls each rope separately out of left, holding them high to show them.*) Because there's still just a little piece ... a middle-sized piece ... and a long piece of rope.

6

ACROBATICS

THE ROPE THAT FLIES WILD

How it looks

    You pick up a rope and a pair of scissors and hold the rope by its top end in your left hand and the scissors in your right hand, as if you were about to perform a rope-cutting trick. But the rope suddenly leaves your left hand and flies up through the air into your right hand. You put the rope back into your left hand, hold the scissors far out to the right, and once again the rope flies through space, across to your right hand.

"That one's too wild to use," you say, as you put the rope and scissors back on the table. "I'd better use a tamer piece." You then take another rope from your pocket and continue with your favorite cut-and-restored-rope routine.

What you need

A 3-foot length of soft clothesline.

Transparent colorless nylon thread. (Designed to blend with backgrounds of any color, this almost "invisible" thread is available at sewing counters in light and dark shades. The *light* shade is best for this trick.)

A small pair of scissors.

White cloth adhesive tape, ½ inch wide.

A needle.

The secret

The rope is pulled through the air from hand to hand by a pulley-like arrangement of the thread and scissors. While the thread is invisible from a short distance, this is not a trick to be shown to a close-up audience. It is self-contained, with no thread attached to your hands or body, and the threading is rigged so you can pick up the rope and scissors to present it at any time in your show.

Thread the needle with a 3-foot length of thread. Sew the thread to what will be the top end of the rope by stitching it through from side to side several times, and then remove the needle. Wrap a band of the white tape around the rope's end to prevent it from fraying and to hold the sewn thread more securely. Bind the bottom end of the rope with a similar band of tape.

Put the scissors points-upward on a table with the *finger-grip* part of the handle at the bottom left. Pass the free end of the thread down through that finger hole and then out to the left. Thread the needle with that end of the thread and push it through the rope from right to left about an inch below the rope's top end. Draw about 3 inches of thread out to the left and remove the needle.

Take a 2-inch length of the white tape and wind the end of the thread around it, sticking the thread to the tape. Then roll the tape upon itself and flatten it into a small button-like tab. (We'll call this the "end tab.")

To set it up for the performance, lay the rope at the left of your table, with its top end vertical and the end tab at the left. Draw the scissors out to the right as far as the thread will allow, and place them to the right of the rope, points toward the front.

What you do

Pick up the scissors with your right hand as you normally would if you were about to cut something, with your thumb through the thumb grip, second finger through the finger grip, first finger against the shank. Lift the scissors a few inches above the table and at the same time take the top end of the rope with your left hand, gripping it between the thumb and inside of the second finger so the little end tab lies horizontally under the thumb. (This is a natural way to pick up the rope and the positioning of the end tab under the thumb is automatic.)

Holding the rope with your left hand and the

THE ROPE THAT FLIES WILD

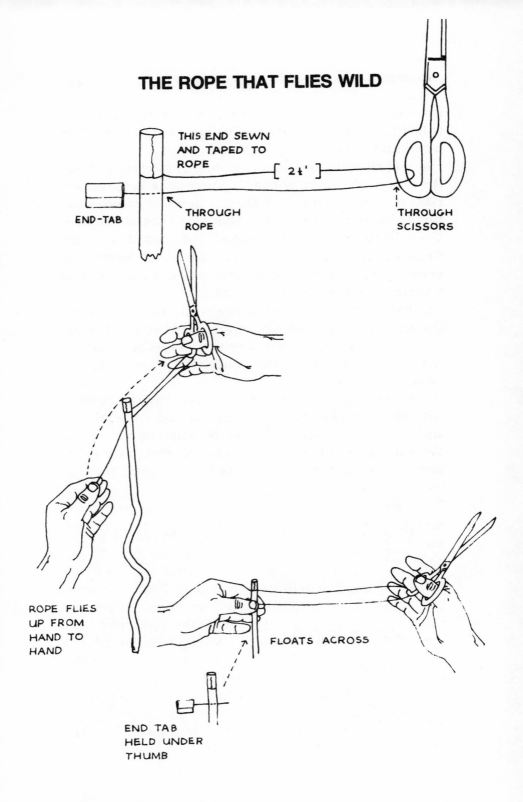

THIS END SEWN AND TAPED TO ROPE

[2½']

END-TAB

THROUGH ROPE

THROUGH SCISSORS

ROPE FLIES UP FROM HAND TO HAND

FLOATS ACROSS

END TAB HELD UNDER THUMB

scissors with your right hand, move away from the table. Keep the rope about waist-high with your left hand and move your right hand up and out toward the front, lifting the scissors high to display them. As your right hand sweeps up and forward, release the top end of the rope from your left hand, keeping the little end tab pressed against the fingers with the thumb. The rope will fly up from hand to hand, drawn by thread. (During this procedure, don't move your left hand at all; keep its fingers as they are. The rope will float up until its top end comes between the right thumb and second finger where they hold the scissors.)

Immediately bring your right hand back down to the left one. Grip the top end of the rope again between the left thumb and second finger, taking it from your right hand. Then, move your right hand with the scissors out to the right as far as the thread will allow. Release the rope from your left hand, keeping the end tab held under the thumb, draw your right hand out toward the right, and the rope will float across from hand to hand.

Bring your right hand back to your left hand and take both the rope and scissors with your left hand. Quickly gather the rest of the rope up into that hand and put the rope and scissors back on the table.

THE RING THAT FALLS UP

How it looks

You take a black ribbon and a brass ring from your pocket, thread the ring on the ribbon, and hold one end of the ribbon in each hand. Tilting your hands up and down, you slide the ring back and forth, so that it falls from the top to the bottom of the ribbon several times.

"When the ring falls *down*," you say, "that's gravity. But when the ring falls *up*...," and as you speak, the ring suddenly slides *up* the ribbon, from bottom to top, "... that's magic!"

What you need

A 20-inch length of black satin ribbon.

A brass-plated ring about 1½ inches in diameter.

Transparent colorless nylon thread. (The *dark* shade is best for this trick.)

A needle.

A small safety pin.

The secret

The method is an old one, used in many tricks of this kind. One end of the thread is fastened to the ribbon, the other end of the thread is attached to the performer. Moving the ribbon forward pulls the thread and causes the ring to rise. But the real secret of this version is in the way the thread is hitched up, so that it extends from below the level of your waist and directly out to the front from the center of your body. This keeps the thread well below the eye-level of the spectators, and centered against the solid background of your body, which helps to conceal it from those who are watching.

Since the reach of each person's arms is different, you will have to experiment to determine what length of thread best suits you, but start with a thread about 3½ feet long. Sew one end of it to one end of the ribbon, stitching it through several times so it holds firmly. Put the other end of the thread through the small hole at the bottom of the safety pin and knot it tightly.

Attach the safety pin inside the belt band at the center of the *back* of your slacks. Now, take the ribbon and pass it through your legs and out to the front, drawing the thread out between your legs. Put the ring into the otherwise empty right-hand pocket of your slacks. Then, roll the ribbon upon itself into a flat coil, starting with the *unthreaded* end, so as to leave the threaded end at the outside of the roll. Slide the rolled ribbon into your pocket on top of the ring.

With the gimmick set up this way, you can move around freely until you are ready to perform the trick. There is no attachment to the upper part of your body to interfere with the use of your hands or your jacket pockets while presenting other tricks.

What you do

Reach into your pocket with your right hand, take out the rolled ribbon, and bring it in front of you. Grip the end of the ribbon between the left thumb and first finger and give it a downward shake so the ribbon unrolls as you remove your right hand.

Keep the ribbon dangling down from your left hand. With your right hand, reach into your pocket again and bring out the ring to hold it high and show it. Thread the ring down over the top end of the ribbon and then hold both ring and ribbon together at the top end with the left thumb and fingers.

Bend forward slightly so you can reach down to

THE RING THAT FALLS UP

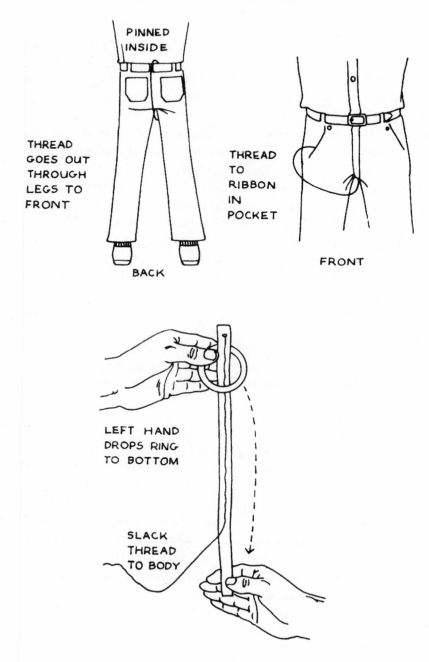

PINNED INSIDE

THREAD GOES OUT THROUGH LEGS TO FRONT

BACK

THREAD TO RIBBON IN POCKET

FRONT

LEFT HAND DROPS RING TO BOTTOM

SLACK THREAD TO BODY

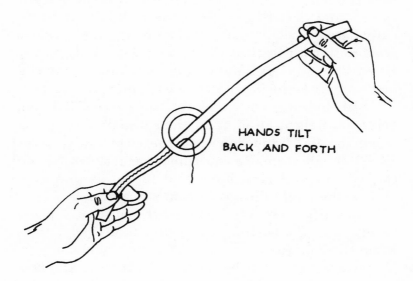

HANDS TILT
BACK AND FORTH

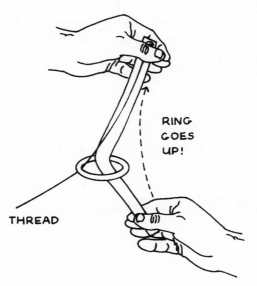

RING
GOES
UP!

THREAD

take the bottom end of the ribbon between the right thumb and first finger. Hold the ribbon taut vertically between your hands and move them both close enough to your body so the thread is slack. Drop the ring from your left hand and let it fall down the ribbon to your right hand at the bottom.

Still holding both ends of the vertical ribbon, bring your right hand up at the same time that you move the left hand down, so the ring again slides from top to bottom. Repeat this several times, tilting the ribbon and ring back and forth, as you say, "When the ring falls *down*, that's gravity."

Now lift your left hand so the ring and right hand are at the bottom of the ribbon, and say, "But when the ring falls *up* ..." Move both hands directly forward from your body, bending the top and bottom ends of the ribbon outward so the thread lifts the ring up the ribbon to the top. Grip the *ring* with your left fingers and drop the top end of the ribbon from your left hand to let it fall free, so the dangling ribbon now is held only by your right hand, as you say, "... that's magic!"

Gather up the ribbon with your right hand, put it back into the right-hand pocket of your slacks, and then take the ring from your left hand and put it away in the pocket with the ribbon.

SPOOKY ACROBATIC KNOTS

How it looks

You tie a large Bow Knot in a rope and hold the

rope by one end so the knot hangs at its center. Suddenly the rope seems to "come alive" and the knot magically unties itself.

Then, you tie a large Overhand Knot, hold the rope hanging down as before, and the bottom end of the rope rises up and spookily passes through the knot to untie the rope again.

What you need

A 2-foot length of soft clothesline.
Transparent colorless nylon thread.
A needle.
A thumbtack.

The secret

These two different knots that visibly untie themselves go well together. The first builds up the effect of the second, and both are worked by the simple means of a thread sewn to one end of the rope and tied at the other end to a thumbtack fastened under the top edge of the table. Secretly pulling up on the top end of the rope unties each of the knots.

Take a 2-foot length of the thread and sew one end of it securely to one end of the rope. Push the thumbtack into the underside of the table you will use when performing, close to its back edge, and knot the free end of the thread to the thumbtack. (The sewing and knotting shorten the thread, but about 1½ feet of it should remain between the end of the rope and the table edge.) Have the rope lying loosely on the table, with its threaded end toward the right.

What you do

Self-untying Bow Knot

Take up the rope near its center with both hands, palms *toward you,* and slide your hands out along it until they are about 8 inches apart. Grip the rope there between the thumb and first finger of each hand, so an end of the rope hangs down from each hand.

Holding it between the thumbs and first fingers, turn both hands palms *upward,* with the two little fingers side by side against the front center of the rope. Close the fingers of both hands down around the rope and turn the fisted hands inward toward each other until their knuckles touch together. This forms a large loop in each hand.

Slide the thumbs down to grip each loop at its base. Cross the left-hand loop over the right-hand loop and then tie the two together just as if tying an ordinary Overhand Knot. The result should be a Bow Knot with two big loops. (It is tied this way to avoid drawing any part of the thread into the knot or entangling it. The thread still runs directly down to the table from the right end of the rope.)

Hold up the rope by its two loops to show the knot, with the two ends hanging at the bottom. Take the left end of the rope between the thumb and first finger of the left hand and lift that hand so the rope hangs down from it, with the knot at its center. Bring the rope straight up above the table until the thread attached to the lower end is taut.

Point to the knot with your right hand and then snap your fingers. At the same time, secretly pull the top end upward with your left hand. This pulls out the two ends and the knot unties. (This should be done quickly, but without jerking the top end up. If the knot has been properly tied, only a slight upward pull is needed.) Hold the dangling rope for a moment and then let it drop from your left hand to the table.

Self-untying Overhand

Pick up the rope again with both hands, your left hand near the unthreaded end and your right hand near the end with the thread. Use both hands to tie a *large and very loose* Overhand Knot near the rope's center, bringing the threaded end out to the bottom. Holding the top end with your left hand, lift the rope above the table until the thread at the bottom is taut.

Point again to the knot with your right hand, and snap the right fingers. But this time, secretly pull your left hand up *slowly* so the audience can watch the bottom end of the rope gradually creep up and visibly pass through the knot to untie it. Hold the rope a moment longer and then let it fall from your left hand and drop back to the table. (Instead of attaching the end of the thread to the table, you may prefer to attach it to yourself. You can use the same sort of a hitch-up previously explained in this chapter for *The Ring That Falls Up* (page 183). Another method, with a slightly longer thread, is to attach the free end to your left shoe by tying it to a shoe strap, buckle, or shoelace eyelet. In either case, you would start with the rope, threaded end down, in your left pocket rather than on the table. At the end of the trick, you would put it away into that pocket again.)

SELF–UNTYING BOW KNOT

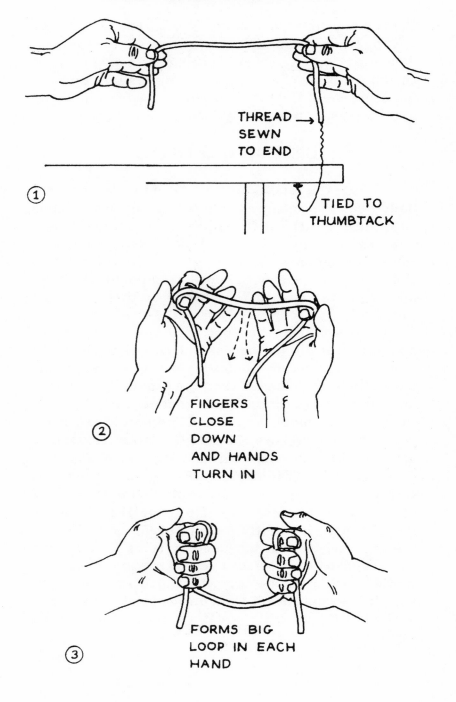

① THREAD SEWN TO END →

TIED TO THUMBTACK

② FINGERS CLOSE DOWN AND HANDS TURN IN

③ FORMS BIG LOOP IN EACH HAND

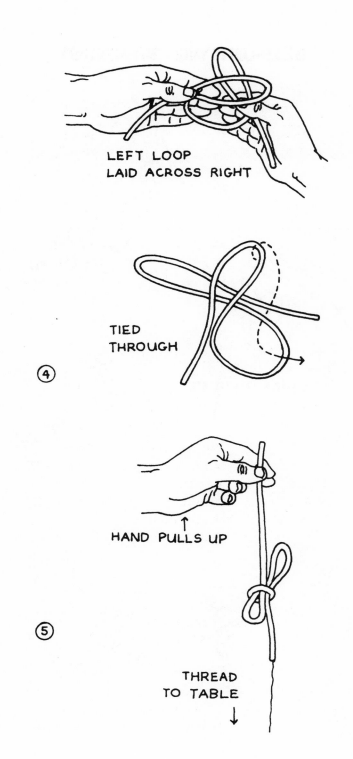

LEFT LOOP
LAID ACROSS RIGHT

TIED
THROUGH

④

HAND PULLS UP

⑤

THREAD
TO TABLE

SELF–UNTYING OVERHAND

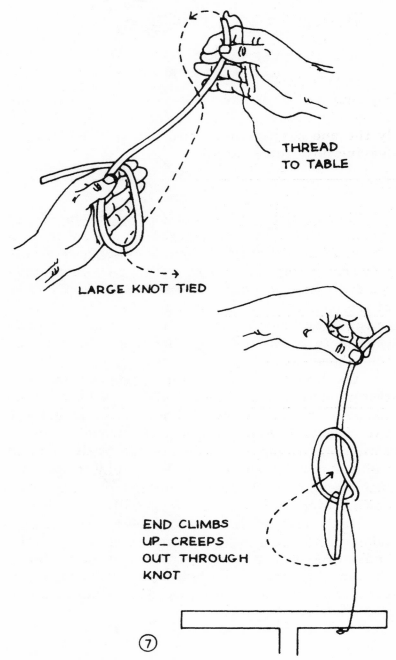

THREAD
TO TABLE

LARGE KNOT TIED

⑥

END CLIMBS
UP_ CREEPS
OUT THROUGH
KNOT

⑦

TOPSY-TURVY ROPE

In this comedy routine, the center of a rope visibly changes into the two ends of it and the ends join to become the center. This happens twice, and finally the one rope changes into two separate pieces, leaving no "center" at all.

How it looks

"For this trick, it is important to hold the rope at its exact center," you say, as you hold up a rope with one hand at its center, so the two ends hang down. "You can always find the center if you hold the middle at the top, because then the two ends have to be at the bottom." You bring your other hand up next to the hand holding the center. "I mean, if the two *ends* were at the *top*, then the *center* wouldn't be there because. . . ."

You break off your sentence as you draw your two hands apart. Suddenly, instead of holding the center of the rope, each hand holds one end, and the two ends that were hanging down visibly join together, so the separate ends are now at the top and the center is at the bottom. Pretending to be confused by what has happened, you say, "It's all upside down. Let me start again."

Running one hand down the rope, you again take it at the center, lifting that up as you drop the ends to the bottom, and say, "If I hold the center at the top, then naturally the two ends are at the bottom." But the same thing happens again. As you draw your hands apart, you are holding two ends instead of the center, and the ends that were at the bottom join to become the center.

"That's still upside down!" You shake your head and look out at the audience. "Would you all please stand on your heads for just a minute—so you can watch this upside down? ... No, wait—I've got it now."

You take the center of the rope with one hand and drape the two hanging ends over the other hand. "If I have two ends at the top and if I also have two ends at the bottom—then I must have *four* ends ... and so I have!" You show that the rope has changed into two separate pieces with four ends. "But now, I don't know where the *center* went," you say, as you throw the ropes down on the table. "And *that* doesn't make any sense at all!"

What you need

Two 2-foot lengths of soft clothesline with their cores removed.

Transparent colorless nylon thread.

Dull-finish (not shiny) transparent tape.

Scissors and a large needle with a big eye.

The secret

The thread runs through the center of the entire lengths of both coreless ropes and is then tied into a large circle, with a space between the ropes, so the ropes slide on the endless loop of thread like two tubes. When the rope's top ends are pulled apart, the bottom ends lift and slide against each other, making it appear that they are joined as one piece.

Both ends of each piece of rope should be cut straight and trimmed clean so the ends will butt together evenly. Bind each end by wrapping transparent tape around it, winding it carefully so the outer edge of tape is even with the cut edge of the rope. Don't tape the ends so tightly that they are squeezed smaller than the rest of the rope; they should remain the same diameter.

Unwind a yard or so of thread from the spool, but leave it attached to the spool. Thread the needle and draw about a foot of thread through the eye so it won't pull loose. Take one of the ropes and push the needle into the hole at one end, where the core was removed.

Work the needle down through the center of the tube-like jacket by pushing it a few inches until the jacket bunches, then gripping the needle through the jacket and holding it while you smooth back the bunched rope. Continue in this manner until you can draw the needle and thread out from the rope's other end. Then, without removing it from the needle, work the same thread down through the center of the second piece of rope the same way, unwinding more from the spool as needed.

When the thread has been passed through both tubes of rope, slide the ropes together on the thread, draw about a foot of thread out at each end, and cut the thread from the spool. Hold both ends of thread together at a point where there will be about 9 inches of thread between the top ends of the two ropes. Tie the threads twice, making the knots with both strands held together, and trim off the excess thread about an inch above the knots. Then, slide one of the ropes around until the knots are inside that rope.

TOPSY-TURVY ROPE

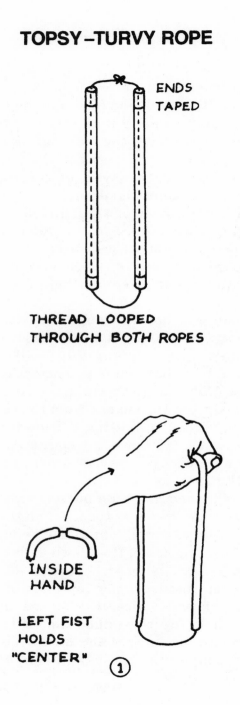

ENDS
TAPED

THREAD LOOPED
THROUGH BOTH ROPES

INSIDE
HAND

LEFT FIST
HOLDS
"CENTER"

(1)

② HANDS DRAW APART

BOTTOM ENDS LIFT AND JOIN

LEFT HOLDS BOTH TOP ENDS

RIGHT SLIDES DOWN TO TAKE "CENTER"

③

SAME MOVES REPEATED

④ RIGHT HOLDS BY "CENTER"

THEN HANDS AGAIN DRAW APART TOP ENDS

continued on next page . . .

TOPSY–TURVY ROPE—continued

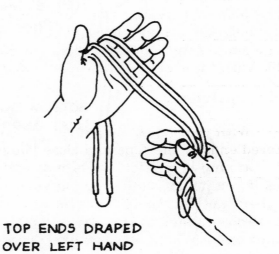

⑤ TOP ENDS DRAPED
OVER LEFT HAND

⑥ TWO
ROPES –
FOUR
ENDS !

Bring the two ropes together at the bottom of the loop of thread, with their lower ends butted against each other to form what would be the center of a single length of rope. Place the rope on your table with that "center" toward the back.

What you do

With your left hand palm-down, pick up the centered ends of the rope and close your fingers into a fist around them. Hold those ends within your hands as if you held a single rope at the center, with the other two ends hanging down at the bottom. Hold the rope up high to show it, as you say, "It is important to hold the rope at its exact center."

Bring your right hand to your left hand. Take one end in each hand, holding the ends upright so they can be seen above the hands, and spread your hands apart as far as the thread will allow. This should be done quickly, but smoothly and gently, as you say, "I mean, if the two *ends* were at the *top*, then the *center* wouldn't be there because. . . ."

Drawing your hands apart visibly lifts the two bottom ends up against each other so they appear to join together. You are now holding the separate top ends of what still seems to be a single rope, but with its center suddenly at the bottom instead of at the top. (You will find that if you give the whole rope a little downward shake as you draw your hands apart, the bottom ends will butt together more evenly.) Pretending to be confused by what has happened, you say, "It's all upside down. Let me start again."

Bring your right hand to your left hand. Place the rope end your right hand is holding beside the end in your left hand and hold both ends with your left hand. Immediately run your right hand down the rope to the bottom. Close your right hand into a fist around the "center" that is now at the bottom, holding those two bottom ends inside your right hand.

Now, lift your right hand high and at the same time drop the ends from your left hand, so that they fall to hang separately at the bottom. As at the start, you seem to be holding a single rope at its center, but this time with your right hand. "If I hold the center at the top," you say, "then naturally the two ends are at the bottom."

Bring your left hand to your right hand, take one top end in each hand, hold them upright, and draw your hands apart as before. Once again, the bottom ends are drawn together so the rope seems to have turned itself upside down, with its center at the bottom and ends at the top. "That's still upside down!" you say, as you jokingly suggest that members of the audience should stand on their heads. "No, wait—I've got it now."

Put both top ends into your left hand to hold them a moment. Close your right hand around both strands of rope and *quickly* run it down to the bottom. Take the bottom ends in your right hand and drop the top ends from your left hand. Turn your left palm toward you and open your thumb and fingers wide. Drape the center of both strands over the top of your left hand, so the top ends hang down separately over the back of that hand, but keep your right hand closed around the bottom ends it is holding.

"If I have two ends at the top and if I also have two ends at the bottom ..." As you speak, secretly spread the two bottom ends in the right hand with your thumb, so they will hang straight and about an inch apart, not curled together, and then let those ends drop and remove your right hand. "... then I must have *four* ends." Instead of "one" rope, you now have two pieces draped side by side over your left hand, with four ends hanging down. Turn your left hand to show it back and front. "And so I have!"

Take the ropes together with your right hand. "But now, I don't know where the *center* went," you say, as you toss them aside on the table. "And *that* doesn't make any sense at all!"